MESSIANIC
EXEGESIS

MESSIANIC EXEGESIS

Christological Interpretation
of the Old Testament in
Early Christianity

DONALD JUEL

Fortress Press   Philadelphia

COPYRIGHT © 1988 BY FORTRESS PRESS

Library of Congress Cataloging-in-Publication Data

Juel, Donald.
  Messianic exegesis.

  Bibliography: p.
  Includes index.
  1. Jesus Christ—History of doctrines—Early church,
ca. 30–600.　2. Bible. O.T.—Criticism, interpretation,
etc.—History—Early church, ca. 30–600.　3. Messiah—
Prophecies.　4. Bible. N.T.—Relation to the Old
Testament.　I. Title.
BT198.J78　1987　232′.1　87-12070
ISBN 0-8006-0840-2

2994D87　Printed in the United States of America　1–840

For my teacher
NILS ALSTRUP DAHL

CONTENTS

ACKNOWLEDGMENTS

This volume represents work done over several years, and my indebtedness to teachers and colleagues is great. Of special importance are my teacher Nils A. Dahl, whose vast knowledge and fertile imagination have given a generation of students an agenda that will take a lifetime to work through; another of my teachers, Judah Goldin, who first introduced me to the mysteries of the midrashim; Geza Vermes, whose learned publications—and whose generosity with his time—contributed to an enjoyable and productive sabbatical year in Oxford; my colleague and friend Alan Segal, whose sage advice and expertise I value highly; the administration and board of Luther Northwestern Seminary, who provided the opportunity and support for a sabbatical leave and time to write; the Aid Association for Lutherans, whose generous support made possible the sabbatical year in England; John A. Hollar and the staff at Fortress Press, whose careful work with the manuscript has greatly improved the quality of the book; my assistant, Jim Hanson, who helped with the less exciting aspects of the project; and my wife, Lynda, whose patience and encouragement have provided support throughout. To all of these, I wish to express my gratitude.

ABBREVIATIONS

CBQ	*Catholic Biblical Quarterly*
GBS	Guides to Biblical Scholarship
HDR	Harvard Dissertations in Religion
HJP	*The History of the Jewish People in the Age of Jesus Christ*
HNT	Handbuch zum Neuen Testament
IDB	*Interpreter's Dictionary of the Bible*
IEJ	*Israel Exploration Journal*
Int	*Interpretation*
JBL	*Journal of Biblical Literature*
JJS	*Journal of Jewish Studies*
JR	*Journal of Religion*
JSJ	*Journal for the Study of Judaism*
JSNT	*Journal for the Study of the New Testament*
JSOT	*Journal for the Study of the Old Testament*
JSOTSup	*JSOT*—Supplement Series
JSS	*Journal of Semitic Studies*
JTS	*Journal of Theological Studies*
MRSBY	*The Mekilta of R. Simeon ben Yochai*
NICNT	New International Commentary on the New Testament
NovT	*Novum Testamentum*
NTS	*New Testament Studies*
RQ	*Revue de Qumran*
SB	Stuttgarter Bibelstudien
SBL	Society of Biblical Literature
SBLDS	SBL Dissertation Series

SBLMS	SBL Monograph Series
SEA	*Svensk Exegetisk Årsbok*
SJT	*Scottish Journal of Theology*
SUNT	Studien zur Umwelt des Neuen Testaments
SWJT	*Southwest Journal of Theology*
TDNT	*Theological Dictionary of the New Testament,* ed. G. Kittel and G. Friedrich, English ed. G. Bromiley
VTSup	*Supplements to Vetus Testamentum*
ZNW	*Zeitschrift für die neutestamentliche Wissenschaft*
ZTK	*Zeitschrift für Theologie und Kirche*

QUMRAN: DEAD SEA SCROLLS

CD	Cairo (Genizah Text of the) Damascus (Document)
1QM	*Milhamah (War Scroll)*
1QpHab	*Pesher on Habakkuk* from Qumran Cave 1
1QS	*Serek hayyahad (Rule of the Community, Manual of Discipline)*
1QSa	Appendix A (*Rule of the Congregation*) to 1QS
4QFlor	*Florilegium* (or *Eschatological Midrashim*) from Qumran Cave 4
4QPB	*Patriarchal Blessings*
4QpIsa	*Pesher on Isaiah* from Qumran Cave 4
4QpPs 37	*Pesher on Psalm 37* from Qumran Cave 4
4QTest	*Testimonia* Text from Qumran Cave 4
11QMelch	*Melchizedek* Text from Qumran Cave 11

INTRODUCTION

The thesis of this book can be summarized in a two-part sentence: The beginnings of Christian reflection can be traced to interpretations of Israel's Scriptures, and the major focus of that scriptural interpretation was Jesus, the crucified and risen Messiah.

The thetical sentence may seem disappointingly commonplace. Some commentary is necessary to explain why it should merit a book-length study. Most would agree, perhaps, that early Christian reflection made use of the Scriptures of Israel, though there is considerable disagreement about the manner in which the writings of Israel were used and for what reason. In his classic study of Christian exegetical tradition, *New Testament Apologetic,* Barnabas Lindars, following the lead of C. H. Dodd, argues that the earliest use of the Scriptures by Jesus' followers was for arguing in behalf of the gospel. I contend that the earliest use of the Scriptures was rather to understand the gospel, to clarify the implications of faith in Jesus for one's relationship with Israel's God and with the world. Why the Scriptures were read and how they were read are questions that deserve more attention, particularly in light of the work done in recent decades on Jewish scriptural interpretation.

As for the second half of the thetical sentence, few would disagree that the major focus of early scriptural interpretation was "christological," meaning that it had Jesus in view. Very few, however, have argued that what stands at the beginning of that reflection and provides a focus and a direction for scriptural exegesis is the confession of Jesus as Messiah. In fact, in most recent studies the image of Israel's expected Messiah plays a minor role in comparison with other salvation figures like the Suffering Servant, the Son of man, the eschatological prophet, Wisdom, or the Righteous Sufferer. The proposal that the confession of Jesus as Messiah is primary is something of a novelty.

The thesis is not my own. I learned it from my teacher Nils Alstrup Dahl, who has offered both a highly detailed and a comprehensive account of christological origins in his various essays and still-unpublished lectures on NT Christology. His subtle—and largely neglected— argument only improves with age. The confession of Jesus as Messiah, he argues, can be derived neither from Jesus' teaching about himself recorded in the Gospels nor from Jewish conceptions of messiahship. The NT itself confirms what is found in Jewish tradition, namely, that "the Messiah" is a royal figure. Yet Jesus does nothing royal. Furthermore, the NT speaks most frequently of Jesus as Messiah-King at the point in his career where he looks least like the expected ruler from the line of David—in the context of his arrest, trial, and death. Dahl argues that the confession of Jesus as the risen Messiah is possible only if Jesus was actually executed as King of the Jews—as a messianic pretender. The transformation of Jesus the Crucified to the risen One becomes messianic only if Jesus was crucified as Messiah. The origin of the confession of Jesus as Christ must be located in the realm of history, not simply within the history of ideas. Events in the last week of Jesus' ministry gave birth to a confession that determined the interpretive agenda for the new religious group born at the resurrection. The scandal of the cross on which Jesus died as King of the Jews provided the focal point for christological exploration of Israel's Scriptures.

It is unnecessary to recapitulate Dahl's arguments in detail. They have been eloquently expressed in a series of essays in his *The Crucified Messiah,* essays soon to appear in a new and expanded collection from Fortress Press. I wish rather to test the thesis by attempting to account for the development of christological interpretation of the Scriptures. The project is necessarily an imaginative exercise. Our present Christian documents contain bits and pieces of interpretive tradition that give evidence of a vast network of exegesis to which we have only limited access. Yet in spite of our limitations, given our knowledge of first-century scriptural interpretation, and given some sense of interpretive traditions available to those wishing to reflect on the career of Jesus, it should be possible to explain the choice of biblical texts to explicate his career, and to show what controlled the direction and shape of the interpretive tradition. That is at least the task I have set myself. If it can be demonstrated that the confession of Jesus as Messiah-King provides the major focal point of exegetical tradition, it will lend greater plausibility to Dahl's proposal and may offer some suggestions for further work both on NT Christology and on the reconstruction of early Christian scriptural interpretation, paralleling work on Jewish exegetical tradition.

The study will focus on a variety of OT passages interpreted messianically in the NT. The task will be to show how the biblical passages are employed and to explain why they were selected to shed light on the career of Jesus the Christ. The biblical passages we will study include standard messianic oracles, like 2 Sam. 7:10–14 and Psalm 110, as well as OT passages that can boast no messianic reading outside Christian literature. Where Jewish interpretations of these biblical texts are available, they will be included both to identify similarities in interpretive technique and to highlight differences in conclusions.

1

MESSIANIC EXEGESIS

Developing an Approach

THE PROBLEM

For I delivered to you as of first importance what I also received, that Christ died for our sins in accordance with the scriptures, that he was buried, that he rose on the third day in accordance with the scriptures, and that he appeared to Cephas, then to the twelve. (1 Cor. 15:3–7)

The familiar words from Paul's first letter to the church at Corinth served as a convenient summary of the "gospel," the message of salvation that so dramatically altered the course of Paul's life and, in time, of world history. The words, which Paul said he "delivered" to the Corinthians, were not his own; they were borrowed from tradition. In opening his argument about the resurrection, he has preserved for all time a short creedal summary that takes us back into the earliest years of the fledgling movement that began among Jesus' followers.

Several aspects of the verses merit comment. Notable first is the structure: four "that"s (vv. 3–5a) followed by four "then"s (vv. 3b–7). We need not join the discussion of the precise extent of the earliest formulation. It is at least clear that Paul's inclusion of himself among the list of those granted appearances of the risen Christ was not part of an originally creedal formulation.

Notable as well is the narrative-like character of the summary. It is hardly a surprise that we should find in other Christian literature entire narratives that tell of Jesus' death, burial, resurrection, and appearances—though, it must be noted, none is an exact expansion of Paul's summary, and all the narratives of Jesus' passion and resurrection are part of a larger story that includes his public ministry.

The creedal summary, though brief, presupposes a history of reflection on the "basic facts" of salvation; it is not a naive report of events. Christ died "for our sins," it reports. The formula with *hyper,* either in the form "for us" or "for our sins," is common in Paul's letters. It appears in statements about Jesus' death in Hebrews, in 1 Peter, and in the Gospel accounts of Jesus' last meal with his followers.[1] The phrase is never explained. Paul assumes his readers will understand what it means. The task is a bit more difficult for us, since we are afforded little more than glimpses of what Paul previously taught. Though we can formulate some general notions about atonement, it is not obvious what images should come to mind. Precisely what did Paul and his contemporaries understand by "for our sins," and where did their ideas come from?

Paul offers at least a suggestion about where to look for answers to such questions: Israel's Scriptures. Jesus' death for our sins, like his resurrection "on the third day," is "in accordance with the scriptures." It is hardly surprising that Jesus' followers should turn to the Scriptures for language to speak about Jesus' death and resurrection. They were, after all, Jews, and like their contemporaries they believed it was in the sacred writings that God's will was to be found. It is probably misleading and certainly anachronistic to speak of the early movement as "Christian." The term appears in the NT only in Acts (11:26; 26:28) and 1 Peter (4:16). In Acts, it is coined not by believers who are part of the sect known as "the Way" but by pagans in Antioch. Most "Christian" groups understood themselves as Jews of some sort. That is certainly true of the groups for whom the four Gospels were written. It is also true of those among whom the first exegetical traditions developed. The "scriptures" of which Paul's creedal summary speaks are Israel's Scriptures; the setting within which they were interpreted by Jesus' followers was determined by Jewish tradition.

The last point is crucial. We cannot understand early formulations of the gospel without knowing something about the Scriptures. But we cannot understand the use of Scripture among Jesus' followers until we know something about Jewish interpretive tradition in the first

---

1. References include Rom. 5:6, 7, 8; 8:32; 14:15; 1 Cor. (1:13); 15:3; 2 Cor. 5:15, 21; Gal. 1:4; 2:20; Eph. 5:2, 25; 1 Thess. 5:10; 1 Tim. 2:6; Titus 2:14; Heb. 2:9; 5:1; 10:12; 1 Peter 2:21; 3:18; Mark 14:24 (Luke 22:19, 20); John 11:50, 51.

century of our era. Biblical exegesis had become an established feature of Jewish religious life. Though there had been no formal canonization of scriptural writings by official representatives of the Jewish community in Palestine or in the Diaspora, there was considerable agreement in practice regarding the outlines of the sacred Scriptures and the nature of the books.[2] For over two centuries Jews had been reading the Torah, the Prophets, and the Writings as sacred texts. Institutionalized suspicion of prophets greatly enhanced the authority of scriptural experts who sought God's will not in visions and dreams but in the sentences and words of the text. Ideological justification for such a scribal approach had been provided: in Sirach, for example, we read that God's Wisdom became incarnate in the Torah.[3] Wisdom "pitches her tent" within Israel and "takes root" among God's elect (24:12). The embodiment of wisdom is quite explicitly identified:

> All this is the book of the covenant of the Most High God,
>> the law which Moses commanded us,
>> as an inheritance for the congregations of Jacob.
> It fills men with wisdom, like the Pishon,
>> and like the Tigris at the time of the first fruits.
>> (Sir. 24:23–25)

The principles inherent in creation, in other words, have become available in the form of the Torah. And scribal interpreters paid attention to the Scriptures as texts, that is, as words and sentences. They developed enormous respect for the precise letters of the text, copying words even when they knew them to be misspelled. Interpretive methods developed that reflected that respect for the precise formulation of the text. By the first century, the process of translation and interpretation was well underway. Traditions of translation and interpretation had developed both on the level of popular synagogue life and on the level of the school. In the next chapter we will have occasion to examine various aspects of postbiblical scriptural interpretation.[4]

Jesus' followers located themselves squarely in that tradition when they used the phrase "in accordance with the scriptures." The

---

2. On canonization, see Schürer, *HJP* 2:314–21; and Sundberg, *Old Testament and the Early Church*. For a different view, see Leiman, *Canonization of Hebrew Scriptures*.

3. See, among other studies, Mack, *Logos und Sophia*.

4. The scholar who is perhaps most interested in the development of traditions in the postbiblical period is Vermes. See the helpful studies in his *Scripture and Tradition* and *Post-Biblical Jewish Studies*.

statements were not intended as ornamentation. Nor may we view the phrases as indicative of missionary efforts to convince "Jews."[5] The first believers were Jews, for whom conversation with the Sacred Scriptures was the primary mode of theological reflection. Exegesis was fundamental to Christian reflection; it was in the language of the Scriptures that Jesus' followers spoke about the "gospel." The study of early Christian exegesis takes us to the heart of the interpretive enterprise, as C. H. Dodd noted in *According to the Scriptures:*

> The attempt to discover just how the Old Testament was employed to elucidate the *kerygma* in the earliest period accessible to us and in circles which exerted permanent influence on Christian thought, is one which we are bound to make in seeking the substructure of New Testament theology.[6]

The particular problem in the case of our confessional summary is to know *what* biblical passages are in view. Where do we read that Christ was to "die for our sins" or to "rise on the third day"? No texts are cited. That in itself is not surprising, since the sentences serve as a summary. We must assume that they presuppose prior reflection on biblical texts and interpretive results. Yet it is quite another matter to identify the texts, the history of interpretation, and the exegetical results. The variety of proposals by scholars indicates that the matter is not at all clearcut; the scriptural roots of "for our sins" and "on the third day" are not obvious.[7] It is by no means self-evident that the Scriptures provide the script for the drama of salvation summed up in these short sentences.

The major complication in tracing the history of the exegetical tradition behind 1 Cor. 15:3–7 is the use of the term "Christ": "Christ died for our sins in accordance with the scriptures." The noun, used here without a definite article, could conceivably be understood as a name. If it were used as a title, we would expect a definite article. In Paul's letters, "Christ" always appears as a reference to Jesus, in such formulations as

---

5. The view is espoused by Lindars in his classic study, *New Testament Apologetic.*

6. Dodd, *According to the Scriptures,* 27.

7. Hengel (*The Atonement,* 49–50) argues that the use of *hyper* seems to derive from Greek antecedents, not biblical, although other features of 1 Cor. 15:3–7 seem to presume interpretation of Isaiah 43 and 53. J. Jeremias (*Eucharistic Words*) argues for the derivation of the whole formula from Isaiah 53. Williams (*Jesus' Death as Saving Event*) argues that the doctrine of Jesus' atoning death was formulated before the scriptural work; he agrees with Kramer (*Christ, Lord, Son of God,* 35–36) that the *hyper* formulations do not seem to have been part of the earliest layers of tradition, but he doubts that Isaiah 53 is the origin of the formulation. The proposals are obviously varied.

"Jesus Christ," "Christ," "Christ Jesus," and "our Lord Jesus Christ" (Rom. 9:5 is the one probable exception).[8] The recipients of Paul's letters could have appreciated what Paul had to say about Jesus Christ without knowing any of the title's background. That by no means rules out the possibility that the term itself, even in Paul's letters, derives from a specific, eschatological interpretation of the Scriptures and that Jewish "messianic" associations of the title were important to Paul.[9]

It is notable that the term is used here at all. Presumably the confession could have stated that "Jesus died for our sins." It does not, however. Remnants of messianic language are associated with Jesus' death and resurrection. The same is true in 1 Corinthians 1, where Paul reminds the congregation that he preached "Christ crucified, to Jews a scandal, to Gentiles foolishness" (1 Cor. 1:23). Paul was certainly aware of the background of the noun "anointed one," *messiah,* in Jewish tradition, even though he makes infrequent explicit reference to that tradition in his letters. The presence of the title in pre-Pauline formulas like 1 Cor. 15:3–7 suggests that Paul's use of the term represents an advanced stage in the development of christological language which must presuppose widespread use of the title in Aramaic-speaking circles, probably in the form of the confession "Jesus is Messiah."[10] Ancient Christian tradition portrayed Jesus as the Messiah who died for our sins and was raised on the third day—in accordance with the Scriptures. The link between Jesus' death and messianic imagery is confirmed by the passion accounts in all four Gospels (see below, pp. 28–29, 93–98).

Our search for the exegetical antecedents of such passages as 1 Cor. 15:3–7 must involve traditions about the anointed One (the Messiah). On the one hand, the scriptural resources for the search seem obvious. The verb "to anoint" is relatively common. Anointing was an important ritual in the installation of kings and priests. Prophets could also be anointed in a figurative sense (e.g., Isaiah 61; 1 Kings 19:16). On the other hand, Christian exegesis developed within Jewish interpretive tradition. How people actually read the Bible in the first century cannot be determined by reading the Scriptures alone. Selection of texts to be read at major festivals, targumic rendering (including both Aramaic and Greek), and the use of scriptural imagery in visionary literature all

8. Dahl, "The Messiahship of Jesus in Paul," in *The Crucified Messiah,* 37–47; and Kramer, *Christ, Lord, Son of God.*

9. See esp. Dahl, "Messiahship of Jesus."

10. Ibid., 41–42; and Kramer, *Christ, Lord, Son of God,* 35.

helped to shape the way people understood the Bible. If we want to know what the term "the anointed One" meant to a Jew in the first century, we need to know not only the scriptural possibilities but also which of these possibilities had been realized within the history of interpretation.

In this context a word about linguistic precision is in order. In 1966, Marinus de Jonge complained about careless use of "Messiah" and "messianic":

> The word "Messiah" is commonly used to denote any figure who brings about future salvation of any kind, regardless as to whether the source in question uses the term or not. The word "messianic" has acquired a correspondingly wider range of meanings, and is even used in connection with passages which do not speak of a future deliverer (let alone one who is actually termed Messiah) at all.[11]

"Messiah" and "messianic," he insists, should be used only when some form of the verb "to anoint" appears in a source.

There are good reasons for requiring such precision. One is to guard against oversimplifying the setting within which early Christianity took shape. Since S. Mowinckel wrote *He That Cometh,* we have reached a greater appreciation of the variety within Jewish eschatological tradition. We can no longer speak of one standard eschatological vision or vocabulary. There are visions of the future in which the term "anointed" never appears. In some such visions, salvation figures might include prophets, in particular Elijah or Moses (neither of whom were called Messiah); in other circles, the great deliverer might be portrayed as a priest; in still others, God himself appears as savior and king. In such cases, the term "messianic" is inappropriate. Jews could speak of someone as a deliverer without referring to him as the Messiah, and they could conceive deliverance without any savior figure at all.

The Messiah is, to be sure, one of the eschatological deliverers in Jewish tradition. With reference to later tradition, for example, the Targumim and rabbinic literature, we can even speak of the Messiah as a stereotyped figure. The noun, with the definite article, refers to a royal figure, usually called the King-Messiah or Messiah-King. The biblical texts from which the portrait of this coming ruler was fashioned include such passages as Isaiah 11; Gen. 49:8–12; Num. 24:17; and Jer. 33:14–26.

---

11. De Jonge, "The Use of the Word 'Anointed' in the Time of Jesus," *NovT* 8 (1966): 132–33.

The matter is more complicated when the question turns to pre-Christian tradition. The absolute "the Messiah" never appears in the OT. The noun is always followed by a modifier ("his messiah," "my messiah," "the Lord's messiah," etc.). The Qumran sectaries could speak of both a royal and a priestly figure as "anointed," though neither is referred to simply as "the Messiah."[12] Usage in the NT presumes a stage in the development of messianic language beyond that of Qumran. Some of the links in that developing tradition still remain unaccounted for.

The sketchy evidence and the complexity of Jewish tradition cannot be used to demonstrate the "relative unimportance of the term in the context of Jewish expectations concerning the future,"[13] however, or to muddy what is in the NT a relatively clear picture. For the NT, as for the later rabbis, "the Messiah" refers to the expected king from the line of David.[14] Though the messianic king was not a standard feature in eschatological visions, the figure itself is fairly consistent.[15] Differences are circumscribed by the royal office. The Messiah can play any of a variety of roles appropriate to a king, but he is a king. The consistency is likewise reflected in the fairly clear set of biblical passages acknowledged as messianic by the sectaries at Qumran, the rabbis, the author(s) of *Psalms of Solomon* 17 and 18, as well as the Jewish sect that came to be known as Christian.[16]

The use of "Christ," the Greek equivalent of *messiah,* in 1 Cor. 15:3 demands that we follow a particular line of investigation in reconstructing

---

12. For an assessment of the evidence from the Qumran material, see van der Woude, *Die messianischen Vorstellungen der Gemeinde von Qumran.* It is unlikely, contrary to van der Woude, that the evidence permits the conclusion that "the Messiah" could have meant more than one figure. Here, see Schürer, *HJP* 2:488–514; and Vermes, *Jesus the Jew,* 130–40, 158–59.

13. De Jonge, "Use of the Word 'Anointed,'" 134.

14. De Jonge himself agrees at this point. See also Vermes, *Jesus the Jew,* 130–40.

15. See the helpful summary of material in Vermes, *Jesus the Jew,* 130–40, 158–59. It might seem unnecessary to say more about a view that most would regard as obvious, were it not for current challenges from K. Berger ("Zum Problem der Messianität Jesu," *ZTK* 71 [1974]: 1–30; "Die königlichen Messiastraditionen des Neuen Testaments," *NTS* 20 [1973–74]: 1–44; "Zum traditionsgeschichtlichen Hintergrund christologischer Hoheitstitel," *NTS* 17 [1970–71]: 391–425 and Harvey (*Jesus and the Constraints*). I do not find their arguments convincing that "the Christ" could be used to speak about a prophetic figure, particularly because of evidence in the NT itself.

16. Such "messianic texts" (i.e., acknowledged by a broad spectrum of Jewish groups as references to the coming king from the line of David) include Gen. 49:10–12; Num. 24:17; 2 Sam. 7:10–14; Zech. 6:12; Isaiah 11; Jeremiah 33; Psalm 2.

the exegetical history behind the verse. Scriptural precedent is claimed for the statement that *Christ* died for our sins and was raised on the third day, and herein lies the problem. It is one thing to suggest that the Scriptures provide categories for understanding the death and resurrection of the man Jesus of Nazareth. It is quite another to speak of the death and resurrection of Jesus the *Messiah* as scriptural. Though martyrdom is not a prominent category in the OT, Jews were able to find resources in their biblical heritage for making sense of the death of the righteous. Wisdom of Solomon 2 represents such an effort, drawing largely on Isaiah 53. In his brilliant essay on the Akedah in Jewish tradition, Shalom Spiegel shows how a story that told how God provided substitution for human sacrifice could provide later generations with a means of finding significance in the death of the righteous.[17] In Geza Vermes's study of the same text in Genesis 22, we observe how the tale of Isaac's binding, read in light of Isaiah 53, could furnish categories for the author of 4 Maccabees to interpret martyrdoms that occurred in the days of Antiochus IV.[18] Christian Maurer and Joachim Jeremias have argued that the image of the servant of God from 2 Isaiah provided Jesus and his followers with the means of comprehending his death.[19] Yet in Judaism none of these interpretive traditions has anything to do with messianic expectation. Isaiah 53 provides a helpful example. Although the verses could be applied to the Messiah in the Targum, every trace of suffering and humiliation is removed from the career of the Servant-Messiah by means of ingenious exegesis (see below, chap. 5). The title Messiah seems particularly ill suited for its role in the passion tradition. It does not suit Jesus' role as preacher and healer, and it certainly does not befit his role as victim of Roman justice. It is difficult to understand how anyone who knew the Bible could say that "Christ died for our sins in accordance with the scriptures."

That is precisely what Paul asserts, however. And the assertion is not his alone. The association of Messiah and death/resurrection is firmly anchored in pre-Pauline tradition. It is most graphically exemplified in the passion accounts in the Gospels. Jesus' ministry in Mark is depicted

---

17. Spiegel, *Last Trial.*

18. Vermes, "Redemption and Genesis xxii: The Binding of Isaac and the Sacrifice of Jesus," in *Scripture and Tradition,* 193–227.

19. Maurer, "Knecht Gottes und Sohn Gottes im Passionsbericht," *ZTK* 50 (1953): 1–38; and J. Jeremias, "pais theou," *TDNT* 5 (1972): 677–717. For a critique of Jeremias, see Hooker, *Jesus and the Servant,* and Juel, "The Servant-Christ," *SWJT* 21 (1979): 7–22.

in thoroughly non-messianic categories, but his trial and death are dominated by royal imagery. Jesus is tried, mocked, condemned, and crucified as "Christ the Son of the Blessed," "King of the Jews," and "Christ, the King of Israel."[20] And although Jesus' death and resurrection are not the sole concern of the evangelists, the events obviously served as the focus of creedal summaries and formed the core of the gospel message. The exegetical history behind 1 Cor. 15:3–7 involves the whole of NT christological tradition and brings us close to the heart of the religious enterprise.

In seeking to reconstruct that history of exegesis, we must recognize that the rules of the game were different in the first century. Like other Jewish biblical interpretation, Christian exegesis was not "scriptural" in a naive sense. Though believers were able to find resources for speaking of Jesus' death in passages like Psalm 22, Isaiah 53, and Genesis 22, a plain reading of the passages would convince no one that "the Christ must suffer and on the third day rise." Interpretation was not restricted to that plain sense, however. Interpreters were free to read Psalm 2 as an eschatological oracle, Nathan's promise to David in 2 Sam. 7:10–14 as messianic; they could view David's psalms as no less prophetic than the writings of Isaiah or Jeremiah. Texts were not bound to their original historical setting; the meaning of words and sentences was not restricted to their immediate literary context. Assertions that something was "in accordance with the scriptures" might presuppose a highly artful, even fanciful, history of interpretation.

Yet even in this setting, the connection between the Messiah and death/resurrection is difficult. No one expected the Messiah to suffer for sins. No one expected the Messiah to rise from the dead, because he was not expected to die. The biblical passages acknowledged as "messianic" in Jewish tradition are consistent in this regard. Attempts to find evidence of a pre-Christian "suffering Messiah" have been unsuccessful.[21] There was a religious vocabulary available to speak about the death of the righteous in Jewish tradition. Christians drew on such resources, just as they made use of traditions about the prophets, particularly eschatological figures like Moses and Elijah. The link with messianic categories, however, is unprecedented. Jesus' followers undertook a creative exegetical enterprise that still requires clarification. How and why were such connections made? What was the role played by biblical texts, and how

---

20. See my study of Jesus' trial before the Sanhedrin, in *Messiah and Temple*.
21. See below, chap. 5.

do the emerging interpretive traditions relate to scriptural tradition in other Jewish circles?

There is a clearer picture of this distinctive "messianic exegesis" in Luke's writings. Unlike Paul and Mark, Luke offers little sense of the tension between partisan and nonpartisan reading of the Scriptures. In Luke 24 at the end of the Gospel, Jesus twice instructs his followers about the scriptural necessity of his death and resurrection as Messiah:

> Then he opened their minds to understand the scriptures. And he said to them, "Thus it is written that the Christ should suffer and be raised from the dead on the third day, and that repentance for forgiveness of sins should be preached in my name to all the nations." (Luke 24:46–47)

The statement serves as a thematic introduction to the missionary speeches in Acts, where assertions about the scriptural necessity of the Messiah's death and resurrection are substantiated by exegesis. In Peter's speech in Acts 2, Psalm 16 is cited as proof that the Christ was not to see corruption (Acts 2:24–31). The argument appeals to Ps. 110:1, Psalm 89 (132), and perhaps Psalm 69 as well. In Acts 8, the evangelist Philip argues that Isa. 53:7–8a refers to Jesus, one who was denied justice and "taken up from the earth" (ascended). Paul's speech in Acts 13 makes use of Psalm 16 and Isa. 55:3 in arguing that Scripture speaks of the death and resurrection of the Messiah. By the time of Justin Martyr's *Dialogue with Trypho the Jew* and the *Epistle of Barnabas,* the arsenal of texts had been considerably enlarged to bolster arguments that "the Christ must suffer and on the third day rise."

But are these texts and these arguments part of the tradition that lies behind the "in accordance with the scriptures" in 1 Corinthians 15? Or are the scriptural arguments in Acts derivative, built upon older foundations of which we are afforded only occasional glimpses? And how are we to relate Luke's almost rationalistic confidence in his ability to argue Jesus' case from the Scriptures with Paul's insistence that his gospel, though in accordance with the Scriptures, remains a scandal to Jews who read the same Scriptures but do not believe? Answering such questions is essential to the task of reconstructing the history of exegesis within early Christian circles which, Dodd insisted, leads to the "controlling ideas" that lie at the heart of Christian theology.

Christianity began not as a scholarly proposal about the meaning of the Scriptures but as a response to events focusing on a particular person, Jesus of Nazareth. The response required a language, and the language of Jesus' followers was that of the Bible (i.e., the OT) as read and interpreted in Jewish circles of the first century. If we wish to understand the language first-century believers used to speak of Jesus, we must have some sense of how they read their Bibles. That enterprise requires attention to at least three areas.

The World of Midrash

The world of first-century scriptural interpretation was very different from our own. The differences can be exaggerated, but for those uninitiated into the mysteries of midrash, rabbinic exegesis or the Habakkuk commentary from Qumran may seem strange. Interpretive techniques may seem playful or highly artificial. If we are to understand early Christian exegesis, however, we must learn the rules of the game.

We are fortunate that a number of first-rate scholars in the field of Judaica have produced studies that open the foreign world to outsiders.[22] The discovery of the Qumran scrolls and their publication have done much to awaken interest in a neglected area of biblical studies. The scrolls, particularly the commentaries, offer dramatic examples of an approach to interpretation foreign to those trained and shaped in modern universities. Our tendency to view texts as windows to a "real" world of events and to locate meaning in the original historical and literary setting of passages contrasts sharply with first-century viewpoints. Interpreters viewed the Scriptures as writings, meaning collections of sacred sentences and words, whose meanings were not bound to an immediate historical or literary context. Like modern interpreters, ancient exegetes were interested in uniting the world of text with their own, but their methods were quite different. In the next chapter we will offer a brief introduction to the hermeneutical world of the first century.

Scripture and Tradition

Vermes has devoted a large portion of his academic career to the search for interpretive traditions that shaped the way Jews read their Bibles.[23] Such traditions were crucial to the life of the religious community, he has argued, because they served as the vehicles for transmission of doctrine:

---

22. In addition to the articles by Bloch and the work of Vermes discussed in the next chap., the recent work by Porton, *Understanding Rabbinic Midrash*, deserves mention as a major contribution by students of Neusner, along with Kugel and Greer, *Early Biblical Interpretation*. For a fuller bibliography, see my notes in chap. 2.

23. See esp. Vermes's two volumes of essays *Scripture and Tradition* and *Post-Biblical Jewish Studies*.

Doctrinal exegesis was similarly influenced by the evolution of Jewish religious thought, and its impact was the more obvious because, in ancient Judaism, systematic theology was unknown, and the establishment, transmission, and development of doctrines and beliefs were effected within the framework of scriptural interpretation.[24]

Such traditions of exegesis had a powerful impact on what people understood the Bible to say. Within religious communities, the faithful do not come to the sacred texts without expectations. Those expectations are shaped by worship and various other forms of tradition. The impact of such tradition would have been much greater in the first century than in our own era, because very few had access to written Bibles. What people knew was what they heard in the temple, in the synagogue, and in set prayers. All but the learned knew the Scriptures in translation— whether in Greek (Septuagint) or in Aramaic (Targumim). Regular use shaped interpretation.

A contemporary example of the interpretive power of tradition is Handel's *Messiah*. Few people have any idea who produced the libretto for the oratorio, and fewer still have any sense of the principles of selection operative in its combination of various biblical texts. Yet those who listen to the great choruses are convinced by a special form of argument that a whole variety of scriptural passages are "messianic." Students of Isaiah may offer whatever arguments they like about the original setting of the lines "For unto us a child is born, unto us a son is given" (Isa. 9:6) or "Surely he has borne our griefs and carried our sorrows" (Isa. 53:4). People know such passages are "messianic"—simply because they are a part of Handel's *Messiah*. If this is true in an age when anyone can own a Bible and most do, when anyone can check a scriptural reference and perhaps find a scholarly opinion in a commentary ready at hand, it is not difficult to understand the force of tradition in earlier times.

What were the favorite texts among Jesus' and Paul's contemporaries? What images came to mind when Psalm 110 was read—or Daniel 7 or Isaiah 53? In the Qumran scrolls, various biblical passages are read as oracles making predictions. The commentator can take it for granted that his readers will understand; no arguments are necessary. The brief commentary on 2 Sam. 7:10–14 from cave 4 is an example of this. Students of ancient Israel have shown considerable interest in Nathan's oracle in its various forms (Psalm 89; 2 Chronicles 17); the tradition of God's promise to David of an everlasting dynasty underwent various

---

24. Vermes, *Scripture and Tradition,* 178.

changes that shed light on political and religious transformations within Israel over a period of centuries. By the first century, however, the oracle had come to be read as a prediction of the coming of the Messiah—the "branch of David who shall arise with the Interpreter of the Law [to rule] in Zion [at the end of] time," as the commentator puts it (4QFlor 11–12). The use of "branch" as a reference to the coming King is taken from Jeremiah 33 and Zechariah 6, passages that are also viewed as "messianic." The commentator at Qumran probably did not himself make the connections between 2 Samuel and Jeremiah 33, nor was he the first to read 2 Samuel 7 as messianic. His own interest in the oracle is evident (see below pp. 61–77), but in large measure his view of the Scriptures is determined by prior exegetical tradition. Knowledge that Nathan's oracle was regarded as messianic prior to Christianity is of considerable significance for understanding early Christian exegesis. In these verses, David's messianic successor is called "son" by God himself, and he is described as David's "seed."[25] Both terms were to become important in Christian tradition. Without some sense of how people read 2 Samuel 7, however, we cannot properly determine the influence of this passage on the use of such language in early Christian circles. Only when we have a sense of the way 2 Samuel 7 was read in non-Christian circles can we determine the direction of distinctively Christian exegesis.

In this volume we will devote space to Jewish interpretive traditions where they are relevant for understanding early Christian exegesis.

Point of Departure

The most important and difficult problem is to determine where to begin and how to proceed. Our interest is principally in the preliterary period in the history of the Christian movement. The exegetical traditions that provide a foundation for the NT writings were largely completed prior to the writing of Paul's first letter and certainly prior to Mark's Gospel. Yet the only access we have to those traditions is through the NT and some later Christian literature.[26] The age of the Epistle

---

25. See below, chap. 3. See also Wilcox, "The Promise of the 'Seed' in the New Testament and the Targumim," *JSNT* 5 (1979): 2–20.

26. Building on the work of Walter Bauer, Koester has shown that 2d-cent. Christian literature is not simply a development or corruption of material from the NT but may represent the evolution of independent traditions (see Koester and Robinson, *Trajectories*). Justin's *Dialogue with Trypho* thus cannot be excluded from the study of early Christian interpretive traditions, though it certainly represents an advanced stage of development.

or the Gospel in which a particular tradition is attested is thus not determinative of the age of the tradition. Later writings give evidence of secondary developments, but they may also preserve ancient tradition not cited in earlier works.

The occasional nature of the NT writings is another complicating factor. Even had there existed written collections of testimonies, as Randall Harris argued, they no longer exist. We have from the first-century Christian movement only letters, narratives, and an apocalypse. We possess no commentaries on OT books, just as we possess no systematic expositions of doctrine.

Paul's letters are a case in point. Paul rarely offers extended examples of the christological interpretation of Scripture that undergird his notions about Jesus and the gospel. Yet we catch occasional glimpses. The rather formalized relative clause in Rom. 4:25 ("Jesus our Lord, who was put to death for our trespasses and raised for our justification") appears to have received its form from an interpretation of Isa. 53:5, 12.[27] Paul's reference to God as one who "did not spare his own Son" in Rom. 8:32 alludes to Gen. 22:15 and may well presuppose an interpretation of the Akedah.[28] The confessional fragment in Rom. 1:2 presupposes a messianic interpretation of 2 Sam. 7:14 or Ps. 2:7, where David's offspring is called son by God himself. In all these cases, Paul does not quote a text. One may ask in some cases whether there is even a conscious allusion intended. The results of interpretation have been incorporated into the language of faith. We can learn a great deal even from these occasional glimpses about the exegetical substructure of Paul's thought and, in many cases, about pre-Pauline exegetical tradition. Fitting the details together into a whole picture requires hypotheses, however, and decisions about where to begin.

An obvious place to begin, of course, is Acts. The narrative includes speeches that incorporate biblical interpretation and are set within the early days of the Christian movement. Scriptural interpretation is part of the missionary enterprise: Peter, and later Paul, seek to convince fellow Jews of the truth of their message by appeal to the sacred text. Dodd, and Barnabas Lindars, choose to begin their reconstructions of early Christian exegesis at this point. Lindars's book begins with Acts 2 and Peter's interpretation of Psalm 16.

---

27. Kramer (*Christ, Lord, Son of God*, 30–32) believes that Paul may have had a hand in formulating the second half of the statement. The issue is complex.

28. See Dahl, "The Atonement: An Adequate Reward for the Akedah?" in *The Crucified Messiah*, 146–60; and Vermes, "Redemption and Genesis xxii."

Acts provides an insubstantial foundation for our reconstruction, however. Martin Dibelius and his students argued that the speeches in Acts should be studied as compositions of Luke the historian and attention paid to their function in the narrative.[29] Recent studies have tended to confirm that view. William Kurz has shown that the "apologetic" pattern characteristic of scriptural exegesis in the speeches in Acts is unique among NT authors and has far more in common with later writers, like Justin Martyr.[30] The highly rationalized approach to scriptural argument shows signs of a sophisticated hermeneutic and a distinctive social setting.[31] Luke's exegesis is neither typical nor primitive. He shares various interpretations with other NT authors, and there are features in the speeches that may be ancient. There is no direct access, however, to the earliest stages of Christian interpretation through Acts. Decisions about a place to begin must depend upon a broader assessment of NT interpretive traditions and a theory about how they fit together.

C. H. Dodd

Much of the interest in early Christian exegesis in the last decade and a half owes its inspiration to the fertile imagination of C. H. Dodd, whose *According to the Scriptures* has had an enormous impact on the direction of NT scholarship. Lindars's *New Testament Apologetic* owes a great deal to Dodd's work. His discussion of the scholarly task and his approach to the problems are still worth examining in some detail. They can aid us in formulating an approach to the task of reconstruction, even if some of his views are untenable.

The task of NT theology, according to Dodd, is to get back to the beginning point of Christian tradition: "The historical study of NT theology, as distinct from dogmatic or systematic theology, is faced by the difficult task of discovering the true starting point of the development which the NT writings exhibit."[32] The starting point, Dodd argues, was the kerygma—the proclamation of certain historical events as salvific. Here he presupposes his earlier work on apostolic preaching:

This apostolic *kerygma* is a basic standard of reference for everything that is set forth as part of the Christian Gospel. It is itself, properly speaking,

---

29. Dibelius, "The Speeches in Acts and Ancient Historiography," in *Studies in the Acts of the Apostles,* 138–85; and Haenchen, *The Acts of the Apostles.* See also Cadbury, "The Speeches in Acts," in *Beginnings of Christianity,* ed. Foakes-Jackson and Lake, 5:402–26.

30. Kurz, "The Function of Christological Proof from Prophecy in Luke and Justin" (diss., Yale Univ., 1976).

31. See my "Social Dimensions of Exegesis: The Use of Psalm 16 in Acts 2," *CBQ* 43 (1981): 543–56. See also below, pp. 82–85.

32. Dodd, *According to the Scriptures,* 11.

pre-theological, and does not bring us very far on the road to that reflective and reasoned presentation of the truth of the Gospel which is Christian theology.[33]

The keynote in early formulations of the kerygma, such as 1 Cor. 15:3–7 and Acts 2, is fulfillment, which only makes sense in light of the prophetic books in the OT. Dodd argues, therefore, that the early formulations in 1 Cor. 15:3 and in Peter's speech presuppose biblical reflection that must lie close to the heart of the theological tradition.

As a way back to that interpretive tradition, Dodd begins with OT quotations or allusions that are found in more than one strand of NT tradition. He takes seriously the observations that led Harris to develop his theory of testimony books but believes the data can be accounted for without recourse to Harris's theory. What best explains the phenomenon of shared quotations, in Dodd's view, is a shared method of exegesis and a common stock of basic texts: "[Paul's] selection of passages seems to be largely dictated by the postulate that certain particular parts of scripture have direct relevance to the events announced in the *kerygma*."[34] His task is to discover that reservoir of texts and to discover why they were selected. He acknowledges the hypothetical nature of such reconstruction:

> By comparison of one passage with others, and of one writer with another, we may be able to draw inferences regarding the general principles which underlie the use of testimonia by these writers, and perhaps to advance to further inferences regarding the employment of the OT by Christian thinkers and teachers in the pre-literary period.[35]

Dodd gathers his list of passages included in the original stock of testimonia and proceeds to group them under three headings: (1) apocalyptic and eschatological; (2) Scriptures of the new Israel; (3) Servant of the Lord and the Righteous Sufferer. The categories offer some glimpse of Dodd's principles of organization. The apocalyptic texts are characterized by the quotation from Joel in Acts 2:

> The employment of these scriptures as testimonies to the *kerygma* indicates that the crisis out of which the Christian movement arose is regarded as the realization of the prophetic vision of judgment and redemption.[36]

It is not surprising that realized eschatology should emerge as the dominant theme in Dodd's reconstruction.

What unites passages in Dodd's third grouping is the image of the servant of Isaiah and the Righteous Sufferer from the psalms. The "plot" provides the consistency. It is important to Dodd's construction that the servant poems from Isaiah, and individual psalms like Psalm 22, were read as wholes. Even if only scattered references appear in a given work, we must presume that the larger passage was in view. This allows Dodd to explain the scattered and sporadic citations of basic texts like Isaiah 53 as arising from an originally unified conception. Individual citations are bits and pieces of a complete

---

33. Ibid., 12.
34. Ibid., 23.
35. Ibid., 28.
36. Ibid., 72.

mosaic that we never glimpse as a whole. The similarity to Rudolf Bultmann's "gnostic redeemer myth" is apparent, and Dodd's views can be subject to the same kinds of attack. Is a consistent interpretation of servant poems given from the beginning, or is a unified interpretation common at the time of Justin Martyr the end product of a lengthy process? Such questions are critical to our whole enterprise.

What holds Dodd's construction together is his view of early Christianity, his own version of Albert Schweitzer's proposal. Schweitzer insisted that the pieces of the puzzle fit together only if we understand everything from the perspective of eschatology—meaning the firm conviction that the end of history was at hand. Only from that vantage point do Jesus' actions make sense. Only the nonoccurrence of Jesus' return and the end of history allow us to understand the production of Christian literature.[37] Dodd agrees in large measure with Schweitzer, but he believes that Jesus' message—and the message of the church—was that the kingdom *had come*. Scripture is read with the sense that prophecies have been fulfilled. What held things together, according to Dodd, was a view of history:

> History . . . is built upon a certain pattern corresponding to God's design for man His creature. . . . It is this pattern, disclosed "in divers parts and divers manners" in the past history of Israel, that the NT writers conceive to have been brought into full light in the event of the gospel story, which they interpret accordingly.[38]

Scriptural interpretation, then, is an argument about and a comment upon a view of history that Dodd is willing to term "biblical":

> The main line of interpretation of the OT exemplified in the New is not only consistent and intelligent in itself, but also founded upon a genuinely historical understanding of the process of the religious—I should prefer to say the prophetic—history of Israel as a whole.[39]

Conversation with Dodd is possible at many levels, since his study is obviously of a piece with the rest of his exegetical and constructive work as an NT historian. We can see clearly where important decisions have been made in each of the three areas outlined for the present endeavor. We can ask, for example, if his proposals are conceivable in light of first-century scriptural exegesis. Serious questions can be raised at this level. Though he may be correct in postulating a core of scriptural passages that were mined by a broad spectrum of Christian groups, his arguments against "atomistic exegesis" cannot be sustained. Christian interpreters, like their Jewish contemporaries, were capable of abstracting a verse or a sentence from its literary context to make a point or to discover a new truth in it. Continuity was provided not by a view of history (here Dodd is highly anachronistic) but by an all-encompassing "truth" that could embrace the meaning of literary units as well as more artfully discovered truths in smaller fragments of Holy Writ.

---

37. The famous view is developed in Schweitzer's *Quest of the Historical Jesus*. The thesis is applied to the whole of Christian dogma by his student Werner, in *Die Entstehung des christlichen Dogmas*.

38. Dodd, *According to the Scriptures,* 128.

39. Ibid., 133.

The relevance of pre-Christian biblical exegesis is likewise apparent. Though no unified interpretation of Psalm 22 or Isaiah 53 is offered in the NT, Dodd argues that the plot in these texts served as a model for understanding Jesus' career. One way to sustain such an argument would be to demonstrate that in Jewish tradition the plots had been worked out in terms of a typical sufferer— whether personified as Israel or as a single figure. If there is no evidence of such unified interpretation, however, it is difficult to rule out the possibility that Christians made use of bits and pieces of psalms or Isaiah 53 until finally a unified interpretation was produced. That would mean, however, that some other explanation would have to be offered for the use of precisely these texts. If there existed no mythic construct such as an apocalyptic Son of man or a Suffering Servant or a Righteous Sufferer, but only the scriptural potential for the construction of such figures, what appear to us as coherent interpretive traditions may well be the product of our imaginations. The so-called plots of Psalm 22 and Isaiah 53 may not have been the starting point for Christian interpretation at all but only a later byproduct. Several scholars have, like Dodd, suggested that Isaiah 61 was important to Christian interpreters because it permitted them to speak about Jesus as "anointed." Does that mean, however, that "Christ" is a term used of Jesus because passages from Isaiah were perceived to be appropriate to him? Or are passages from Isaiah appropriate because Jesus is confessed as the Christ? Our knowledge of postbiblical exegesis in the pre-Christian era has an important bearing on such questions.

That leads once again to the matter of starting points and approach. Dodd chooses to begin with shared quotations and allusions. That means ignoring possible deposits of earlier traditions that are not quoted, however. The use of the term "seed" to speak of Jesus derives from an interpretation of Psalm 89 and 2 Samuel 7, yet in the passages where it is used, no reference is made to either text. We must begin with quotations and allusions we can find, but there is no guarantee that they will provide a starting point for the history of exegesis. Scriptural terminology that has become part of a standard vocabulary cannot be excluded from consideration. Dodd exhibits a preference for material in Acts, but his reasons can in most cases no longer be accepted. And finally, when pressed about the ultimate starting point for the history of scriptural interpretation exhibited by the NT, he can only suggest that this "creative interpretation" of the Scriptures probably began with Jesus himself.[40] Making Jesus an advocate for a view of history that generates a profoundly distinctive interpretation of Scripture and tradition does not solve the problems Dodd laid out in his provocative study. His invitation to the scholarly world deserves further response.

A PROPOSAL

The focus of this study is Christian interpretation of the Scriptures; to be more precise, it is christological interpretation of the OT. We possess

---

40. Ibid., 110. See also J. Jeremias, *New Testament Theology,* 288–93, inter alia; and Chilton, *A Galilean Rabbi.*

letters and narratives (e.g., the Gospels, Acts, the Apocalypse) written by people who believed Jesus to be the one sent by God to redeem the world. Their convictions were expressed in a variety of ways. Basic to all speech about Jesus, however, is the language and imagery of the OT. Our task is to understand how that scriptural language was used to speak both about Jesus and about the significance and implications of his ministry. Jesus' own understanding of the Scriptures, if that can even be determined, is of relevance only as it is crucial to our understanding of the exegesis of the community of believers.

Study of christological exegesis is an approach to NT Christology that has certain advantages over traditional approaches. The study of christological titles has frequently given the false impression that the first believers had available to them a number of distinct eschatological constructs, each with a particular label like "Son of man," "Son of God," "Lord," or "Christ." In fact, the titles frequently overlap in meaning to a considerable extent, and the alleged construct to which the titles refer may even prove to be the product of scholarly creativity in the present. The "apocalyptic Son of man," for example, probably did not exist in the imaginations of first-century Jews and Christians (see below, pp. 165–70).

Acknowledging the scriptural roots of christological language provides greater control over scholarly imagination. The categories employed by the first believers came from the Scriptures. That does not mean, as we have seen, that expressions like "Son of God" or "prophet" meant only what they meant in their original setting in the OT. Influences from the environment had been brought to bear on the scriptural texts during the centuries after they were written. We have some insight into that process, however, and by observing how certain biblical texts and images were handled in pre-Christian interpretive traditions, we can gain a more accurate impression of what options were available to those who wished to reflect on the meaning of Jesus' ministry. In light of that traditional exegesis, we can observe how texts are often used in the NT, noting what is distinctive about Christian interpretation; we can determine why particular passages were selected as appropriate to Jesus, how the biblical material was harmonized in sketching portraits of Jesus, and what "controlling ideas" are discernible in the history of exegesis.

Any history of christological exegesis should probably speak in terms of a logical rather than a chronological development. The somewhat rigid chronological scheme employed by Reginald H. Fuller, according to which an eschatological orientation is typical of an early period and "high" Christologies of a later period, fails to acknowledge that from the very first, people spoke about Jesus differently in various settings.[41] The language appropriate to prayer and praise was not the same as language used in confessions of faith and preaching or exhortation. The high Christology of Paul's hymn in Philippians 2 can boast an antiquity perhaps as great as that of the confessional summary in 1 Cor. 15:3–7, and both may be older than the "lower" prophetic Christology found in Luke-Acts. There were developments, and we may reasonably attempt to discern some order in the evolution of Christology. Perhaps the most we can hope for, however, is some logical ordering of various developments in areas of hymnic, confessional, and parenetic tradition.

Where do we begin? In fact, a choice has already been made. We have begun with a look at the confessional tradition behind 1 Cor. 15:3–7, for reasons which are perhaps obvious. The confessional summary highlights central features of the "gospel." Jesus' crucifixion and resurrection were the foundation of Christian preaching and Christian faith. The events were understood by NT authors as the decisive moments in Jesus' ministry and marked a transition from one time to another that could only be described by means of eschatological categories. It is hardly surprising that these events likewise provided the locus for much of the scriptural interpretation that characterized the first decades of the religious renewal. The use of the formula "according to the scriptures," which appears almost exclusively with statements about Jesus' death and resurrection, only underlines the point.

Similarly, we have noted the prominence of the title Messiah in traditions about Jesus' death and resurrection. Werner Kramer has shown that the term "Christ" is used with terms like *kēryssein, euaggelion,* and *pistis/pisteuein,* where the title Lord does not appear, settings in which death/resurrection references predominate.[42] The remarkable concentration of royal imagery in the four accounts of Jesus' death in the Gospels provides support for the analysis of material found principally in Paul's letters. We begin our study of christological exegesis, therefore, by focusing on the crucified and risen Messiah.

Lindars makes a similar decision in *New Testament Apologetic,* with one difference: he chooses to begin with traditions about the resurrection.

---

41. The two studies that have employed the most structured chronological approach to Christology are those by Fuller (*Foundations of New Testament Christology*) and Hahn (*Titles of Jesus in Christology*).
42. Kramer, *Christ, Lord, Son of God,* 133–50.

In the very first phase after the Resurrection there was probably some uncertainty exactly how what had been accomplished in Jesus should be interpreted. It was clear that all he had said and done had been triumphantly vindicated, in spite of apparent failure. His preaching that the coming kingdom was near proved to be true. Since he had risen from the dead, it was evident that he would still take the lead in the kingdom. In other words, there could be no doubt that he was to be identified with the Lord's Messiah.[43]

The instincts are good, but the logic is faulty at crucial points. It is not clear that Christians believed "all that he had said and done had been triumphantly vindicated." Jesus had been vindicated, but much was uncertain. Among the uncertainties was the "nearness" of the kingdom. What does Lindars's statement mean? What did Jesus' followers think about the kingdom? And regardless of our answer to that question, Jesus' vindication would not have convinced anyone that he was Messiah—as Schweitzer argued many years ago:

How can the appearances of the risen Jesus have suggested to the disciples the idea that Jesus, the crucified teacher, was the Messiah? Apart from any expectations, how can this conclusion have resulted for them from the mere "fact of the resurrection"? The fact of the appearance did not by any means imply it. In certain circles, indeed, according to Mark 6:14–16, in the very highest quarters, the resurrection of the Baptist was believed in; but that did not make John the Baptist the Messiah.[44]

Jesus' resurrection by itself would have convinced no one that he was the Messiah, since no one expected the Messiah to die or to be raised from the dead. The resurrection would have been understood as proof of his messiahship only if a messianic claim were already an issue, only if messiahship were somehow at stake at his death. That is, in fact, precisely what the Gospels suggest: Jesus was executed as a pretender to royalty, as King of the Jews.

The argument has been forcefully made by Nils Dahl in "The Crucified Messiah."[45] The extraordinary force of Jesus' personality and authority has left its mark on christological tradition. His ministry of healing and teaching cannot, however, serve as the basis for the claim that he is Messiah. The NT makes no such claim. Nor can the claim be derived from Jesus' own teaching and exegesis. Such a derivation must rely on arguments from silence and ignore the NT's portrayal of Jesus'

---

43. Lindars, *New Testament Apologetic,* 32.
44. Schweitzer, *Quest of the Historical Jesus,* 343.
45. Dahl, "The Crucified Messiah," in *The Crucified Messiah,* 10–36.

remarkable caution regarding a messianic claim. In biblical tradition, the confession of Jesus as Messiah is bound up with his last days in Jerusalem. The one certain historical fact is that he was executed as King of the Jews, a charge that was construed in political terms by the Romans and in religious terms by the Jewish leadership. In Mark's passion narrative, when Jews speak the terms are "the Christ, the Son of the Blessed" (Mark 14:61) and "the Christ, the King of Israel" (15:32); the formulation "King of the Jews" is Roman. Though the Gospels display extraordinary reserve about Jesus' attitude toward messiahship throughout his ministry, they all agree that when the question was put to Jesus, "Are you the Messiah?" he did not deny it. It is in the context of those last days in Jerusalem that the royal title emerges publicly as a potential estimate of Jesus. On the basis of such a possibility, Jesus was executed as a messianic pretender. And for that reason his resurrection can be understood as God's vindication of the crucified Messiah.

Dahl's hypothetical reconstruction can explain why messianic imagery and the title Christ should be so closely associated with Jesus' death: that is the historical occasion for their rise to prominence in Jesus' ministry. Apart from Acts 3, Jesus is called Christ not in anticipation of his coming reign but with reference to his death and his vindication on the third day.

What lies at the heart of Christian tradition and christological exegesis is the confession of Jesus as the crucified and risen Messiah, a confession that involves considerable tension between Jesus the Christ and the traditional messianic figure that was part of Jewish eschatological scriptural exegesis. Christian interpretation of the Scriptures arose from the recognition that Jesus was the expected Messiah *and* that he did not fit the picture. The lack of a pre-Christian Jewish concept of a suffering Messiah provides one of the first agenda items for the small circle of believers. The slogan "in accordance with the scriptures" expresses the conviction that the God who raised the crucified Messiah from the dead is the God of Abraham, Isaac, and Jacob, whose promises somehow find their confirmation in Jesus of Nazareth. The extensive exploration of the Scriptures generated by faith in Jesus the Messiah is what we will examine in subsequent chapters of this book.

I intend this volume to be a contribution to the contemporary discussion of NT Christology, a conversation that involves systematic theologians as well as biblical scholars. At the end I will comment on the further implications and relationships to other christological studies.

Alternative Opinions

Before proceeding to the investigations, however, a word is in order about a view, espoused by at least two prominent scholars, that explicitly rejects a proposal such as the one made here. The proponents of the alternative opinion are A. E. Harvey, in his interesting volume *Jesus and the Constraints of History,* and Klaus Berger, whose two essays, "Die königlichen Messiastraditionen" and "Zum traditions-geschichtlichen Hintergrund christologischer Hoheitstitel," have had a profound impact on Edward Schillebeeckx's widely read and massive proposal.[46]

Both Harvey and Berger find the confession of Jesus as Messiah particularly troublesome. They are familiar with the concept in Jewish tradition and thus know its apparent inappropriateness as a designation for Jesus. Approaching the accounts of Jesus' trial and death from the perspective of Jesus' ministry, Harvey finds the Gospel accounts inherently improbable if they are taken to suggest that Jesus accepted the designation Messiah. In addition, he does not believe Jesus' followers could have found the title useful either. In support of his views he quotes Schillebeeckx, who in turn is heavily dependent upon Berger:

E. Schillebeeckx has recently drawn attention to the sheer improbability of the Christians, immediately after the resurrection, having been able, not merely to claim that the crucified Jesus was the Messiah (if "Messiah" meant a victorious Davidic leader) but to have coined, and persuaded others of, an entirely new meaning for that term. He writes: "Without already existing models it was out of the question for a triumphalist, Jewish messiah concept to be reshaped within a few years by the Christians into a suffering Messiah."[47]

How seriously can we take Schillebeeckx's skepticism? Common sense is certainly not to be despised. Views about what was or was not possible, however, must arise from historical study. Proposals must be tested in light of the "constraints" of language and tradition—the very point of Harvey's book! Harvey's arguments in support of his views of the Gospel accounts derive from his study of Jewish eschatological tradition. He argues not simply that eschatological beliefs were fluid in first-century Jewish communities but that there existed no clarity whatever with respect to the title Messiah (an argument made also by de Jonge):

The title was apparently not a common one, nor would it necessarily have carried much meaning unless qualified and explained; and the expectations of Jews, though they certainly included in many quarters a lively longing for a new . . . supernatural age, did not necessarily specify an individual who would help bring it into being.[48]

Harvey is correct in pointing to various eschatological traditions within Judaism that display little interest in redeemer figures. His comment about the

---

46. For the works of Harvey and Berger, see n. 15 above. See also Schillebeeckx, *Jesus: An Experiment in Christology.*

47. Harvey, *Jesus and the Constraints,* 137.

48. Ibid., 45.

lack of clarity regarding the designation Messiah, however, is incorrect. We have already noted the familiar constellation of biblical texts acknowledged as messianic by a wide variety of Jewish groups. In *Jesus the Jew,* Vermes nicely summarizes evidence that the "Lord's Anointed" from the line of David was a recognizable figure in pre-Christian tradition.[49] The seventeenth and eighteenth *Psalms of Solomon* sketch a detailed picture of the expected king, features of which are recognizable in the Qumran scrolls, in the benediction of the morning prayer, and in the *Testament of Judah,* as well as in later rabbinic and targumic traditions.

The most important evidence, however, is the NT itself. In his concern to demonstrate a consistency in Jesus' ministry from beginning to end, Harvey must ride roughshod over the passion narratives. All four evangelists leave no doubt how the title Messiah is to be understood at this point in the story. The imagery in the passion traditions is consistently royal.

The matter is perhaps clearest in Mark's account of Jesus' death. The predominant feature of his narrative is irony, as I have argued elsewhere.[50] The irony is possible because the reader knows something that participants in the story do not: Jesus is the Messiah. Jesus' response to the question of the high priest, "Are you the Christ, the Son of the Blessed?" leaves no ambiguity: "I am; and you will see . . ." (Mark 14:61–62). It is equally obvious that Jesus' opponents recognize he does not fit the category of Messiah. They regard the appellation as comic, absurd, blasphemous, and seditious. Thus Jesus is mocked, tried, condemned as the King of the Jews or Christ the King of Israel. The Roman garrison pays mock homage to the King. The irony is that those who mock speak the truth. They are the agents of his investiture; they hail him as King with their taunts. They testify to a truth hidden from them, and thus fulfill Jesus' predictions and what is written in the Scriptures as Mark understands them. The tension crucial to the narrative depends upon the truth of the claim that Jesus is the Messiah *and* upon the apparent inappropriateness of that claim. Jesus' enemies, both Jewish and Roman, know very well that "Messiah" means "king"—and that Jesus seems anything but royal. Even if we had no access whatever to first-century Jewish tradition, we would have to infer from Mark that for Jews, the Messiah meant something very specific that made it difficult to imagine that Jesus could be the long-awaited deliverer from the line of David.

The problem to which Harvey points—the non-messianic ministry of Jesus and his messianic death—is a real one. His solution is untenable. His attempt to explain the use of "anointed" from traditions about prophetic figures is ingenious, but it cannot be sustained by evidence from the NT or from Jewish tradition. Apart from the two occurrences of "anointed ones" used of the prophets in the Qumran scrolls (CD II, 12; VI, 1), prophets are not referred to as the Lord's anointed in eschatological tradition. And even at Qumran, no single prophet is called the anointed One or the Lord's Anointed (singular). Without some striking new piece of evidence, there is little reason to disagree with Vermes that the

---

49. Vermes, *Jesus the Jew,* 130–40.
50. Juel, *Messiah and Temple.*

definite "the Messiah" could have been understood in NT times only as a reference to the coming King.[51]

What stands at the heart of the kerygma—and thus at the beginning of Christian tradition—is the surprise that God's Messiah should appear as one who died on a cross. The resurrection did not efface the problem but placed it squarely in the path of those who sought to follow the crucified and risen Christ. God had vindicated the one who died as the King of the Jews. Their task was to understand how such things could be and what the implications were, and it led them into the Scriptures with a specific agenda. The character of those explorations was determined largely by the interpretive world of which the first believers were a part. To the nature of that interpretive world we now turn.

---

51. Vermes, *Jesus the Jew*, 139, 159. For a review of evidence in the NT, see Kramer, *Christ, Lord, Son of God*, 203–15; and Dahl, "Messiahship of Jesus."

2

RULES
OF THE GAME

Biblical Interpretation in
the First Century C.E.

THE NEED FOR EXEGESIS

By the time of Jesus, Judaism had become a religion of the book. That had not always been the case. The production of a national literature probably began with the rise of the monarchy and the creation of an elite capable of producing and appreciating literary works. The nation's earlier history left an indelible impression on literary productions, but without the organization of the cult and the support of an educated class by the monarchy little would ever have been written down. Subsequent centuries witnessed the composition and collection of various kinds of material, from narratives to legal codes to liturgical material and prophetic oracles. Study of that impressive body of literature has offered a picture of Israel's place in the larger family of nations in the ancient Near East and of the nation's evolution over a period of many centuries.

It was in the postexilic period that Israel's religion came to be bound so closely to sacred writings. The priestly redaction of the Pentateuch and the composition of Chronicles were critical moments in the transformation that occurred. Chronicles was a rewriting of earlier historical books. Many of the characteristics of later biblical interpretation can be observed in the method of the chronicler.[1] By the time of Ezra, a scholarly

---

1. Among studies of textual adaptation within the Scriptures, Sandmel's "The Haggadah within Scripture," *JBL* 80 (1961), is perhaps one of the best-known

tradition appears to have been established. Ezra is described as a priest and a scribe, "learned in matters of the commandments of the Lord and his statutes for Israel" (Ezra 7:11); he "had set his heart to study the law of the Lord, and to do it, and to teach his statutes and ordinances in Israel" (Ezra 7:10). His major reform included public reading of the law (Nehemiah 8).[2]

There is much we do not know about the Persian and the Hellenistic periods in Israel's history, the centuries that witnessed the editing of the Torah, the editing and collecting of the prophetic corpus, the cessation of literary production, the collection of "sacred writings" and the attribution of sacred status to that material, the rise of scholarly interpretation and a class of learned scribes. The importance of this era for understanding the subsequent history of Israel can scarcely be overestimated. It is no surprise that the era should have been subjected to such intense investigation in the last decades.[3]

By the first century, biblical interpretation had become an essential feature of Jewish intellectual life. Scholarly interpreters of the written tradition had largely replaced the priests as guardians of the heritage and experts on legal matters. They had developed an elaborate hermeneutical mechanism with which to make sense of sacred texts, to fit them into a harmonious whole, and to apply them to the realities of life in the Greco-Roman world. Specific interpretive traditions had grown up, some with roots far back into the postbiblical era and beyond. Exegesis had become a primary mode of intellectual discourse.

The need to interpret written texts, of course, had been felt long

---

essays. See now Fishbane, *Biblical Interpretation in Ancient Israel.* Also helpful are the chaps. by Kugel in Kugel and Greer, *Early Biblical Interpretation.* From the enormous and growing body of material on midrash, the following are especially useful: R. Bloch, "Methodological Note for the Study of Rabbinic Literature," in *Approaches to Ancient Judaism,* ed. Green, 1:54; idem, "Midrash," in ibid., 29–51; Porton, *Understanding Rabbinic Midrash;* Vermes, "Bible and Midrash: Early Old Testament Exegesis," in *Post-Biblical Jewish Studies,* 59–91; Schürer, *HJP* 1:90–99, vol. 2; Le Deaut, "Apropos a Definition of Midrash," *Int* 25 (1971): 259–82; and Seeligman, "Voraussetzungen der Midrashexegese," *VTSup* 1 (1953): 150–81.

2. The point is not so much the centrality of law as such as the importance of legal tradition in the form of sacred texts.

3. Among important studies of the intertestamental era are Hengel, *Judaism and Hellenism;* Vermes, *Scripture and Tradition;* idem, *Post-Biblical Jewish Studies;* Nickelsburg, *Jewish Literature between the Bible and the Mishnah;* Stone, *Scripture, Sects, and Visions;* Schürer, *HJP;* and Kugel and Greer, *Early Biblical Interpretation.* A helpful collection of primary sources is provided in Nickelsburg and Stone, *Faith and Piety in Early Judaism.*

before the final editing and collecting of works that were to become Sacred Scriptures.[4] The collection of scriptural works, however, greatly spurred the development of learned method. This is particularly true of the Torah, which, certainly since the time of Ezra, was acknowledged as the special source of revelation from God. It offered the faithful a picture of what it meant to be the people of God. The holy texts were read on the Sabbath and at religious festivals. But even by the time of Ezra, translations were required, since few people understood biblical Hebrew. The great reading of the law, which began Ezra's reform, had to be accompanied by interpretation. Ezra's colleagues

> helped the people to understand the law, while the people remained in their places. And they read from the book, from the law of God, clearly; and they gave the sense, so that the people understood the reading. (Neh. 8:7–8)

The need for Targumim—translations or paraphrases in the vernacular—demanded that the *meturgemanin* (the translators) understood the Hebrew. They could hardly translate what they did not understand. Unusual Hebrew words had to be explained; cryptic passages had to be interpreted; some contexts had to be supplied for laws or rules whose original setting had long been forgotten; crude phrases or religiously unacceptable concepts, like anthropomorphisms, had to be dealt with so as not to offend the faithful. Geza Vermes terms the response to such basic requirements "pure" exegesis, necessary simply to understand the written text.[5]

Translation included more than finding suitable Aramaic or Greek terms for the Hebrew. It also involved accommodation to a new setting. Laws had to be applied to a society that was very different from the original for which the laws were intended. Decisions had to be made about matters that were not covered in the Torah. To serve as a guide for life, the Scriptures had to be "actualized" in the experience of the faithful. In the area of "applied exegesis" as well (to use Vermes's term), creative responses were demanded of the learned interpreters of the Scriptures. The result was the development of exegetical method and traditions of interpretation.

The response to the need for biblical interpretation assumed several forms. One was a rewritten biblical text. *The Biblical Antiquities* of

---

4. See Vermes, "Bible and Midrash"; note also the comments by Porton (*Understanding Rabbinic Midrash,* 5–6, 10 nn. 14–16). One of the clearest examples is in Dan. 9:2, 24, where the seer is shown that the reference to seventy years of desolation in Jeremiah (25:11, 12; 29:10) means seventy weeks of years.

5. Vermes, "Bible and Midrash," 63–80.

Pseudo-Philo and the *Genesis Apocryphon* are examples. Biblical stories were retold, but with characteristic embellishment and necessary "corrections."[6] Careful examination of the corrections and the embellishments demonstrates that these compositions depend upon the kind of interpretive work attested in the more familiar forms of interpretation (e.g., midrashim and Targumim).

Another response was allegorical exegesis. This technique of interpretation is known from the commentaries of Hellenistic philosophers and is best exemplified in the work of Philo of Alexandria. Texts were read as elaborate pointers to another realm. Philo read Abraham's migration, for example, as an allegorical account of the migration of reason from the realm of the senses (symbolized by Ur of Chaldea, the region known for the practice of astrology) to the realm of pure thought (symbolized by the promised land). The techniques—the use of etymology, the employment of conventional symbolism—were also practiced by interpreters of dreams and by students of Homer who discovered hidden realms of meaning in his writings (originally defending them against charges leveled by Plato).[7] Robert Hammerton-Kelly has produced an interesting piece on Philo's technique which offers some insight into the method. Though allegory permitted interpreters almost unlimited freedom to derive meaning from texts, there was method in the procedure as well as a tradition of conventional symbols, and the text exercised some constraints on the imagination. Allegorical exegesis is not common in NT or rabbinic writings, but there are examples. Galatians 4:21–31 is an example from the NT; the Song of Songs is consistently treated as an allegory in rabbinic writings, describing the relationship between God and Israel using the image of lovers.

A third form of interpretation was the Targum, a paraphrase of the Hebrew into the vernacular, which we noted briefly above. We possess only Aramaic Targumim, but it is possible that Greek versions existed as well; they would have been rendered unnecessary, however, by the translation of the whole Bible into Greek—the Septuagint. The practice is traced to the time of Ezra. Targumic traditions evolved gradually and

---

6. For analyses of "rewritten Bible," like the *Biblical Antiquities* of Pseudo-Philo, see Vermes, *Scripture and Tradition*, 67–126.

7. The standard work on allegorical exegesis is R. Hanson's *Allegory and Event*. See also Christiansen, *Die Technik der allegorischen Auslegungswissenschaft bei Philon von Alexandria*, and Hammerton-Kelly, "Some Techniques of Composition in Philo's Allegorical Commentary with Special Reference to *De Agricultura*," in *Jews, Greeks, and Christians*, ed. Hammerton-Kelly and Scroggs, 45–56.

were written down only centuries after the Common Era.[8] In many cases, the Targumim are fairly literal translations. Often, however, the translations—or paraphrases—presuppose creative interpretations of the Hebrew known from other exegetical literature, employing techniques shared with the learned community. One of the most striking examples of creative exegesis and interpretive freedom is known from the Targum on Isaiah, a passage that will be discussed later. The famous "servant poem" beginning in Isa. 52:13 is consistently applied in the Targum to the Messiah. The interpretation is possible because the Hebrew "servant" is used, elsewhere in the Scriptures, of the Messiah. In the Targum's version of the poem, the suffering is transferred to the enemies of the Messiah, and he, God's exalted servant (52:13), appears triumphant throughout. The reinterpretation is accomplished by clever changes in the language (see below, chap. 5).

The Targumim are important as evidence of interpretive traditions often shared with the larger community and attested in rewritten Bible versions, in Philo's allegorical exegesis, or in early Christian, Qumran, or rabbinic tradition. But our major source of information about scriptural interpretation is a body of commentaries called the midrashim. It is to these that we now turn.

MIDRASHIC EXEGESIS

The most frequently used term to describe biblical exegesis in the postbiblical era is "midrash"—from the Hebrew *darash,* "to seek," "to interpret." The term is used in several different ways. It refers first to a body of literature, the midrashim, scriptural commentaries or collections of individual reflections on biblical material which began to appear in the fifth century. Second, the term is used to speak of a particular comment on a biblical phrase or verse—a midrash. Finally, the word is used more loosely to speak of the approach to scriptural interpretation characteristic of "midrashic" literature.

An impressive body of scholarly literature has appeared in the last decades that focuses on midrash. The interest was generated in large measure by the publication of the Dead Sea Scrolls. The fresh body of

---

8. On the Targumim, see Schürer, *HJP* 1:99–113 (note the extensive bibliography); McNamara, *The New Testament and the Palestinian Targum to the Pentateuch;* idem, *Targum and Testament;* Bowker, *The Targums and Rabbinic Literature;* Chilton, *Glory of Israel;* and York, "The Dating of Targumic Literature," *JSJ* 5 (1974): 49–62.

evidence regarding the character of first-century Judaism has stimulated a thorough reappraisal of earlier pictures of rabbinic Judaism, or "normative Judaism." Central to that reappraisal is scriptural interpretation. The abundance of exegetical writings in the Qumran library and the distinctive features of Qumran exegesis have stimulated interest in the use of Scripture in postbiblical Judaism, a matter of importance for students of the NT as well as of rabbinic Judaism.[9]

The learned discussion of midrash has been difficult to follow, largely because scholars are interested in different features of the overall problem. This is apparent even in the various attempts to define the term. Addison Wright made an initial contribution in his work *The Literary Genre Midrash*. Coming to the problem of definition from his study of the Gospel of Matthew, Wright was concerned to establish some precision in terminology. He argued that "midrash" should be understood largely as a category describing a literary genre defined by external features. It refers to a kind of literature—a literature about literature, a "work that attempts to make a text of Scripture understandable, useful, and relevant for a later generation."[10] His proposal has not met with the approval of most students of scriptural exegesis, because it speaks of midrash in too narrow a fashion. Father R. Le Deaut, noted for his studies of the Akedah and the "poem of the four nights" in the *Palestinian Targum* on Exodus, responded to Wright that if we are to speak of "midrash" only as a literary genre, the term will be inappropriate for the time of the NT and earlier. The midrashic collections of various types began to appear only in the fifth century, and the precise form of interpretive comments common to the collections owes much to the rabbinic schools in which they developed.[11] The particular interpretations, however, and the approach to the scriptural text may be typical of earlier periods. Le Deaut believes that the terms should be extended to include method as well as literary form:

> The term *midrash* expresses the conviction that the ultimate answer is to be found in searching the scriptures where it will be revealed to whoever knows how to search.[12]

---

9. Vermes, "The Impact of the Dead Sea Scrolls on Jewish Studies during the Last Twenty-Five Years," in *Approaches to Ancient Judaism,* ed. Green, 1:201–14; and Vermes, *The Dead Sea Scrolls.* See also Fitzmyer, "The Contribution of Qumran Aramaic to the Study of the New Testament," in *A Wandering Aramean,* 85–114.

10. Wright, *The Literary Genre Midrash,* 74.

11. Le Deaut, "Apropos a Definition."

12. Ibid., 270.

As one interested in pre-mishnaic times, Le Deaut wants to explore what is implied in the "how to search."

Still another perspective is characteristic of those interested primarily in rabbinic literature, who are concerned to allow for a proper estimate of the contribution of the schools to the literary deposit we now know as the midrashim. Gary Porton, a student of Jacob Neusner who has studied traditions about rabbinic authorities and the formal characteristics of rabbinic tradition, has been impressed by the distinctive changes wrought by sages in the decades and centuries following the Bar Kokhba war. He is furthermore concerned to emphasize the distinctive features of reflection within the Jewish community. Certain forms of argument were shared with other sages in the Greco-Roman world. What is special about midrash is the attachment to a text:

> In brief, I would define midrash as a type of literature, oral or written, which stands in direct relationship to a fixed, canonical text, considered to be the authoritative and the revealed word of God by the midrashist and his audience, and in which this canonical text is explicitly cited or clearly alluded to.[13]

Such precision is important, he believes, because it serves as a safeguard against anachronism. Commentaries produced by rabbinic schools cannot be used uncritically to reconstruct a picture of Jewish interpretation in the pre–Bar Kokhba era.[14] Significant innovations were introduced by rabbinic sages, which form-critical analysis can disclose. Neusner himself has argued, for example, that midrashic collections assembled by rabbinic schools, like *Sifra,* owe their distinctive shape and features to the innovative mentality that produced the Mishnah.[15] The differences between these midrashim, on the one hand, and scriptural commentaries at Qumran, on the other, signal differences between the respective societies and can serve as evidence of the striking changes in Judaism that occurred with the production of the Mishnah.

Yet formal questions are not the sole considerations in the study of postbiblical scriptural interpretation. The rabbinic midrashim still share both an approach to the scriptural text and specific interpretive traditions with Qumran commentaries, targumic literature, and the

---

13. Porton, "Defining Midrash," in *The Study of Ancient Judaism,* ed. J. Neusner, 62. See now Porton, *Understanding Rabbinic Midrash.*

14. Neusner, "The Use of Later Rabbinic Evidence for the Study of First-Century Pharisaism," in *Approaches to Ancient Judaism,* ed. Green, 1:215–28; and Vermes, *Jesus and the World of Judaism,* 58–88.

15. Neusner, *Midrash in Context,* 103ff.

NT. It is this world of shared approach and interpretive traditions that is of the greatest interest to us.

The work of Vermes, influenced by that of Renée Bloch, is perhaps the most relevant to the study of messianic exegesis. Vermes speaks of midrash in the broad sense as the "study and exposition of the written word in school and synagogue."[16] He is particularly interested in the historical development of midrashic tradition, and he traces interpretive traditions through various bodies of literature. Antecedents of traditions found in late rabbinic works can be detected in pre-Christian times by careful study of datable material, like the Qumran scrolls, Philo, Josephus, and intertestamental works. Creative exegesis developed early, and once formulated, particular interpretations could dominate for centuries the way a passage was read. Vermes's study of the Dead Sea Scrolls has convinced him that the "Qumran interpreters took over from pre-sectarian Judaism a body of exegetical tradition already fully developed and in advance of the purely literal significance of the Scripture."[17] Of this tradition, he states,

> The disclosure of a body of interpretive tradition prior to, and free from, any sectarian bias is one of the most important contributions made by Qumran literature to our knowledge of Palestinian religious thought.[18]

Various groups within the Jewish community, from the Qumran sectarians to authors of apocalypses, early Christians, and the rabbis, were heirs of this heritage. The distinctive features of each group emerge in their use of that heritage, not in the development of a whole new hermeneutical approach to the Scriptures. The interpretive ethos within which various circles worked remained remarkably stable from prebiblical times until well into the Middle Ages.

Defining the Midrashic Method

At the most elementary level, midrash is explanation and explication of the Scriptures. In rabbinic commentaries, considerable effort is expended simply in making clear what the text says. We can assume that such explanations were sought from the moment the texts became important as texts. Words often need to be explained. In Exod. 12:13, for example, a verb with the consonants *psh* is used. The verb is translated "skip over": "And when I see the blood, I will skip over you, and no

---

16. Vermes, *Post-Biblical Jewish Studies,* 38. See Bloch, "Midrash."
17. Vermes, *Post-Biblical Jewish Studies,* 46.
18. Ibid., 47.

plague will fall upon you to destroy you." The literal meaning hardly seems appropriate to the context, so it is "enriched" by appeal to its usage elsewhere in the Scriptures. One opinion is credited to Rabbi Ishmael:

> The word *pasachti* means nothing but protection, as it is said, "like birds hovering, so the Lord of hosts will protect Jerusalem; he will protect Jerusalem; he will protect and deliver it, he will spare (*pasoach*) and rescue it" (Isa. 31:5).[19]

The technique is familiar to all who have used a concordance. Meaning is determined by context. The use of a word in a setting where the meaning is clear can shed light on a usage where the meaning is less clear. Scripture is interpreted by Scripture.

In Exod. 14:27, we read that Pharaoh pursued the Israelites with "six hundred picked chariots and all the other chariots of Egypt with *shalishim* over all of them." The word *shalishim* requires explanation, since it apparently means "third ones." The commentary on Exodus furnishes an explanation by means of analogy with another scriptural passage, as a first step:

> "And *shalishim* over all of them." The word "shalishim" means mighty men, as in the passage, "captains (*shalishim*) and councillors, all of them riding upon horses" (Ezek. 23:23).[20]

The usage in Ezekiel clearly indicates that the word is a military term and can thus clarify the usage in Exodus. It does not matter that Ezekiel is a prophetic work and Exodus part of the Torah. Both belong to the same scriptural world.

A more creative interpretation is credited to Simon ben Gamaliel, who plays on the root meaning of the term:

> It [*shalishim*] refers to the third man on the chariot. Formerly there had been only two who drove the chariot, but Pharaoh added one more so as to pursue Israel faster.[21]

Modern lexicons speculate that the meaning may well be due to the practice of having three on a chariot. The practice was unfamiliar to people at the time of Simon ben Gamaliel. He uses the linguistic possibilities to dramatize the story as well as to clarify. The tendencies lead to even more inventive readings:

---

19. *MRSBY* 1:56.
20. Ibid., 202.
21. Ibid.

Another interpretation: "And *shalishim* over all of them." This means that there were three of them against each Israelite. Some say there were thirty against each one. And some say three hundred against each one. But how did Pharaoh know how many of the Israelites had died during the three days of darkness and how many of them went out to Egypt? He got out their registers and on the basis of these registers he sent forth armies against them.[22]

Interpretation moves from explanation to heightening the dramatic to the creation of legends that sometimes become part of an exegetical tradition. The possibilities of such creative exegesis are limited only by the imagination of the exegete. Every such comment, however, takes its cue from specific features of the text and depends upon some interpretive mechanism, whether etymology, wordplay, analogy, or the like. These interpretive mechanisms constitute what we would term midrashic method.

Though the explanation and harmonization of scriptural texts were important in rabbinic academies, the Bible was read and studied first of all because it was understood as the Word of God addressed to the present as well as the past. Midrash was the vehicle by which meaning was actualized in the present. Because the primary interest of sages was ethical, and because their ethical conception was based on a legal model, they devoted much of their time as exegetes to explication and application of the Torah. For scholars engaged in deriving principles for the faithful to live by, and in seeking ways to justify specific legal decisions, halakah was primary. Various interpretive mechanisms permitted the extension and application of specific laws by means of inference and analogy. Because exegesis was a community enterprise, rules of argument were required. Lists of such principles, or *middoth,* gradually appeared as hermeneutics became more self-conscious. The first list of seven principles is attributed to Hillel; a list of thirteen is attributed to Ishmael; and finally a list of thirty-two *middoth* is attributed to Eliezer ben Jose ha-Gelili.[23] The lists have always held a prominent place in discussions of rabbinic midrash and frequently provide the point of departure for definitions.

The list attributed to Hillel established principles (*middoth*) for legal argument, making possible the extension of scriptural law to new

---

22. Ibid.
23. Hillel's seven are reported in *t. Sanh.* 7.11; Ishmael's eleven are enumerated in the introduction to *Sifra;* Rabbi Eliezer's thirty-two are found in the *Mishnat de R. Eliezer* (the last list is characterized as appropriate for haggadah). On the exegetical rules, see Schürer, *HJP* 2:343–44.

situations. The first rule, *qal vahomer,* allows for inference from the less important to the more important (or vice versa). In 1 Corinthians 9, Paul quotes Deut. 25:4, which states, "You shall not muzzle an ox when it treads out the grain," to prove that evangelists deserve their wages. If God is concerned about a fair share of the crop for the working oxen, the argument goes, how much more is he concerned about a fair share for those bringing in the harvest in his kingdom. The form of argument is one of the most common in midrashic literature.

The second is also common. *Gezerah shawah* establishes the principle of analogy, based largely on identity of wording in distinct scriptural passages. Both principles are common forms of argument outside midrashic literature as well. Rhetorical forms common to the Greco-Roman world were adapted to the distinctive mode of legal and theological discussion among Jews, namely, scriptural exegesis.

The problem with using the lists as a means of defining midrash is that they are by no means exhaustive of interpretive techniques or rules. Furthermore, some of the principles appear not to have been widely used even by the rabbis to whom they are attributed. Porton, in his thorough study of traditions associated with Rabbi Ishmael, demonstrates that only five of the sage's alleged thirteen *middoth* are employed in his recorded exegetical comments, and that the vast majority of comments make use of either *qal vahomer* or *gezerah shawah,* the two procedures credited to Hillel and common in Greco-Roman literature.[24] Most of the rules were employed prior to the formulation of lists, but the production of the lists presumes a stage in hermeneutical reflection considerably later than the era of the sages to whom they are attributed, and thus later than the period of interest in our study. Defining midrash only by appeal to the lists of *middoth* limits appreciation of the actual operation of interpretation and imposes on earlier times the perspective of later rabbinic schools.[25]

Equally important, it is only the latest of the lists, the thirty-two *middoth* of Eliezer, that purpose to apply primarily to nonlegal midrash (haggadah). The lists of Hillel and Ishmael focus on legal interpretation (halakah). The NT contains virtually no halakhic midrash, a fact of considerable significance in any comparison between early Christian

---

24. Porton, *Traditions of R. Ishmael.*

25. Neusner has argued that even the shape of rabbinic commentaries is largely dependent upon a mode of thinking reflected in the composition of the Mishnah— and thus that these "midrashim" are clearly "rabbinic," meaning products of the religious school that produced the Mishnah.

and later rabbinic institutions. While halakah may more accurately reflect the perspective of those who eventually established rabbinic
courts, haggadah reveals aspects of Judaism more important for understanding the origins of early Christianity, as Bloch observed in her pro-
grammatic article on midrash:

> Indeed, it is obvious that *aggadah* is the aspect of rabbinic literature which
> is the most interesting for the study of the Old and New Testaments, Chris-
> tian origins and ancient Christian literature, and which is most important
> for the understanding of the living religious content of Judaism. Further-
> more, the *aggadah*, essentially homiletic in nature, represents an intrinsi-
> cally religious meditation on immutable sacred texts; it is much less subject
> to fluctuation, to adaptation to ever-changing circumstances, than is the
> *halakah*, whose nature is essentially *practical.* Thus the *aggadah* has a much
> more stable nature, one more apt to conserve extremely ancient traditions.
> To a far greater extent than halakhic literature, the *aggadah* allows one to
> distinguish the constant elements and the evolutions in ancient Jewish tra-
> dition and to situate both of these in the larger framework of the history of
> religions, particularly in relation to Christianity. . . .[26]

Haggadic midrash is better described than defined. Born in liturgical
settings, it is homiletical in nature. Comments are intended to draw a
moral or illustrate a great truth. The occasion for such a comment can
be an unusual word, an apparent redundancy (the sages believed no
word in Scripture is redundant), an unexpected turn in the narrative, or
even an apparent contradiction between two passages. A mechanism
connects the comment with the text, whether a wordplay, an analogy, or
an inference. Comments are usually restricted to a word or a phrase,
though they may arise from larger units as well.

In the commentary on Exodus, known as the *Mekilta,* a variety of
alternative interpretations of Exod. 14:15 are offered. The verse reads,
"The Lord said to Moses, 'Why do you cry to me? Tell the people of
Israel to go forward.'" That the verse has attracted attention is not
difficult to understand, for it seems out of place. In the preceding
verses, the little band of escaped slaves finds itself trapped by
Pharaoh's army. Their escape has been cut off by the wilderness and
the sea. In panic, they cry to God—and attack Moses for leading them
to certain death. Moses responds with a brief exhortation, promising
that God will rescue them and destroy the Egyptians. At that point,
God says to Moses, "Why do you [singular] cry to me?" It is the people, not Moses, who have been crying to God. Why does God address

---

26. Bloch, "Methodological Note," 54.

Moses? Furthermore, to whom else should one cry out if not to God? The words demand some explanation if one is at all curious about the meaning of the Scriptures.

One solution to the problem, common among interpreters, is to supply what seems to be missing in the text. Additional information makes sense of what otherwise seems strange: Moses has obviously himself been praying, which must explain why he has given no marching orders. Rabbi Eliezer says,

> The Holy One, blessed be He, said to Moses: "Moses, my children are in distress, the sea forming a bar and the enemy pursuing, and you stand there reciting long prayers; 'wherefore criest thou unto me?'"[27]

God's words to Moses now make sense. Moses has been praying when he should be taking action. Give the order to march! The commentator cannot resist the opportunity to attach a moral to his explanation of the text:

> For R. Eliezer used to say: There is a time to be brief in prayer and a time to be lengthy.

This is clearly a time to be brief.

Several later commentators adopt the same procedure for making sense of the verse: they supply additional information to interpret God's words to Moses. Other commentators, however, probe more deeply into the logic of the scene. They too presume that Moses has been praying to God; they too sense a reproof in God's response. Why would God reproach Moses for calling out for help? Perhaps because he should have been more confident of deliverance himself. Such reasoning leads to an exploration of possible reasons for confidence. Why should God have provided escape for the band of runaways? Why could they have expected anything from him? Several explanations follow, among which is the following:

> Simon of Kitron says: "For the sake of the bones of Joseph I will divide the sea for them." For it is said, "And he left his garment in her hand and fled" (Gen. 39:12). And it also says, "The sea saw it and fled" (Ps. 114:3).

The cryptic remark must be deciphered, not because it is esoteric but because everything is taken for granted. Arguments and scriptural quotations are abbreviated because they were intended for members of a community who knew the procedures and the biblical passages. We must work to understand what the bones of Joseph have to do with the

---

27. *MRSBY* 1:216.

parting of the sea, and what citations from Genesis and a psalm have to do with a passage in Exodus.

Note first that in seeking to understand the unusual verse in Exodus 14, Rabbi Simon looks elsewhere into the Scriptures. Scripture is viewed as a whole; the truth to which its constituent parts point is the same consistent truth.

Note also that curiosity has played an important role in the development of the tradition. The verse quoted from Psalm 114 with the intention of shedding light on Exodus 14 itself arouses curiosity. Literally translated, it reads, "The sea saw and fled." The psalmist speaks about the exodus, using poetic images. But why these images? Why, for example, is there no object for the verb "to see" in Psalm 114? English translators avoid any difficulty in interpretation by rendering the verse, "The sea looked and fled." That is not quite the sense of the Hebrew. One expects an object with the verb "to see." What did the sea see? Rabbi Simon has an answer: the sea saw the bones of Joseph.

His answer is ingenious, for it solves another problem that must provoke curiosity. The narrator in Exodus makes a point of telling how Moses brought the bones of Joseph along when he left Egypt:

> And Moses took the bones of Joseph with him; for Joseph had solemnly sworn the people of Israel, saying, "God will visit you; then you must carry my bones with you from here." (Exod. 13:19)

Why should that be important to mention in the narrative? It provides some information about Moses, one of Joseph's extended family, who takes oaths seriously. But Rabbi Simon had a better answer: the bones of Joseph were essential for what was to happen at the sea. God's parting of the sea was a reward to Joseph for his piety. When the sea saw the bones Moses had brought along, it "fled."

The verb in the psalm is the crux of the interpretation. It is not simply a poetic image, according to Rabbi Simon. The same verb appears in the story of the attempted seduction of Joseph by the wife of Potiphar, one of Pharaoh's officers. Joseph successfully resists her advances until one day, when he encounters her in the house alone:

> But one day, when he went into the house to do his work and none of the men of the house was there in the house, she caught him by the garment, saying, "Lie with me." But he left his garment in her hand, and fled, and got out of the house. (Gen. 39:11-12)

The spurned woman uses the garment to get her revenge on Joseph, and he ends up in prison. Once again, God does not abandon him but uses the evil deed to good advantage, as Joseph is available to interpret important dreams. Nor does God forget Joseph's refusal to commit adultery. Because Joseph "fled" from sin, says Rabbi Simon, the sea "fled" at the sight of his bones. Moses had every reason for confidence as a descendant of such a meritorious ancestor, particularly since he had brought the bones of Joseph with him out of Egypt.

Rabbi Simon's comment on the verse from Exodus is the result of an elaborate interpretive construct. It serves to clarify several unusual features of the biblical text, the ingenuity is entertaining, and he makes a homiletical point about the rewards of morality. At a more basic level, his comment affords a glimpse of the world the faithful inhabit—a world in which there are many enemies bent on Israel's destruction but in which God is ultimately in charge, a God who is not capricious but who rules with justice and mercy and will deliver his people from danger.

The world is constructed with raw materials taken from the Scriptures. Various mechanisms provide connections that hold scattered verses together—like the common occurrence of the verb "to flee" in Psalm 114 and Genesis 39, together with the mention of Joseph's bones in Exodus 13. The exercise itself is important, for it convinces both the interpreter and the audience that the Scriptures make sense, that they are part of the one truth, and that those Scriptures disclose a world in which God's will can be known and obeyed with confidence.

Midrash and Method

Midrash must be approached in various ways. It involves particular procedures for deriving meaning from texts; thus we may examine its interpretive method. But the enterprise is only possible because of shared convictions about meaning and the unity of the biblical world, we may thus examine basic convictions. Finally, the midrashim arise from a need to make clear and to edify and to apply; we study midrash also as a religious enterprise.

Midrash was considered a learned undertaking. Interpretation followed certain rules, even if they cannot be spelled out precisely in a particular list. The need for some settled approach arose in the first place because scriptural interpretation was a community enterprise. In the halakah, means had to be devised for deciding between competing interpretations. What counts for evidence? How is a case to be argued? Similar questions were discussed in rhetorical schools in the Greco-Roman world. In the domain of midrash, arguments focused on the sentences and words of Scripture. The imaginative lore of the preachers likewise remained close to the biblical text or at least took its cue from something in Holy Writ.[28] Rabbi Simon makes his case by appeal to the occurrence of the verb "flee" in Gen. 39:12 and Ps. 114:3 alike. Another interpretation of the dividing of the sea in the *Mekilta* observes that according to Exod. 15:21, the sea "was split"—as a reward for the meritorious deed of Abraham, who "split" the wood in preparation for offering his son on the altar in obedience to God's command (Gen. 22:3).[29]

Few students of the Scriptures today would find such arguments convincing, though the ingenuity of the rabbinic sages is impressive. That, however, is hardly the point. We must appreciate the relationship between imagination and the constraints of the text in the midrashic process. Clever interpreters could often make the biblical text say precisely what they wanted. But midrash is more complex than that. Biblical words or concepts were not employed merely to lend a sacred aura to ideas that had already been formulated independently. Biblical material did affect the shape of religious expressions and reflection, even if the texts exercised a control of a different sort than we presume should be the case in contemporary exegesis.[30] And however we may evaluate the appropriateness of midrashic productions, we must reckon with the fact that scriptural interpretation was the primary mode of theological reflection. If we are interested in Jewish thought—what we might call doctrine—we must look to exegetical traditions and appreciate their dynamics.[31]

> Doctrinal exegesis was similarly influenced by the evolution of Jewish religious thought, and its impact was the more obvious because, in ancient Judaism, systematic theology was unknown, and the establishment, transmission, and development of doctrines and beliefs were effected within the framework of scriptural interpretation.[32]

---

28. Not all midrash was word-for-word or line-for-line commentary. See, e.g., the homiletical midrashim, discourses only loosely tied to the text.

29. *MRSBY* 1:218.

30. The relationship of the text to the reader is a matter basic to all hermeneutical reflection. The "control" exercised by the text in midrash is different from the kinds of control exercised in so-called historical-critical study. The views of Stendahl ("Interpretation," *IDB*) are naive; they suggest that a "descriptive" reading permits the text to shape interpretation. See Kelsey, *Uses of Scripture,* and Keifert, "Mind Reader and Maestro: Models for Understanding Biblical Interpretation," *Word and World* 1 (1981): 153–68.

31. For works that show how midrash works and that offer some sense of its dynamics, see Goldin, *Song at the Sea;* Spiegel, *Last Trial;* Vermes, *Post-Biblical Jewish Studies;* and Porton, *Understanding Rabbinic Midrash.*

32. Vermes, *Scripture and Tradition,* 178.

Scholastic and Sectarian Interpretation

The focus of this book is christological exegesis. The general thesis is that we cannot understand the evolution of Christology without appreciating the place of exegesis, and that we cannot understand early Christian exegesis without knowing something about the way people read the Bible in the Jewish world of the first century of our era. One problem, to which we have alluded, is that the major sources used to reconstruct "first-century exegesis" are products of rabbinic schools. The midrashic collections, the midrashim—in particular, commentaries on the books of the Pentateuch—were edited no earlier than the fifth century; some of the collections were assembled only in the Middle Ages. The problem of using rabbinic materials for reconstructing the setting out of which Christianity arose has become far more serious in light of the Qumran scrolls and the growing appreciation of how creative the rabbinic movement was. Scholars like Bloch, Vermes, and others have offered ways of dating rabbinic traditions for those especially concerned with Christian origins. Their success in demonstrating the antiquity of various interpretive traditions proves that the sources can be used for historical reconstruction, with proper attention to the difficulties.

Rabbinic Midrash

Having cited examples of midrash from rabbinic commentaries, I would like to suggest a few differences between rabbinic midrashic literature and what we encounter in the NT. Many of the differences relate to setting: rabbinic midrashic collections are scholastic literature, produced by and for schools. This setting has left its impress.

Striking, for example, are the number of interpretive comments in the midrashim whose sole function is to explain the text. Virtually all of the exegesis we know from Qumran and early Christianity is "interested," in the sense of interpreting the Bible for religious reasons. Though Vermes is certainly correct that the desire to explain the text is basic to interpretive traditions, the preponderance of such comments in the rabbinic midrashim—and their absence in Qumran and the NT—demands some comment. Neusner makes an instructive observation: we should be impressed as we read rabbinic literature, he insists, by

a concern for the close and careful explanation of words and phrases. We may well be struck by the interest in the mere facts of the meaning of words and phrases, the meaning of which was already known. The very facticity of discourse should not be missed. . . . For the numerous passages in the collections of exegeses in which theological exegeses—through apologetics, dogmatics, mere homiletics, or historical anachronism—dominate are outweighed by the still more numerous ones of a different sort. In these more common exegeses there is a clear claim that any reasonable and informed person must read things in this way and not in some other.[33]

Neusner suggests that this desire to explain is part of a large religious project:

> The apologetic use of this second sort of reading of the ancient verses of Scripture, the one we may characterize as philological or, at least, other-than-theological, is now to be specified. It makes possible a second sort of discourse. If the theological passage is to address the insider, the philological kind (in the mind of the insider at least) speaks to the world at large. This other, general mode of discourse about Scripture serves to persuade the insider that outsiders, reasonable and informed people, may well accept what the exegete has to say. A powerful apologetic—addressed, self-evidently to the believer—thereby emerges. What we say about Scripture's meaning is reasonable and demonstrable, not merely to be believed by a private act of faith. It is to be critically examined, assented to by shared reason. So the claim of the exegete to provide mere facts supplies the most powerful apologetic. Transforming convictions into (mere) facts serves to reinforce the faith of the believer, beyond all arguments from revelation, let alone historical confirmation.[34]

Rabbinic Judaism was a rationalizing enterprise. Peter Berger calls Diaspora Judaism the "triumph of rationality"—meaning the imposition of rational structures on reality.[35] The enterprise did not begin with the second-century rabbis. Sirach had already provided an ideology for such an undertaking when he described the "books of the law" as the embodiment of God's eternal wisdom (Sir. 24:23). The need to harmonize the whole of the Scriptures is apparent from earlier times.[36] The enterprise was carried out in rabbinic circles, however, and is a marked feature of their midrashim. The self-conscious use of interpretive principles and discussions of hermeneutics display a confidence in reason and logic to disclose the truth within the Scriptures that is not found at Qumran and rarely in the NT. This feature once again has something to do with the scholastic setting of the tradition. Similarly, the playfulness of interpretation, the concern to preserve a variety of opinions, and the

33. Neusner, *Midrash in Context,* 123.

34. Ibid., 122–23.

35. P. Berger, *The Sacred Canopy,* 120; Juel, "Social Dimensions of Exegesis: The Use of Psalm 16 in Acts 2," *CBQ* 43 (1981): 551.

36. Vermes classifies harmonization as "pure" exegesis; see his *Post-Biblical Jewish Studies,* 69–74.

lack of preoccupation with opponents are signs of an established institution and contrast sharply with the "sectarian" character of Qumran and NT midrash.

Qumran Exegesis

Among the scrolls discovered in the caves near Qirbet Qumran are numerous examples of scriptural exegesis. They range from commentaries on biblical books, to small collections of interpretive comments on several passages, to interpretive comments that are part of instructional material. From the number of biblical manuscripts and commentaries discovered in the caves, it is obvious that scriptural interpretation was a preoccupation among the sectaries.

The contrast with known midrashim in rabbinic schools is striking. There is a singleness of purpose and outlook, even of form, among the commentaries that has led scholars to propose a separate classification for Qumran exegesis. It is called pesher, from the consistent use of the word *pishro*, "interpretation." The standard form of a comment is to quote a biblical verse or phrase, then follow it with a comment introduced by "its interpretation . . ." The rabbis collected midrashim; the Qumran sectaries collected pesherim.

The Qumran pesherim, to cite one difference, do not preserve a variety of interpretations of a given verse. There are no "other opinions." One view is offered. The only valid interpretation of the Torah is held to be that of the sect's teacher and founder, the Teacher of Righteousness.[37] Of particular importance to the priestly community was interpretation of cultic regulations. Fundamental differences separated the group from the priestly faction in power, like adherence to a solar rather than a lunar calendar. The apparent intransigence of both parties led to a split and the departure of the Essene priestly group into "exile." In the view of the sectarians, there could be no compromise on matters of halakah. The interpretation of their teacher was the only valid one. The commentaries reflect that view. The stringency of their halakhic views is reflected in the community's code: those who disobeyed a commandment, as interpreted by the teacher, were expelled from the community.

Equally striking is the eschatological emphasis. Whereas the rabbis spoke of the essential timelessness of the Torah, the Qumran group stressed the nearness of the end of days. They believed they were witnessing the dawning of those days and that they would play a special role

---

37. For a balanced study, see G. Jeremias, *Der Lehrer der Gerechtigkeit.*

in the events of the end time. Their time is one of both fulfilled prophecies and renewed expectations. Typical is a comment from the commentary on Habakkuk (1QpHab):[38]

> [Behold the nations and see, marvel and be astonished; for I accomplish a deed in your days but you will not believe it when] told (i, 5).
> [Interpreted, this concerns] those who were unfaithful together with the Liar, in that they [did] not [listen to the word received by] the Teacher of Righteousness from the mouth of God. And it concerns the unfaithful of the New [Covenant] in that they have not believed in the Covenant of God [and have profaned] His holy Name. And likewise, this saying is to be interpreted [as concerning those who] will be unfaithful at the end of days. They, the men of violence and the breakers of the Covenant, will not believe when they hear all that [is to happen to] the final generation from the Priest [in whose heart] God set [understanding] that he might interpret all the words of His servants the Prophets, through whom He foretold all that would happen to His people and [His land]. (1QpHab II, 2–10)

Notable as well in such comments is the conviction that the Scriptures speak mainly about the sectarians and their history. The term "wicked" is read as "wicked priest"; "righteous" means "teacher of righteousness." In Habakkuk 2:8 the "murder of men and the violence inflicted on the land, the city, and its inhabitants" points to the persecution of the sect:

> Interpreted, this concerns the Wicked Priest whom God delivered into the hands of his enemies because of the iniquity committed against the Teacher of Righteousness and the men of his Council. . . . (1QpHab IX, 9–10)

Scriptural interpretation is portrayed as a prophetic enterprise, possible only to those inspired by the Spirit of God. The scriptural books are viewed as mysterious, books whose meaning can be grasped only by one gifted of God. The instructions given Habakkuk in 2:1–2 are interpreted in this way:

> And God told Habakkuk to write down that which would happen to the final generation, but He did not make known to him when time would come to an end. And as for that which He said, "That he who reads may read it speedily," interpreted this concerns the Teacher of Righteousness, to whom God made known all the mysteries of the words of His servants the Prophets. (1QpHab VII, 1–5)

The confidence of the sectarian interpreters in the ability to discern the mysteries embedded in the texts is reflected in the lengths to which

---

38. Quotations from the Qumran scrolls are taken from Vermes, *The Dead Sea Scrolls in English,* unless otherwise noted.

they were willing to go to find the "truth" that applied to themselves. Creative wordplay is supplemented by the choice of alternative readings and occasionally by the change of letters in words.[39] Of the procedure Vermes says,

> Dogmatic assumptions govern the whole process and prompt an existential interpretation of Scripture. The history and teaching of the community were announced in prophetic writings; the latter must in consequence be explained by the former.[40]

F. F. Bruce made the same point when he insisted that the sectarians sought the harmony of scriptural texts in the experience of the sect rather than in the texts themselves.[41]

It is possible to overstate the differences between pesherim and midrashim, however, or at least to misunderstand the differences. The conclusion that Qumran or rabbinic exegetes do greater violence to the scriptural text is a matter of taste. The scribes who began the practice of inserting marginal notes with suggestions about how a written word ought properly to be read (*qere* and *kethib*) were capable of changing letters to suit their own views—and their suggestions became part of printed Bibles! The use of present experience as a hermeneutical key to the exposition of a text is hardly unique to the sectarians, though their single-minded rendering of the Scriptures in light of their own history is unparalleled. The distinctiveness in this case is a matter of degree. The notion that the Scriptures contain mysteries that must be explained, common among Qumran interpreters, was probably inherited from apocalyptic tradition. We can observe the same approach to the interpretation of prophetic writings in Dan. 9:1-2, 20ff., where the seer is granted a heavenly revelation enabling him to understand that the seventy years of exile in Jer. 29:10 really meant seventy weeks of years. The rabbis were equally adept at uncovering new possibilities in familiar texts, though their hermeneutical terminology may be different. Once again, what is unique at Qumran is the consistency of the interpretive program aimed at uncovering secrets in the text. Finally, the notion that the Scriptures speak about the last days was certainly not a conviction

---

39. On the use of textual variants by interpreters, see Stendahl, *The School of St. Matthew;* on the possibility of a changing of letters, see the striking example in the comment on Ps. 37:20 in 4QpPs 37, where "enemies," *oyive,* of the Lord is changed to those who "love," *ohive,* the Lord.

40. Vermes, *Post-Biblical Jewish Studies,* 46.

41. See the influential study of scriptural exegesis at Qumran by Bruce (*Biblical Exegesis in the Qumran Texts*).

held only by those exegetes within the Qumran group. They were heirs to an exegetical tradition that had already identified numerous biblical passages like Psalm 2, Num. 24:17, Deut. 18:15–20, Isaiah 11, and 2 Sam. 7:10–14 as oracles pointing to the distant future.[42] What is special is the sect's version of the oracles, reflecting the interrelationship between scriptural tradition and the history of this little group.[43]

There are major differences between pesherim and midrashim, but they relate not so much to the methods of interpretation as to formal differences arising from different settings. The pesherim are products of a sectarian society whose outlook was decisively shaped by an awareness of being outsiders. Interpretive work was necessary both to spell out the way of life that distinguished the sectarians from their opponents and to account for the details of their unique history. They could afford little playfulness in their exegesis. Nor could they afford the luxury of exegesis for its own sake. There were matters they had to understand about their history, cases that had to be argued. And it is hardly accidental that interpretation is portrayed as a matter of revelation rather than reason. They were well aware that the most sophisticated arguments would never convince outsiders of their views. Central to their own hermeneutical reflection were not the principles of intellectual discourse but the insurmountable barriers to communication that seemed to defy rational solution. True understanding, they knew, could only be revealed.

That does not imply that their own exegesis was irrational or that the sectarians operated without principles of intellectual discourse. Exegesis was still a community enterprise at Qumran. Cases could be argued from the Scriptures, at least within the sect. And the means of dealing with texts were not very different from those employed by the rabbis. We will consider two examples.

A small fragment of a comment on Isaiah has been preserved, known as 4QpIsa. It is included among fragments of one of several works on Isaiah. The focus is the famous oracle in Isaiah 11 about the "branch from the stump of Jesse":

> "And there shall come forth a rod from the stem of Jesse and a Branch shall grow out of its roots. And the spirit of the Lord shall rest upon him, the spirit of wisdom and understanding, the spirit of counsel and might, the spirit of knowledge and of the fear of the Lord. And his delight shall be

---

42. Vermes, *Post-Biblical Jewish Studies,* 45–46.

43. Dahl, "Eschatology and History in the Qumran Texts," in *The Crucified Messiah,* 129–45.

in the fear of the Lord. He shall not judge by what his eyes see, or pass sentence by what his ears hear; he shall judge the poor righteously and shall pass sentence justly on the humble of the earth" (Isa. 11:1–3).

[Interpreted, this concerns the Branch] of David who shall arise at the end [of days] . . . God will uphold him with [the spirit of might, and will give him] a throne of glory and a crown of [holiness] and many-coloured garments . . . [He will put a sceptre] in his hand and he shall rule over all the [nations]. And Magog . . . and his sword shall judge [all] the peoples.

And as for that which He said, "He shall not [judge by what his eyes see] or pass sentence by what his ears hear"; interpreted this means that . . . [the Priests] . . . As they teach him, so will he judge; and as they order, [so will he pass sentence]. One of the Priests of renown shall go out, and garments of . . . shall be in his hands . . .

Though the small fragment is badly damaged, enough remains to catch the drift of the exegesis. The *nezer*, "stem," of Isa. 11:1 is identified as the *zemach David*, the "Branch of David who shall arise at the end of days." The interpreter presumes that Isaiah is not speaking about an ordinary king but is speaking about the great deliverer to arise at the end time. The title Branch of David presumes a prior history of interpretation, in the process of which links have been established between passages like Zech. 3:8; 6:12; and Jer. 23:5; 33:15. The texts all refer, according to the interpreter, to *the* King to come.

That interpretation of Isa. 11:1 is shared with other wings of the Jewish tradition. In all likelihood the messianic reading of the famous oracles was firmly established before the Essene movement was born. The interpreter does not have to argue that the oracle is eschatological; that can be presumed. The "secret" in the passage has to do with the relationship of this royal figure to other eschatological personages, specifically to a priest. The exegete knows that the oracle speaks of more than one eschatological figure, based on his reading of the words "his eyes" and "his ears." According to the exegesis, Isa. 11:3 does not suggest that the coming ruler will judge by second sight. It means that he will not be able to judge on his own but will require the assistance of others. And who are the others? "One of the priests of renown." It is not surprising, given the constitution of the Qumran sect, that there should be some bias against lay leadership in favor of priestly guidance. The interpretation of Isaiah is not without justification, however. For in Zechariah 6 and in Jeremiah 33, the one known as the Branch is portrayed as ruling with a priestly figure. The oracles in Jeremiah and Zechariah, understood as eschatological, can thus offer an interpretation of what is meant in Isaiah 11 by "will not judge by what *his* eyes . . . or *his* ears . . ." The Messiah will depend upon priests—

probably one priestly figure (known elsewhere in the scrolls as the Anointed of Israel, and Interpreter of the Law). The traditions that underlie this reading are common to Christian and rabbinic tradition, and the techniques—close reading of the text, interpreting Scripture in light of Scripture—are familiar as well.

The interpretation of Num. 21:18 in the Damascus Document may serve as another example of familiar interpretive method. The verse in Numbers 21 reads, "The well which the princes dug, which the nobles of the people delved with a rod . . ."

The interpretive comment is,

> The well is the law, and those who dug it are the converts of Israel who went out from the land of Judah and were exiled in the land of Damascus; all of whom God called princes, for they sought him and their glory is denied by no man. And the *mehoqeq* is the Interpreter of the Torah, as Isaiah said, "He has made a tool of His work" (Isa. 54:16). And the nobles of the people are they that come to dig the well with the help of the *mehoqeq's* precepts that they may walk in them during all the time of wickedness, and without which they shall not succeed until the coming of the Teacher of Righteousness at the end of days. (CD VI, 4–11)

The song Israel sang is read as an oracle with a cryptic message that refers to the history of the sect. The meaning of the verses is extracted, however, through familiar means. The word "rod," *mehoqeq,* in Numbers can also mean "leader" or "lawgiver." By means of a play on the word, the interpreter refers the term to someone identified as the Interpreter of the Law who serves as God's tool. That is followed by a reference to Isaiah 54, where the "tool" God will fashion serves an important role in establishing God's people when the times of punishment are over. The "well" in Numbers is identified as the Torah—an identification shared with other interpretive traditions and thus not unique to Qumran. The distinction between "princes" and "nobles" seems to refer to different generations of the sectaries. The historical founder of the sect, here identified as the Interpreter of the Law, establishes precepts that are considered valid until the coming of an eschatological figure, here called the Teacher of Righteousness.

What is distinctive about this interpretation is neither method (wordplay, reading Scripture in light of Scripture, etc.) nor even certain interpretive traditions (e.g., the equation of Torah with the well in Numbers 21), but the application to the history and experience of the sect. The exegesis was not offered as an argument calculated to convince outsiders but was expected to be persuasive to insiders who knew certain fundamental secrets and who knew the rules of interpretation. Discovering the mysteries of the Scriptures required the inspiration of the Spirit, particularly apparent in the career of the teacher who founded the sect. But interpretation still required attention to the sacred texts. Analogies and wordplay still provided the means of expressing the truth and of finding one's way through the maze of scriptural possibilities.

The differences between midrashim and pesherim should be understood properly. They are largely formal differences, arising from distinct social settings, which may be classified as scholastic and sectarian. The categories help to underscore important differences between types of exegetical literature and between approaches to exegesis, but they cannot be pressed. Lengthy debates about whether a particular exegetical comment within the scrolls should be termed a midrash or a pesher are not very helpful.[44] Differences among various approaches to interpretation within postbiblical Jewish tradition should not obscure similarities. Rabbinic midrash, Qumran pesher, and NT scriptural exegesis belong within a common ethos in which texts are read in particular ways. The various groups shared specific interpretive traditions as well as an approach to texts. Differences among commentaries at Qumran may reflect the degree to which common tradition has been appropriated to the special needs of the group at various stages in its history. At some points, the distance between sectarian exegesis and the inherited tradition may not be as apparent. Though the eschatological midrashim from cave 4 that we shall analyze in the next chapter may seem less distinctively Essene, they are part of the scriptural tradition at Qumran. The characteristics of pesher ought not to be formulated exclusively from the commentary on Habakkuk. The distinctiveness of Qumran scriptural exegesis can be appreciated properly only when it is seen against the background of the similarities that encompass early Christian, Essene, and rabbinic exegesis. To quote Vermes again,

---

44. Rigid distinctions between midrash and pesher have sometimes been overdrawn. See Brooke's discussion of the differences between midrash and pesher in his *Exegesis at Qumran,* 36–44, 154–55 (and notes). See also his "Qumran Pesher: Towards the Redefinition of a Genre," *RQ* 10 (1981): 483–503. G. Jeremias (*Der Lehrer der Gerechtigkeit,* 270) makes a similar distinction between pesher and more midrashic exegesis that he argues is typical of the Damascus Document. Bruce (*Biblical Exegesis in the Qumran Texts*) was one of the first to draw such clear distinctions between the form of interpretation practiced at Qumran and that among rabbinic exegetes, and the differences are exaggerated—or perhaps insufficiently explained—even here.

The disclosure of a body of interpretative tradition prior to, and free from, any sectarian bias is one of the most important contributions made by Qumran literature to our knowledge of Palestinian religious thought.[45]

It is that "Palestinian religious thought," particularly as it relates to exegesis and exegetical tradition, which is of importance in our understanding of early Christian exegesis.

Early Christian Exegesis

At first glimpse, the NT is very different from the rabbinic and the Qumran literature. It contains not a single commentary. It is made up of letters, narratives, and an apocalypse. Behind the formal differences, however, lie notable similarities. Biblical interpretation plays a central role in NT literature, as it played a role in preliterary tradition. Paul's letters include extended arguments that reveal hermeneutical expertise (Galatians 3; Romans 4; 9—11). The Letter to the Hebrews offers sophisticated scriptural arguments on christological themes (Hebrews 1—2; 6—10). Almost a dozen OT quotations in Matthew, introduced by a particular formula, reveal the activity of a school, perhaps the work of "scribes trained for the kingdom of heaven" (Matt. 13:52). The speeches of Peter and Paul in Acts evidence similar expertise in scriptural interpretation, often with a distinctly "scholastic" tone.[46]

Even where specific biblical passages are not cited, exegesis—and the results of exegesis—are very much in evidence. The phrase "in accordance with the scriptures" is used at the earliest stages of tradition. Language used to speak about Jesus is uniformly scriptural in origin. Echoes of interpretive traditions can be heard everywhere.

Exegetical activity belongs clearly to the larger world inhabited by the Qumran sectarians and the later rabbis. Familiar techniques are in evidence. Paul uses the *qal vahomer* argument (argument from the lighter to the heavier) in 1 Corinthians 9 to prove from Deut. 25:4 (Do not muzzle a treading ox) that apostles deserve support from congregations. His allegorical method in Galatians 4 is reminiscent of Philo's. Careful attention to words, analogy, atomistic exegesis of scriptural texts, eschatological reading of historical texts—all are common coin in the NT as in other Jewish interpretive tradition. Shared traditions of interpretation are present as well. Like the sectarians at Qumran,

---

45. Vermes, *Post-Biblical Jewish Studies,* 47.
46. Regarding the scholastic tone in the speeches of Acts, see my "Social Dimensions of Exegesis," 549–50, 554–55.

Christian exegetes read 2 Sam. 7:10ff. and Psalm 2 as messianic oracles (see below, pp. 77–88). Prior reflection on the Akedah in Genesis 22 was an important source of atonement imagery (see below, pp. 85–87).

Overall, NT scriptural interpretation is more like the "sectarian" exegesis at Qumran than the "scholastic" exegesis in rabbinic literature.[47] Eschatological convictions pervade everything: the prophetic dimensions of the Scriptures are central; the present is understood as the last days and as a time of fulfilled promises (1 Corinthians 10:11; Acts 2; Matthew 1—2; Luke 1—2; etc.). There is little time for playfulness or humor; relevance of Scriptures to the present leaves no opportunity to pursue mere curiosities for their own sake. In Paul and in John, it is explicitly stated that inspiration is required for a proper understanding of the Scriptures (2 Corinthians 3; John 6). Gospel writers do not preserve different interpretations of a particular passage—though the mere fact that the NT contains four Gospels instead of one attests a tolerance of variety unknown at Qumran.

The greatest difference between early Christian exegesis and other forms of Jewish scriptural interpretation is the impact made by Jesus. That is only to state the thesis, however; it does not explain the precise shape of the tradition. That is the task of our study. We will examine what impact Jesus had on interpretive tradition as well as how the scriptural heritage influenced the shape of Christology. What is the interplay between persons, events, interpretive traditions, and the scriptural texts that we know as Christian exegesis? It is to that question we now turn.

---

47. Ibid. The topic invites further study.

3

CHRIST
THE KING

Christian Interpretation
of 2 Samuel 7

Deciding where to begin a study of christological exegesis may seem relatively simple. C. H. Dodd, for example, chose to begin with explicit quotations that occur with the greatest frequency and are attested in multiple strands of NT tradition. Yet such a choice may not take the occasional nature of the NT writings with sufficient seriousness. The NT contains not a single essay on Christology, not one christological commentary on an OT book or even a portion of a book. It includes narratives, letters, and an apocalypse; even the earliest of these was composed well after most of the basic exegesis of the OT had been completed. Paul's letters give evidence of a wealth of interpretive traditions, only a small portion of which he chooses to quote or comment on explicitly. The notable absence of christological exegesis in his letters reveals less a lack of interest in the topic than a general approval of the formulations he inherited from the tradition. There may well be OT passages that were foundational to the development of exegetical constructions that are never cited, either because their presence could be taken for granted or because their major function was to provide links with other, more readily applicable portions of the Scriptures.

That suggestion is not new. Dodd himself was among those who argued for the fundamental significance of the servant poems in Isaiah within Christian exegetical tradition despite the relative paucity of citations. The absence even of allusions to the poems in the passion narratives has not deterred scholars from arguing for their importance both in the shaping of the narratives and in the development of views of atonement. The weakness of such arguments is that they build on silence; there is little to exercise constraints on the imagination of the interpreter. The absence of citations and allusions to Isaiah 53 in the passion narratives should be taken as an indication that the text had little to do with the development of the narratives. Later use of the famous passage as a passion text is more likely the product of Christian interpretation than its source.[1] Beginning with explicit citations at least provides some control over imagination.

Yet such risks notwithstanding, reconstruction of christological exegesis in its earliest stages cannot rely solely on such criteria as frequency of citation. The choice of a point of departure must arise from an imaginative proposal that seeks to comprehend the tradition as a whole. That is the case in Dodd's work as well. He begins with texts that speak of the present in terms of fulfilled prophecies, consistent with his understanding of the Christian message in terms of realized eschatology. He relies heavily on the early speeches in Acts because he regards them as outlines of the apostolic preaching in early stages of the church's life. Barnabas Lindars largely concurs, giving as an additional reason for beginning with Acts his theory that Christian exegesis of the Scriptures arose in the context of missionary argumentation—apologetic, as he terms it. Those themes would have been dealt with first that were central to the kerygma —like Jesus' resurrection and death, which is precisely what he finds in Acts 2 and 3.

I would like to suggest an alternative. Based on clues explored in chapter 1, I want to begin with the confession of Jesus as the crucified and risen Messiah (with stress on the messianic office). The thesis will look something like this: convinced that Jesus was the promised Messiah, Christians undertook the task of reflecting on the gospel of his death and resurrection in light of the Scriptures.[2] What came first was not apologetic argument but scriptural reflection whose goal was to understand the gospel and its implications. If my proposal is tenable, it should be possible to find evidence that royal texts, meaning OT passages acknowledged as messianic in postbiblical Jewish tradition, have played a critical role in the development of Christian exegesis. We will begin with one such text, God's promise to David through the prophet

---

1. See below, chap. 5.

2. The approach is suggested by Dahl in several of his essays, particularly those in *The Crucified Messiah.*

Nathan, as recorded in 2 Sam. 7:10–14 (with parallels in 1 Chronicles and Psalm 89).

2 SAMUEL 7 IN THE QUMRAN SCROLLS

The promise to David of a dynasty, as recorded in 2 Samuel and Psalm 89, is of enormous importance for those interested in tracing the development of royal ideology in ancient Israel. There is little evidence that the verses were of great consequence in the eyes of postbiblical interpreters, at least judging by explicit citations. There is no apparent reference to the oracle in the whole of intertestamental literature, in Philo, or in Josephus. The rabbis either ignore the text or studiously avoid it. Even in the NT, there is only one explicit citation of the verse and perhaps a half dozen allusions. The choice of such a passage as a starting point is obviously not motivated by widespread use.

One clue to the possible importance of the text is the use of particular imagery in the NT: Jesus is frequently designated "seed" and "Son of God." Both terms appear together in Nathan's oracle:

When your days are fulfilled and you lie down with your fathers, I will raise up your offspring [*sperma,* "seed"] after you. . . . I will be his father, and he shall be my son. (2 Sam. 7:12b, 14)

That the use of "seed" and "son" for Jesus presupposes a messianic interpretation of Nathan's oracle will be the burden of this chapter's argument. Second Samuel 7 belongs to the basic stock of messianic oracles whose interpretation provides a foundation for NT christological development.

Another reason for beginning with this passage and its interpretation is that we are in the remarkably fortunate position of possessing a detailed commentary on the critical verses from 2 Samuel, from the sectarians at Qumran. As the lines from the "Midrash on the Last Days" (4QFlor) make clear,[3] Christians were not the first to read the promise to David as a messianic oracle. The text, in fact, suggests that the Qumran community likewise inherited a messianic reading of the oracle

---

3. The designation is that of Vermes (*The Dead Sea Scrolls in English*). Despite the awkwardness of his unique system of identifying scrolls, his translation is used unless otherwise noted, because of both its quality and its accessibility. On 4QFlor, see also Allegro, ed., *Discoveries in the Judean Desert of Jordan V: Qumran Cave 4;* Strugnell, "Notes en marge du volume V des Discoveries in the Judean Desert of Jordan," *RQ* 29 (1970): 163–276; Yadin, "A Midrash on 2 Sam. vii and Ps. i–ii (4Q Florilegium)," *IEJ* 9 (1959): 95–98; and most recently, Brooke, *Exegesis at Qumran.*

from earlier times and made use of the passage to find a special word for themselves. Christian and Qumran interpreters shared a basic approach to the verses, but their exegesis led in rather different directions. Close comparison of midrashic traditions permits greater insight into the particularity of Christian exegesis of this royal text. In what way did the confession of Jesus as Messiah depend upon texts like 2 Sam. 7:10–14? How was the language of Christian confession shaped by the oracle? Where did the interpretive tradition lead? This is where we begin our study.

Qumran Exegesis of Nathan's Oracle (4QFlor)

The discovery of manuscripts in caves near the Dead Sea that began in the late 1940s has had an enormous impact on the study of first-century Judaism and early Christianity. The reason is not that the tiny sect, probably Essene, was a major factor in Jewish life in first-century Palestine, nor that the group or its writings had any direct influence on early Christians. The scrolls are important because they provide insight into aspects of postbiblical Jewish tradition in the Christian and pre-Christian era that were previously unknown.

A good example is the document 4QFlor. The page, pieced together from twenty-six fragments, contains a midrash on 2 Sam. 7:10b–14 and the opening lines of Psalms 1–2. The remaining fragments are virtually impossible to identify, though there may have been comments on selected verses from Deuteronomy 33 and on Numbers 24.[4] The midrash reads Nathan's words to David as a prediction of the coming Messiah at the end of days, and it quotes, without hesitation, the words of God according to which he will call the Messiah his "son." The midrash offers a striking comparison with the opening chapter of Hebrews, where both 2 Sam. 7:14 and Ps. 2:7 are quoted to speak of Jesus the Messiah as God's son. With the publication of the midrashic fragment, textbooks that spoke about messianic language in postbiblical Judaism have had to be rewritten.[5]

Interpreting the midrash is not without problems. The text has no clear beginning and ending. The problem is most serious at the beginning, where the almost illegible first half of the opening line makes it difficult

---

4. Brooke, *Exegesis at Qumran,* 80–84.

5. The emphatic statements regarding the impossibility of understanding "the Son of God" as messianic language in the first century, made by such scholars as Haenchen (*Der Weg Jesu,* 512) and Schweizer (*The Good News According to Mark,* 324), are representative of a view that must now be revised.

to determine the antecedent of the initial comment. Interpretation of the whole, therefore, must remain speculative. Nevertheless, we can learn a good deal from the small midrash that will shed light on Qumran exegesis, postbiblical tradition, and Christian use of 2 Samuel 7.

Context within the Dead Sea Scrolls

Various types of literature have been identified among the scrolls: biblical manuscripts, manuscripts of apocryphal and pseudepigraphical works, commentaries, and others more difficult to classify (1QS, the Temple Scroll, CD, etc.). 4QFlor is largely in a category by itself. It is a comment on specific biblical selections, not on a biblical book, like the commentary on Habakkuk. The extant fragments include comments on 2 Sam. 7:10b–14 and lines from Ps. 1:1 and 2:1–2. The omission of most verses from Psalm 1 only highlights the selectivity of the interpreter. There is evidence of selective interpretation of biblical texts (e.g., the small fragment, also found in cave 4, known as "Patriarchal Blessings," an interpretation of Jacob's testament in Genesis 49), though there is not another example of a series as in 4QFlor. Biblical passages are selected and quoted serially in 4QTest (Deut. 5:28–29; Deut. 18:18–19; Num. 24:15–17; Deut. 33:8–11; Josh. 6:26), but without comment.

The most helpful things that can be said about the genre of this midrash arise from simple description. It is interested in the exegesis of eschatological passages, presumably more than one. It may be that one feature shared by the texts is focus on eschatological deliverers, though little can be said with certainty. The questions are dealt with at some length—and without firm conclusions—by George Brooke.

Text

The complete text of the midrash cannot be established. There are holes in the manuscript at several points, and some of the writing is illegible.[6] In a few cases, more than one reasonable reconstruction of a reading is possible. Even where the text is visible, there can be disagreements about letters. In at least one case, the disagreement has an important bearing on interpretation of the whole midrash (see the brief discussion of *todah* and *torah* below, p. 67). In this particular instance the letters are so similar that there is no way to distinguish between them with certainty. Arguments must depend upon context; some circularity in argumentation is unavoidable.

---

6. A glimpse at the facsimile in *Discoveries in the Judean Desert,* ed. Allegro, is a useful introduction to an interpretation of the midrash.

The text on which the translation is based is the standard edition in *Discoveries in the Judean Desert of Jordan V: Qumran Cave 4*, edited by John Allegro. There are included emendations suggested by John Strugnell, Geza Vermes, and George Brooke.

Translation

The translation is taken principally from George Brooke's *Exegesis at Qumran*, with emendations from Vermes's *Dead Sea Scrolls in English:*

". . . and his enemies [will not disturb him] any more; neither will a son of wickedness afflict him any more as formerly and as from the day that I commanded judges to be over my people Israel." That is the house which [he will build] for him in the latter days, as it is written in the book of [Moses], "The sanctuary, O Lord, which thy hands have established; The Lord will reign for ever and ever": that is the house to which shall not come [even to the tenth generation and for]ever, Ammonite nor Moabite nor bastard nor stranger nor proselyte for ever, for his holy ones are there. [His glory shall] be revealed for ever; continually it shall be seen over it. And foreigners shall not make it desolate again, as they desolated formerly the sanctuary of Israel because of their sin. And he promised to build for himself a sanctuary of men [*miqdash adam*], for there to be in it for him smoke offerings before him, works of thanksgiving [read *todah* instead of *torah*]. And that he said to David, "And I will give you rest from all your enemies," that means that he will give rest to them from all the sons of Belial who cause them to stumble in order to destroy them [through their errors], just as they came with the plots of Belial to cause to stumble the sons of light, and in order to devise against them plots of wickedness so that they [might be caught] by Belial through their [wicked] error.

"And the Lord declares to you that he will build you a house. And I will raise up your seed after you, and I will establish the throne of his kingdom for ever. I will be his father, and he will be my son": he is the Branch of David who will stand with the Interpreter of the Law, who [will rule] in Zion in the latter days as it is written, "And I will raise up the booth of David which is fallen": he is the booth [or, Branch] of David which was fallen, who shall arise to save Israel.

Analysis of the Commentary

Interpretation of the verses begins with a short comment, "That is the house which will be built at the end of days," followed by a citation of Exod. 15:17. The form of the comment departs from norm in the scrolls. The word *pishro* is not used; the comment begins with a pronoun. The same occurs in line 3 ("That is the house which . . ."), in line 11 ("That is the Branch of David who . . ."), and in line 12 ("That is the *sukkath* of David which . . ."). The only variation is in line 7, where the relative *asher* functions in much the same way, relating the comment to a previous word or phrase. The departure from the common form in the scrolls is striking, but it is perhaps not as significant as some commentators suggest.[7]

In general, the movement of the comments is clear. The first two comments speak about something in the passage that is identified as "the house." The third comment focuses on God's promise to "give rest." The last comment identifies the "seed" promised David as the coming Messiah, the Branch of David. Several lines from 2 Sam. 7:10–14 have been omitted in the commentary, upon examination, intentionally.

When it comes to detail, understanding the commentary is more difficult. It is unclear, first, what we are to understand as the antecedent of the first "that" ("That is the house . . ."). There would be little problem if we could be confident that what preceded the comment was a citation of 2 Sam. 7:10a: "And I will appoint a place for my people Israel, and will plant them, that they may dwell in their own place, and be disturbed no more." The obvious candidate for antecedent would be the term "place." The comment could be understood as a specification of that place: it is the "house" of which Exod. 15:17 speaks, the "sanctuary" God promised to build with his hands. There is good biblical precedent for such an interpretation of *maqom;* in Deuteronomy, it is a regular designation for the temple. Exodus 15 was understood as a prediction of the temple under Solomon (and of an eschatological temple) in postbiblical tradition.[8] The use of the verb "to plant" in both Exodus 15 and 2 Samuel 7 provides a link between the verses. The simplest explanation of the initial comment is that it seeks to identify the "place" mentioned in 2 Sam. 7:10a as the future temple.

One difficulty with this interpretation is that the word "enemy" seems clearly present in the first line of the manuscript, thus preceding the interpretive comment, and the word is not found in 2 Sam. 7:10a. It seems inherently unlikely that the word "enemy" has been inserted into the biblical citation, as suggested by Brooke.[9] Several reconstructions of the opening of the midrash can be offered, with consequently differing proposals regarding the antecedent of "that." Little is to be gained by such speculation here. The equation of "place" (2 Sam. 7:10) and "house" and "sanctuary" (Exod. 15:17) suggests that the point of the comment is to establish a link between "place" and temple, to be identified in what follows with the "house" God promises David in the oracle.

---

7. Brooke, *Exegesis at Qumran*, 139–43.
8. See the discussion of the passage in Goldin, *Song at the Sea*.
9. Brooke, *Exegesis at Qumran*, 97–99.

The use of "house" ("That is the house," line 2) must come from 2 Sam. 7:11 (quoted in line 10): "The Lord declares that the Lord will build you a house." Nathan's oracle actually speaks of two houses, one that God will build for David, and one that David's seed will build for God (v. 13). The mention of a second house is not cited by the Qumran interpreter. The omission is significant. Without v. 13, there is only the house that God will build—the same building mentioned in Exod. 15:17 as the "sanctuary." Despite the suggestion of many interpreters that the sectarian interpreter understands all of the building imagery as a reference to the community, the evidence seems to point to an equation of "place" in 2 Sam. 7:10 with the "house" in 7:11, and the identification of both as references to the temple God will build with his hands.

Major effort is invested in describing entrance requirements for this coming temple: "This is the house where there will not enter . . ." The list of those excluded seems drawn first from Deuteronomy 23, which lists entrance requirements for the *qahal adonai* (the assembly of the Lord). There may also be imagery drawn from Ezekiel 44, which discusses the restored temple God shows Ezekiel in a vision. The reason for including these features in the comment cannot be found in Nathan's oracle but must be sought in the preoccupations of the interpreter. The whole existence of the Essene sect was tied to ritual purity and a stubborn refusal to compromise on cultic regulations regarded as fundamental. In sketching a picture of the future, the practice and structure of the sectarian group are projected onto the screen. It is Ezekiel's picture of the temple, not Isaiah's, that serves as blueprint. The rules for the congregation in Deuteronomy 23 become rules of admission to the temple God will build.

The preoccupation with the "rest" promised David can likewise be understood from the experience of the group at Qumran. The highly figurative explanation given the line from Nathan's oracle ("I will give you rest from your enemies") reflects their stormy history. Though we cannot decipher the figurative language with any precision, we can understand its force. The promise of rest at the end of days was important to the beleaguered sectarians excluded from the cult of Israel, who could hope for changes of the sort only God could provide.

Determining precisely what the sectarians find in the oracle is difficult also because of an enigmatic expression and an ambiguous word. The "house" that God plans to build is identified as a *miqdash adam* in line 6, which has been variously translated as a "man-made sanctuary,"[10] a "sanctuary among men,"[11] and a "sanctuary [composed] of men."[12] The purpose of this sanctuary is to provide a place where sacrifices can be offered to God—either "works of Torah" (reading *torah* in line 7) or "thank offerings" (reading *todah* in line 7). The resh and daleth are indistinguishable. Does the strange passage suggest that God will provide a substitute for the actual temple in the form of a human community in which obedience to the Torah will serve as a replacement for bloody sacrifices in the temple? Or does it simply take God's promise as pointing to the building of a temple among his people, in which proper thank offerings will be made? If the latter is seen as more probable, is this future temple to be a replacement for the current structure in Jerusalem? Answering the questions properly would require a lengthy discussion and an elaborate justification that would nevertheless remain hypothetical. I tend toward the latter interpretation, in any case. It seems likely that the interpreter has in mind a real temple to be built at the end of days. Nowhere in the scrolls is the community understood as a permanent replacement for the temple, even if there is some spiritualization of sacrificial imagery necessary to work out a view of atonement while corrupt priests preside at invalid sacrifices for the present.[13] That the exegete understands Nathan's oracle to speak about a temple to be built at the end of days seems even more likely in view of the concluding comment on 2 Sam. 7:14.

The last comment, which follows an abridged citation of vv. 11b–14, identifies the seed promised David as the Messiah: "This is the Branch of David." The designation "branch" is familiar from Jer. 23:5 and 33:15; it appears also in Zech. 3:8 and 6:12, where it is used to speak of the coming king. The interpreter takes for granted that these prophetic passages are messianic, as do the rabbis.[14] The identification is made easier by the omission of several phrases from 2 Samuel 7 that might tend to suggest that the seed promised David was literally one of his offspring (i.e., Solomon). The omission of "And when your days are fulfilled and you lie down with your fathers," "seed which shall come forth from your body," and "He will build a house for my name" is particularly striking.

---

10. Allegro, ed., *Discoveries in the Judean Desert,* 289.

11. Klinzing, *Die Umdeutung des Kultus,* 82–83.

12. Brooke, *Exegesis at Qumran,* 92.

13. See Vermes, *The Dead Sea Scrolls in English,* 45–46; and Klinzing, *Die Umdeutung des Kultus.*

14. Juel, *Messiah and Temple,* 172–182.

The comment betrays no embarrassment regarding the use of father-son imagery in v. 14. That is notable only in light of later targumic and rabbinic tradition that took great pains to ensure that the imagery from this text be understood as figurative.[15] Later tradition was hesitant to use "son" to speak of the Messiah; the Qumran interpreter shows no such reservations. Though the title Son of God is not used of the Messiah here, such usage is surely conceivable.[16]

The identification of the "seed of David," whom God will call his "son," as the Messiah, the Branch of David, does not seem to be what is of greatest interest to the commentator. The distinctive feature of his comment is the introduction of a figure about which Nathan says nothing: the Interpreter of the Law. For the identity of this eschatological figure expected to appear with the Messiah and for an explanation of his seemingly unwarranted appearance in the exegetical comment, we shall have to look elsewhere among traditions of the Qumran sectaries.

INTERPRETER OF THE LAW

The identity of the mysterious second figure is not spelled out in the midrash. The exegete presumes his audience will understand the reference. As outsiders, we can only try to locate information crucial to the identity of the Interpreter elsewhere. In fact, the epithet occurs elsewhere twice, both times in the Damascus Document (CD). In both cases it is employed as part of an interpretive comment on a biblical text.

The first occurrence is in CD VI, 7. The context is a comment made about the foundation of the community. According to the commentator, the birth of the movement constitutes the fulfillment of Num. 21:18:

---

15. Levey, *The Messiah* (on Ps. 2:7); Juel, *Messiah and Temple,* 108–9 (for a discussion of the Targumim on 2 Samuel 7 and 1 Chronicles 17).

16. Fitzmyer has published a widely known but heretofore inaccessible fragment from Qumran ("The Contribution of Qumran Aramaic to the Study of the New Testament," in *A Wandering Aramean,* 102–14), in which an unidentified figure is called both Son of God and Son of the Most High God. Though Fitzmyer is correct that there is no justification for identifying the figure with the Messiah, and thus that the fragment does not provide a basis for speaking of "the Son of God" as a messianic designation, he seems to overstate the case (pp. 105–7). The text is clearly royal and, as Hengel states, "not completely alien to Palestinian Judaism" (*Son of God,* 45). The placement of a midrash on Psalms 1—2 immediately following the messianic interpretation of 2 Sam. 7:10–14 in 4QFlor lends greater probability to the suggestion that "the Son of God" was understood as royal—and messianic—language in postbiblical Jewish circles.

The well which the princes dug,
which the nobles of the people delved with a rod . . .

The interpretive comment is,

The well is the Law, and those who dug it are the converts of Israel who went out from the land of Judah and were exiled in the land of Damascus. God called them all princes, for they sought Him and their renown was disputed by no man. And the stave is the Interpreter of the Law, of whom Isaiah said, "He makes a tool for His work" (Isa 54:16). And the nobles of the people are those who come to dig the well with the Mehoqeq's precepts, that they may walk in them during all the time of wickedness, and without which they shall not succeed until the coming of the Teacher of Righteousness at the end of days.

The truth hidden in the prophetic passage has been extracted largely through "inspired" wordplay. The word "stave," *mehoqeq,* can also mean "leader" or "lawgiver." The text is read to refer to a figure, known as the "lawgiver," who is the tool of God with which the well in Num. 21:18 is dug. The well, according to rabbinic as well as Qumran exegesis, is the Torah.[17] The distinction between princes and nobles seems to designate different generations of sectaries. There may be a wordplay in the comment on "prince," though it is not at all obvious (the relationship would have to exist between *sar,* "prince," and *darash,* "seek").

The interpreter reads Num. 21:18 as a prophecy that has been fulfilled. The Scriptures promised that a "lawgiver" would come whose efforts in delving the Torah would provide the foundation of a community. The prophecy has been fulfilled. The precepts of the founder will suffice "until the coming of the Teacher of Righteousness at the end of days." In this passage, "Interpreter of the Law" refers to a historical figure of the past, "Teacher of Righteousness" to a coming figure.

The reference to the "Interpreter of the Law" in CD VII, 15–19 is more difficult. The enigmatic expression occurs again in an interpretation of a biblical verse, this time from Amos:

"You shall take up Sakkuth your king, and Kaiwan your star-god, your images which you made for yourselves; therefore I will take you into exile beyond Damascus," says the Lord, whose name is the God of hosts. (Amos 5:26–27)

The threat is transformed into a promise by creative exegesis. First, the interpreter omits the initial verb ("you shall take up") and replaces it

17. Vermes, *Scripture and Tradition,* 53 n. 6.

with the verb from the second clause ("I will exile"). The two names of the gods are read as other nouns (*Sakkuth* is read as *sukkath,* "booth"; *Kaiwan* is read as a derivative of *kun,* meaning perhaps "bases of statues" [Vermes]). The promise now reads, "I will exile the tabernacle of your king and the bases of your statues from my tent to Damascus." The comment follows:

> The Books of the Law are the "tabernacle" of the king; as God said, "I will raise up the tabernacle of David which is fallen" (Amos 9:11). The "king" is the congregation; and the "bases of the statues" are the Books of the Prophets whose sayings Israel despised. The "star" is the Interpreter of the Law who shall come to Damascus; as it is written, "A star shall come forth out of Jacob and a sceptre shall rise out of Israel" (Num 24:17). The "sceptre" is the Prince of the whole congregation, and when he comes "he shall smite all the children of Seth" (Num 24:17).

Some of the interpretive moves have precedent and thus were not unique to the Qumran exegetes. The LXX, for example, has also read the apparent name of the god (*Sakkuth*) as the construct of *sukkah,* translating *skenē,* interpreting rather freely, "And you will take up the tent of Moloch." The question is more complicated with the second Hebrew term, which the LXX renders as *Raiphan,* reading it as a name. The Qumran exegete takes this word to be a noun, though it is not certain what he made of the strange Hebrew construction. André Dupont-Sommer, also deriving the word from the verb *kun,* translates it "faithfulness" or "fidelity."[18] His translation, "faithfulness of his images," makes little sense, however. Vermes derives the term from *kun* as well but takes it to mean "bases" of their images. Whatever the strange reading, the interpreter takes the oracle to mean that the Law and the Prophets—the sacred writings—will provide the foundation for the community that will be led by God into exile in Damascus.

The Hebrew *cocab elohechem* is omitted from the citation of Amos by the commentator, yet its presence must be presumed. The comment "The star is the Interpreter of the Law" can only be understood as an interpretation of that *cocab,* "star." The exegete explains what is meant by "tent," "king," the "bases of their images," and finally *cocab elohechem.* The Hebrew is read not as "their star-god" but as "the star of their god." The star is identified by appeal to another scriptural text:

> A star has journied out of Jacob and a sceptre is risen out of Israel (Num 24:17).

---

18. Dupont-Sommer, *The Essene Writings from Qumran,* 134 n. 3.

Once this passage is cited, the interpreter feels obliged to identify the scepter mentioned in Balaam's oracle as well: "The sceptre is the Prince of the whole congregation," a designation of the Davidic Messiah who will "smite all the children of Seth" when he comes.

The "star" from Amos, then, is called the Interpreter of the Law. The link with Balaam's oracle makes it virtually certain that the Interpreter is viewed as an eschatological figure. It is possible that in the opinion of the sectaries, this eschatological figure has already come. This is the view of Dupont-Sommer, who translates, "And the Star is the Seeker of the Law who came to Damascus." Vermes, however, chooses to translate the verb as a future: "The star is the Interpreter of the Law who will come to Damascus." Vermes's translation seems the more likely. The identification of the scepter from Numbers 24 as the "Prince of the whole congregation" distinguishes the royal figure from the "star" (see the use of "scepter" for the expected offspring of Judah in Gen. 49:10). The coming of the royal figure is still awaited, which suggests the same is true in the case of the "star." Most likely, therefore, the "star" designates the anointed high priest who figures so prominently in the eschatological visions of the sectaries. The coming high priest is thus designated the Interpreter of the Law.

This interpretation is not without problems. First, the interpretive comment ("The star is") must refer to Amos 5, where the "star of their god" seems to be exiled with the tent of the king and the bases of the images. Thus, "Interpreter of the Law" might more likely be taken as a reference to the historical teacher who founded the sect, thus in line with CD VI, where the Interpreter provides precepts necessary "until he comes who shall teach righteousness at the end of days." Further, if the star is identified as the eschatological high priest in distinction from the anointed Prince, the passage provides an exception to the rule in CD, where the two Messiahs of Aaron and Israel have merged into one figure (see esp. CD XII, 23; CD XX, 1). This passage cannot be read as a reference to one figure known both as "star" and as "sceptre."

The issue cannot be settled by alleged consistency in terminology. The expression "Teacher of Righteousness" (or "he who teaches righteousness") is used both of a historical figure and of one whose coming is still expected. In CD VI, the Interpreter of the Law is a historical figure whose work is preliminary to that of the Teacher who will come at the end of days. The founder of the sect, identified here as the Interpreter of the Law, is not the eschatological Teacher of Righteousness. In 1QpHab I, 13, however, the designation "Teacher of Righteousness" is used to speak of the historical founder of the sect. The same is true in CD I, 11 and in CD XX, 32. The same ambiguity attends the designation "the Priest" (eschatological: 1QSa II, 19; 1QM X, 2; historical: 1QpHab II, 8; 4QpPs 37 II, 15).[19] The mere use of epithets cannot, therefore, determine whether our passage in CD views the Interpreter of the Law as the historical teacher who founded the sect or as the eschatological priest whose coming the community still awaited.

An attempt to provide a satisfactory solution to the problem in CD could lead us far afield, and it might not succeed in any case. The reference in CD VII retains a certain ambiguity. It is tempting to read the passage as an identification of the "star" with the eschatological priest who will be known as the Interpreter of the Law, a figure yet to come whose career is viewed as parallel to that of the historical priest-teacher who founded the sect. He is paired with the "sceptre"—the royal Messiah from the line of David who also will play a role in the decisive events still in the future. If that is the case, what we observe is that the epithet "Interpreter of the Law" is used in a manner similar to that of "Teacher of Righteousness": both are functional epithets that can be used to speak both of historical and of eschatological figures. There was a historical priest whose interpretation of the law provided the foundation for a new religious community, a priest to whom the text from Hosea 10:12 was applied, as well as the text from Numbers 21 (CD VI, 2–11). Likewise the sect looked forward to a future time when another priest, the anointed high priest, would play a decisive role in the last days. His career was fitted out with the trappings of an earlier ministry, that of the historical teacher. He too could be called the Teacher of Righteousness and the Interpreter of the Law. It was the career of the historical priest that provided some direction and shape for the later history of biblical exposition among his followers—in the case of our passage, not in terms of specific legal opinions but in terms of functions that decisively shaped the way the community viewed the role of priest.

The ambiguity that attends the use of "Interpreter of the Law" in CD VII is absent from 4QFlor. The comments on Nathan's oracle look to the future. The Interpreter is an eschatological figure whose career parallels that of the Branch of David. The exegesis of Numbers 24 in CD VII fits such an interpretation as this, distinguishing as it does two salvation figures. Nathan's oracle in 2 Samuel 7 is clearly not the source of such a view. What we find in the reference to the Interpreter of the Law in

---

19. Dahl, "Eschatology and History," in *The Crucified Messiah,* 180 n. 31.

4QFlor are deposits of an earlier, elaborate history of exegesis. Our task, if it is possible, should be to reconstruct that history of exegesis so as to understand why the phrase "Interpreter of the Law" should have been inserted into the comments on 2 Samuel 7 and how the epithet could have been used both for a historical and for an eschatological figure.

The sectarians did not create their images of the future de novo. They began with interpretive traditions inherited from earlier generations and shared with other branches of the Jewish family. The selection of scriptural texts in 4QTest, for example, provides evidence of such inherited tradition. The eschatological texts include Deut. 18:18–19; Num. 24:15–17; and Deut. 33:8–11. Three distinct eschatological figures are identified. The first is the prophet like Moses from Deuteronomy 18, familiar from Samaritan and early Christian tradition. In some strains of Jewish tradition, the prophecy was understood as a reference to Elijah, as also was Hosea 10:12 (the "one who teaches righteousness").[20] The sectarians read the oracle as a prediction of an eschatological figure. In their construction of the future they made little of the prophet, however. The figure is not mentioned in CD. One reason is perhaps that prophetic functions within the community were exercised principally in the interpretation of the Scriptures, an enterprise in which both leaders and ordinary members of the sect had a share. Little was left for a prophet to do. The tasks assigned Elijah by the rabbis—teaching, for example—were reserved for priests.

The scepter from Balaam's oracle in Numbers 24 was understood as a reference to the Davidic Messiah. This interpretation was shared with all branches of the Jewish community. It presumes a link with Gen. 49:10 ("The scepter shall not depart from Judah, nor the ruler's staff from between his feet"), a passage likewise acknowledged as messianic elsewhere in Jewish tradition. The scrolls say more about the role assigned the Davidic Messiah than about that assigned the prophet like Moses, though their exegesis is not creative. Comments depart little from what is included in the biblical texts. The Davidic Messiah was expected to play a role in the great battle against the children of darkness (Num. 24:17: "It [the scepter] shall crush the forehead of Moab and break down all the sons of Sheth"). He is viewed essentially as a deliverer. And it is about this figure, says the commentator, that 2 Sam. 7:10–14 speaks.

---

20. On Hosea 10:12 as a reference to Elijah in talmudic and post-talmudic literature, see Ginzburg, *Eine unbekannte jüdische Sekte,* 303ff.

The identification of the Messiah as the Branch of David presumes links with other biblical passages, like Jeremiah 23 and 33, as well as Zechariah 6:

> Behold, the days are coming, says the Lord, when I will fulfil the promise I made to the house of Israel and the house of Judah. In those days and at that time I will cause a righteous Branch to spring forth for David; and he shall execute justice and righteousness in the land. In those days Judah will be saved and Jerusalem will dwell securely. And this is the name by which it will be called: "The Lord is our righteousness."
>
> For thus says the Lord: David shall never lack a man to sit on the throne of the house of Israel, and the Levitical priests shall never lack a man in my presence to offer burnt offerings, to burn cereal offerings, and to make sacrifices for ever. (Jer. 33: 14–18)
>
> Thus says the Lord of hosts, "Behold, the man whose name is the Branch: for he shall grow up in his place, and he shall build the temple of the Lord. It is he who shall build the temple of the Lord, and shall bear royal honor, and shall sit and rule upon his throne. And there shall be a priest by his throne, and peaceful understanding shall be between them both." (Zech. 6:12–13)

Read as oracles pointing to the last days, the prophecies speak of the Davidic King as the Branch. Both passages also refer to a priestly figure, however, who has a place in the eschatological vision. Such passages could be related to Numbers 24 ("star" and "scepter") and to the promise to Levi in Deuteronomy 33. Other texts could be gathered to fill out the career of the priestly figure.

This is clearly what occurred at Qumran. Unlike the Davidic Messiah, however, the eschatological priest is depicted in nontraditional ways. Traditional passages quoted by the rabbis as applying to a priest who will come at the end of days are rarely quoted. The priest's role in presiding over the temple sacrifices is seldom mentioned. More important was his expected role in blessing the meals and the troops in the days to come, and his role as an interpreter of the law.

In Deut. 33:10, Moses speaks about the role of the priests as interpreters of the tradition: "They shall teach Jacob thy ordinances, and Israel thy law." For the sectarians, that was decisive, not simply because the idea was scriptural but because it reflected the experience and practice of the sect. Within the group, as within the earlier Jewish community, it was priests who served as teachers of the law and guardians of the tradition. Their interpretation of the law distinguished the Qumran group from others and was responsible for their exile from Jerusalem. They looked forward to a time when they would again preside at sacrifices (1QM and the Temple Scroll). In the meantime, their task was to preserve the tradition and to ensure a proper reading of the law.

In what little we know about the interrelationship among eschatological deliverers in the visions of the sectaries, it is again both Scripture and experience that are decisive. In their view, the priestly figure would take precedence over the royal (1QSa II, 11–22; compare the role of the Prince in 1QM V, 1 with that of the Priest in 1QM XV, 4–15, 1QM XVI, 13, and 1QM XVII, 9). Exegetical warrants for such a view could be discovered in surprising places. In 4QpIsa, as noted above, the interpreter offers an insider's view of what is meant by the sentence of the famous messianic oracle in Isaiah 11 that says of the Shoot from the stump of Jesse, "He shall not judge by what his eyes see, he shall not decide by what his ears hear":

> And as for that which He said, "He shall not [judge by what his eyes see] or pass sentence by what his ears hear"; interpreted, this means that . . . [the Priests] . . . As they teach him, so will he judge; and as they order, [so will he pass sentence]. One of the Priests of renown shall go out, and garments of . . . shall be in his hands . . . (4QpIsa, frag. D)

According to this reading, the text says that the Davidic Messiah will not judge by what "his" eyes see nor decide by what "his" ears hear. He will rely on others. Scriptural passages like Zechariah 6, Jeremiah 23 and 33, and Deuteronomy 33 provide information about the ones on whom he can rely: it is priests who must judge and interpret, perhaps even the Interpreter of the Law par excellence, the priest who will arise at the end of days to stand with the Branch of David.

In 2 Sam. 7:10–14 nothing is said about such a priestly figure. The oracle predicts the coming of a king—perhaps of the King. The identification of that figure as the Branch of David, and the inclusion of another figure identified as the Interpreter of the Law presuppose a whole history of exegesis on which the commentator draws, a history that tells us a great deal about the history and experience of the Qumran sect as well as about interpretive traditions prior to the sect.

Summary

It goes without saying that the vision of the future sketched by the sectaries at Qumran did not arise from the Scriptures without some creative assistance. At times the secrets of the text could be extracted only with considerable struggle with the words, even the letters, of the biblical passage. At the same time, the raw material out of which such visions were constructed came from the Bible; the mode of reflection was exegetical. Furthermore, eschatological visions were not born full grown like some Athena, to be projected back onto the biblical texts.

The Scriptures provided images with which to conceive the future; prior interpretive tradition shaped the way the Qumran community approached basic questions and what texts were given consideration. Even at Qumran, reflection involved genuine conversation with the Scriptures.

Second Samuel 7 was one of the fundamental texts that spoke of the longed-for future. The reason for Nathan's oracle's being regarded as an eschatological passage probably lies in the history of the oracle's interpretation prior to the birth of the Qumran community. The exegete obviously feels no need to argue for an eschatological as opposed to a historical reading of the passage. What is notable about the exegesis in 4QFlor is not that the oracle is read as a messianic prophecy but how it is so interpreted. The exegete assumes that there is an order behind the multiplicity of biblical texts and images, an order that links them into an intelligible whole. His task is to discern that order and make it explicit, either to understand an aspect of the sect's history or to offer a glimpse of what lies ahead—all this in addition to the task of ordering public and private life in accordance with the Torah. The construction of a whole picture is the result of combinations of various scriptural texts, done in the context of prior interpretive tradition as well as in light of the unique history and outlook of the sect.

The commentator was not the first to identify the "seed" promised David as the Branch of David. The use of images from other scriptural passages to make sense of 2 Samuel ("Branch of David" from Jeremiah and Zechariah; "tent of David" from Amos 9) follows customary ways of working with written texts and relating them to one another. Other Jewish interpreters would have had little difficulty identifying the seed promised David with the Branch, or linking the figure with other images from Numbers 24 or Isaiah 11.

Though the interpreter is interested in 2 Sam. 7:10–14 as a prediction of the Davidic Messiah, he is more interested in the promise of a "place" and "rest from enemies" than in the figure of the Messiah himself. The promises have more immediate significance and strike closer to home— though here as well, the exegete does not simply read ideas directly out of the words of the passages but employs scriptural analogies to extract the hidden meaning of "place" and "rest" (citing Exod. 15:17; Deuteronomy 23; Ezekiel 44; etc.). And most characteristic, the exegete cannot mention the Davidic "Prince" without also mentioning the anointed Priest—identifying him as the Interpreter of the Law—though there is no hint of such a figure in 2 Samuel 7. Passages like Jeremiah 33 and Zechariah 6 are more central to the community's exegesis.

The unknown author of the little commentary on 2 Samuel 7 found in Nathan's oracle an occasion for reflection on the relationship of the sectarian community to the outside world in the days to come. Promises of rest and deliverance were also observed. Early Christians found promises and important information in the oracle as well. There are matters on which Qumran and Christian exegetes agreed. The very different direction of interpretation in Christian circles, however, provides a helpful means of comparing the two groups and of identifying the unique features of early Christian exegesis.

2 SAMUEL 7 IN THE NEW TESTAMENT

On the basis of casual observation, it would be difficult to argue that Nathan's oracle was a text of major importance to the early Christian movement. The NT does not contain a commentary on the passage. In fact, the only actual citation from the passage is in Heb. 1:5, where 2 Sam. 7:14 is quoted. The list of allusions is somewhat longer. The references to David's "seed" in John 7:42 and Acts 13:23 allude to 2 Sam. 7:12 (and perhaps to Ps. 89:4 as well). The words of the angel in Luke 1:32–33 are formulated with the promise to David in mind: "He shall be called the son of the Most High" (2 Sam. 7:14); "And the Lord God will give to him the throne of his father David" (2 Sam 7:12–13, 16). A few other passages might be added, but the list is in any case modest. The explicit quotations and allusions do not demonstrate the fundamental significance of the oracle in early Christian exegesis, but they provide at least a starting point.

The Son of God

The Letter to the Hebrews

Hebrews, one of the most polished compositions in the NT, contains an impressive collection of highly sophisticated scriptural arguments. The letter opens with the first of a series of arguments calculated to prove the superiority of the "Son" through whom God has spoken "in these last days." The argument turns on the name given the revealer:

> When he had made purification for sins, he sat down at the right hand of the Majesty on high, having become as much superior to angels as the name he has obtained is more excellent than theirs. (Heb. 1:3b–4)

In the list of biblical quotations that follows, the revealer is identified as God's Son by means of citations from Ps. 2:7 and 2 Sam. 7:14. In vv. 8–9, he is identified as "God" by means of a citation of Ps. 45:6–7, verses that speak both of his kingship and of his "anointing" by "God, your God." In v. 10 he is called Lord in the citation from Ps. 102:25–27. Though the word "Lord" is not included in the quotation of Ps. 110:1, it is implied.

The string of passages is the result of a highly developed exegetical tradition linking various biblical texts, some of which were part of the tradition from the earliest days. The dominant imagery is royal. It is not simply that Psalm 45 speaks of thrones and "anointing," or Psalm 110 of sitting at God's right hand. The citations from Ps. 2:7 and 2 Samuel 7 are taken from oracles in which God addresses the king-to-come as "my Son." The reference to this revealer as firstborn in v. 6 underscores the royal origin of the imagery: the epithet is taken from Ps. 89:27, a psalm that speaks explicitly of God's "Messiah" as David's heir. In this psalm as well, the relationship between God and the King is described in terms of father-son imagery (Ps. 89:26). In Hebrews at least, the title of Son that provides a thematic introduction to the opening section is a royal title— that is, it is language used to speak of the Messiah-King.

Prior to the discovery of the Qumran scrolls, the phenomenon was difficult to explain. As late as 1968, Ernst Haenchen could assert that "Son of God" was never used as a designation for the Messiah in Jewish circles.[21] Based on extant Jewish evidence, his assertion was warranted. The Targumim on 2 Sam. 7:14, 1 Chron. 17:13, and Ps. 2:7 take pains to avoid the implication that "son" is anything but a figure of speech (e.g., 1 Chron. 17:13: "I will love him as a father loves a son, and he will love me as a son loves his father").[22]

The commentary fragment from cave 4 discussed above has changed our perception of the matter considerably. The fragment demonstrates that Nathan's oracle was interpreted messianically in pre-Christian Jewish circles and that there was no apparent embarrassment about the father-son imagery. Though the midrash on Psalms 1–2 that follows in 4QFlor is unfortunately broken off, the reference to God's "begetting the Messiah" in 1QSa II, 11–12 indicates that Ps. 2:7, in which God addresses the king as "my son," was likewise understood as furnishing stock messianic language. The publication of J. T. Milik's long-awaited fragments indicates that "Son of God" and "Son of the Most High" could be used as epithets for the king—though in extant literature they were probably not used of the Messiah outside the NT.[23]

---

21. See n. 5 of the present chap.
22. See n. 15 of the present chap.
23. See n. 16 of the present chap.

Although the Letter to the Hebrews cannot be classified as very early in its exegesis, there is in the logic of these opening citations a clue to the use of "Son" in earlier tradition.

The Baptism of Jesus

The same association of son and king can be found in the Synoptic accounts of Jesus' baptism. The focus of all the accounts is the *Bat Qol:* "You are my son, my beloved, with you I am well-pleased" (we may take Mark's version as the earliest). Virtually all the phrases can be accounted for in the OT, an appropriate source of language for a voice from heaven. The clearest parallel is God's declaration in Ps. 2:7: "You are my son; today I have begotten you." The declaration also fulfills God's promise to David: "I will be his father, and he will be my son."

Messianic oracles are not the only source of language for the baptismal voice. It is difficult to miss an allusion to Isa. 42:1 LXX:

Behold my servant, whom I uphold,
  my chosen, in whom my soul delights;
I have put my Spirit upon him,
  he will bring forth justice to the nations.

Joachim Jeremias once argued that behind the "Son" in Mark 1:11 was an original *pais theou,* "child (or servant) of God."[24] What lies at the basis of the baptismal tradition, he argued, was the image of Jesus as the Servant of the Lord. Such an argument is difficult to sustain. The use of *huios* for *pais* would be unusual in any case. And in the NT, *pais* is not even a title. It occurs only in Acts, where it appears as royal terminology, primarily in the context of prayers. In Peter's prayer in Acts 4, David is referred to as "our father David, thy servant" (Acts 4:25). In the same prayer, the opening verses of Psalm 2 are cited and applied to the opposition of Herod and Pilate to the Lord's Anointed, "thy holy servant Jesus" (Acts 4:27). If anything, therefore, *pais* is a term used to speak of royalty, not a title in its own right. And as both Psalm 2 and 2 Samuel 7 make clear, the king can be called God's *huios.*

There are additional difficulties with Jeremias's interpretation. The allusion to Isaiah 42 in Mark does not derive from the LXX. The translation of *bechir* in Isa. 42:1 as *eklektos,* as in the LXX, seems more common than Mark's *agapētos* (though see Matt. 12:18).[25] There is

---

24. Jeremias, "pais theou," *TDNT* 5 (1972): 701–2.

25. Stendahl (*The School of St. Matthew,* 110) regards the *agapētos* in Matthew 12 as taken over from Mark and speaks of it as a possible "retained targumic rendering" (n. 6). Gundry (*Use of the Old Testament,* 30) notes a parallel to "beloved" in *Targ. Ps.* 2:7. Chilton (*A Galilean Rabbi and His Bible,* 125–31) seeks to derive the phrase

reason to suppose that the term "beloved" may derive from an interpretation of Genesis 22, where Isaac is called Abraham's "beloved" son (LXX). We know from elsewhere in the New Testament that Genesis 22 was an important text for Christian interpreters (see below, pp. 85–88). There seems little reason to believe that Isa. 42:1 represents the very earliest feature of the baptismal scene. Particularly since it has now been demonstrated that such oracles as Psalm 2 and 2 Samuel 7 were read as messianic prior to the Christian era, it seems most reasonable to locate the scene in royal ideology. Images from Isaiah and perhaps Genesis have been enlisted in filling out the career of the one God calls Son. It is possible, as I shall argue below, to explain the development of tradition in this direction; it is not possible to understand why an original *pais* should be changed to a *huios,* transforming a "servant oracle" into one declaring Jesus' messianic identity.

At least in Mark, the messianic associations of "Son of God" are apparent. Particularly striking is the scene before the Jewish court, where the high priest asks Jesus in that climactic scene, "Are you the Christ, the Son of the Blessed?" (14:61)—to which Jesus replies, "I am, and you will see . . ." The question and response occur as part of a trial dominated by royal imagery.[26]

The link between "Son" and "Messiah" established in the Letter to the Hebrews is present in Mark as well. There is evidence in Paul that the tradition likewise predates the earliest of the Gospels.

Pre-Pauline Tradition

The early character of the association between king and sonship is established by the confessional fragment to which Paul makes reference in Rom. 1:2–4: ". . . which he promised beforehand through his prophets in the holy scriptures, the gospel concerning his Son, who was descended from David according to the flesh and designated Son of God in power according to the Spirit of holiness by his resurrection from the dead, Jesus Christ our Lord." It is unnecessary to engage in the debate about the precise structure of the ancient fragment and Paul's modifications of it.[27] The reference to being "designated" to sonship indicates that

---

"in whom I am well pleased" from the Aramaic rendering of *bechir* elsewhere in the Targum on Isaiah (esp. 41:8–9; 43:10), though Mark's version could not have been derived from the rendering of 42:1.

26. Juel, *Messiah and Temple,* 77–83.

27. Cf. Käsemann, *Commentary on Romans,* 10–14.

it is conceived as an office into which one is installed. The royal character of the office is established by the reference to descent from David.
There is no contradiction between being descended "from [the seed of]
David according to the flesh" and "designated Son of God." What hap-
pens after the resurrection does not cancel what came before. On the
contrary, in 2 Samuel 7, it is the promised offspring of David who will be
installed in office and called son by God himself.[28] Nathan's oracle, with
Psalm 2, seems to furnish the pattern for the confessional fragment.[29]

Results

One source of language used of Jesus as God's Son is messianic oracles like 2 Samuel 7 and Psalm 2. That cannot be the only source. The
absolute "the Son" in Jesus' teaching, particularly in his parables, and
his (related) use of "Abba" in addressing God, cannot be derived from
messianic ideology. Nevertheless, to a greater degree than normally assumed, "Son of God" is an epithet used of Jesus because he is Messiah.
That is the logic in the Hebrews passage, in Mark 1:11; 14:61; and Rom.
1:2-4.

Hebrews is important for other reasons as well. In the opening chapter, the identity of Jesus as Messiah is important as a presupposition for
the author's argument. Its significance is its ability to make possible a
wider association of biblical images—like the use of "Son" and "Lord"
to speak of Jesus. The images are then developed further, and the specifically messianic (royal) overtones fade into the background. "Son of
God" becomes the basis of reflection on Jesus' relationship with the
Father and a way of understanding his relationship with other heavenly
beings.

The logic cannot be reversed. The confession of Jesus as Christ is not
derivable from use of "the Son" by Jesus. And the title Messiah is
not subject to further development in the way "Son of God" is—as, for
example, in Johannine tradition. "Christ" becomes a virtual second
name. The confession of Jesus as Messiah is the presupposition of NT
theology, not necessarily its content. Messianic oracles like 2 Samuel 7
have provided a basis for speaking of Jesus as God's Son, even if the
connections lie buried deep in the tradition.

---

28. Loevestam (*Son and Savior;* "Die Davidssohnfrage," *SEA* 27 [1962]: 72–82)
has argued that, for the author of Acts and for Mark, Jesus' resurrection is understood to be the fulfillment of God's promise to David of an offspring whose throne
would be established forever.

29. Kramer, *Christ, Lord, Son of God,* 108–10.

The Seed[30]

Unlike the Qumran exegete, Christian interpreters were interested in the imagery used to speak of the Messiah in 2 Samuel 7. The use of father-son imagery to speak about the relationship between God and the king to arise at the end of days became important. Traditions about the Son of God developed in various directions. Christians also focused on the use of "seed" to speak of the Christ. There is nothing unusual about the term; it means simply "offspring." It can be used to speak of a single offspring, or it can function as a collective noun to designate all offspring, that is, lineage. An example of this second usage can be found in the passage already cited in Rom. 1:3, where God's son is descended *ek spermatos Dauid* (from the line of David).

The use of the singular "seed" in 2 Samuel 7:12 and Ps. 89:4, 29, 36, however, made possible a distinctive line of argument regarding the identity and career of the Messiah. Because the Messiah can be called seed, other scriptural passages can be enlisted in describing his career. Though Peter's speech in Acts 3 is not the earliest example of this line of argument about the seed, it is a useful place to begin, because the exegesis is so explicit.

Acts 3:11–26

The speeches in the opening chapters of Acts are of enormous importance in the overall plan of the book. In the speeches, the author constructs a framework within which the story is to be understood. In Acts 2, Peter shows from the sign of the outpouring of the Spirit that a new time of repentance is at hand, when "all who call upon the name of the Lord will be saved" (Acts 2:21, quoting Joel 2:32). In Acts 3, Peter demonstrates the power of faith "in the name of the Lord" by healing a lame man, while also warning his audience that those who do not heed the invitation to repentance will be "rooted out" of the people of God. Stephen's speech in Acts 7 completes the framework by locating the division that the apostles' preaching creates among Jews within Israel's own history.[31]

Equally important is that the speeches construct the framework through interpretation of biblical texts. They flesh out Jesus' thematic

---

30. Wilcox, "The Promise of the 'Seed' in the New Testament and the Targumim," *JSNT* 5 (1979): 2–20.

31. Dahl, "The Story of Abraham in Luke-Acts," in *Jesus in the Memory of the Early Church,* 66–86; Jervell, *Luke and the People of God,* 41–74; and Juel, *Luke-Acts,* 69–77.

statement in Luke 24:44–47 that his death and resurrection as Christ, as well as the preaching of repentance and forgiveness to all nations, "has been written." In the speeches we see the biblical proof. The speech in Acts 3 takes a few terms from Exod. 3:6 and Isa. 52:13, and quotes Deut. 18:16–20 (in abridged and modified form) and Gen. 22:18. It is the last text, which speaks of Abraham's "seed," that is of particular interest.

The speech makes use of a variety of christological images. Jesus is called, at various points, "servant," *pais,* as well as the "holy and just one," the "author of life," the "prophet like Moses," and the "seed of Abraham." The theme of scriptural fulfillment dominates the speech. To be more precise, it is the theme of God's fulfillment of messianic promises that dominates the speech. The basic christological image is still the Messiah:

> But what God foretold by the mouth of all the prophets, that his Christ should suffer, he thus fulfilled. (Acts 3:18)

> . . . that times of refreshing may come from the presence of the Lord, and that he may send the Christ appointed for you, Jesus, whom heaven must receive until the time for establishing all that God spoke by the mouth of his holy prophets from of old. (3:19b–21)

The point is worth stressing. It is the scriptural program for "the Christ" of which Jesus speaks twice in Luke 24 that forms the thematic introduction to Acts. The centrality of Jesus' identity as Messiah-King is stressed in Peter's speech in Acts 2, in his prayer in Acts 4:24–30, and in Paul's speech in Acts 13.

The problem is that one of the scriptural prophecies Peter quotes is from Deuteronomy 18, where God promises through Moses a prophet like Moses whom he will raise up at a future time. Jesus is identified as that prophet (Acts 3:22–26) while also being Messiah. In prior tradition, "prophet" was not the same as "Christ." The figures are clearly distinguishable in the eschatological expectations at Qumran and among Samaritans. Even in Luke's Gospel (9:18–22) the difference between prophet and Christ is presumed in the disciples' response to Jesus' question about what people thought of him. The people regard him as a prophet; Peter's response "[You are] the Christ of God" follows Jesus' question "But who do *you* say I am?" The *hymeis de* presupposes there is a difference between what the people and the disciples think.

In Luke-Acts, however, Messiah and prophet have been harmonized. One means is the use of Isaiah 61 in Luke 4:17–19, read at Jesus' inauguration at the synagogue in Nazareth. He is the Messiah; earlier chapters have established that. He has been anointed by the Spirit at his baptism. The use of the verb "anoint" in Isaiah 61 ("The Spirit of the Lord is upon me, because he has anointed me") makes it possible to attribute to the anointed One functions normally ascribed to prophets—like teaching and healing. Jesus can be both King and a prophet like Moses.[32]

The identification of Jesus as the prophet from Deuteronomy 18 is important for what implications can be drawn about the dispute taking place in the Jewish community regarding the preaching of the apostles. Jesus is shown to be the sign by which membership in the people of God is determined (Luke 2:34–35). Those Jews who refuse to heed the words of Jesus as spoken by his apostles forfeit their birthright and no longer deserve the name of Israelite. They have been "rooted out" of the people. The speech insists that the days of which Moses spoke have arrived.

The threat in Deuteronomy is matched by a promise from Genesis: "And in your seed shall all the families of the earth be blessed" (Gen. 22:18). The term *ethnē,* "nations," has been changed to *patriai,* "families," probably to ensure that Peter's Jewish audience be included in the promise. In good midrashic form, the promise is interpreted almost word for word: "God, having raised up his servant, sent him to you first, to bless you in turning every one of you from your wickedness" (Acts 3:26). The comment suggests that God has kept his word to Abraham by "raising up his servant" (the term *pais* has already been used to speak of Jesus in 3:13, where it is surely part of an allusion to Isa. 52:13). God has sent him as a "blessing"—referring to "blessing" in Genesis, interpreted by Peter as an offer of repentance and forgiveness. "You," Peter's Jewish audience, is given pride of place among the "families of the earth."

What remains unexpressed is the justification for reading "seed" in Genesis as a genuine singular instead of a collective noun, and referring it to a specific figure—Jesus, God's Servant. The mechanism is obvious enough: the noun is singular. The critical unexpressed link in the exegetical argument, on which everything depends, is the use of "seed" in 2 Samuel 7 and Psalm 89. As Messiah, Jesus is David's seed; by analogy, he may be understood as the seed promised Abraham by whom the families of the earth will be blessed.

An assertion that a link was established with Genesis 22 by means of the use of "seed" in the passage and in royal oracles requires some

---

32. Luke's harmonizations of the traditions are very different from those encountered in John's Gospel, on which see Meeks, *The Prophet-King.* I have discussed the speech of Peter in more detail in an article, "Peter's Speech in Acts 3," which is to appear in a Festschrift for Henry Fischel.

substantiation, which will be provided by Gal. 3. Alternative routes to the famous story of Isaac's binding are possible. One might argue that it is Jesus' identity as Servant of the Lord that established the link based on the thesis that Isaac had been identified as the Isaianic servant in pre-Christian tradition (on the use of servant material from Isaiah, see chap. 5). It seems unlikely that there existed any separate identification of Jesus as Servant of the Lord at any stage in the tradition, and it is at least the case that in Acts, "servant" is used of Jesus only as language appropriate to the king (Acts 4:25, 27, 30). It is probable that behind the identification of Jesus as the seed promised Abraham in Acts 3 is his prior identification as the seed promised David. The argument is substantiated by Paul's use of Genesis in Galatians 3, and the antiquity of the tradition employed by Luke is likewise guaranteed.

Galatians 3

Much of this chapter in Paul's Letter to the Galatians is devoted to a detailed scriptural argument about faith and the law. It is designed to prove Paul's point that faith in Christ excludes works of law, notably circumcision. The argument is intricate, and there is still no agreement among commentators about its logic.[33] The portion of the argument in which we are interested, however, is clear, and it depends upon the identification of Jesus as the "seed" from Gen. 22:18.

The critical section is Gal. 3:13–14. Having established the opposition between faith and law by means of citations from Hab. 2:4 and Lev. 18:5, and having relegated all who do not do the law to the curse pronounced in Deut. 27:28, Paul argues for the redeeming power of faith by citing Deut. 21:23 ("Cursed is anyone who hangs on a tree"), which he understands in light of Genesis 22. Jesus takes the curse of the law upon himself, thus redeeming all who are under the curse. The image that lies behind the conception of Jesus' death is that of the ram offered as a substitute for Isaac. The implications of this death are likewise understood in light of Genesis 22. Verse 14 is a paraphrase of Gen. 22:18: ". . . that in Christ Jesus the blessing of Abraham might come upon the Gentiles, that we might receive the promise of the Spirit through faith."

The expression "blessing of Abraham" is taken from Gen. 28:4, where it appears in Isaac's blessing of Jacob: "May he give the blessing of Abraham to you and to your seed." God's promise to Abraham in Genesis 22 is read in light of the earlier promise in Genesis 15, where Abraham

---

33. One plausible reading has been proposed by Dahl in "Contradictions in Scripture," in *Studies in Paul,* esp. 169–77.

"believed God, and it was reckoned to him for righteousness." Most important is the substitution of "in Christ Jesus" for "in your seed." The interpretation exploits the use of the singular of *sperma:*

> Now the promises were made to Abraham and to his offspring. It does not say, "And to offsprings," referring to many; but, referring to one, "And to your offspring," which is Christ." (Gal. 3:16)

The identification of "seed" and "Christ" coincides with what we have observed in Acts. Paul rarely uses *Christos* as a title for a figure distinct from Jesus Christ, but the titular significance is apparent here. Any doubts can be dispelled by the paraphrase of an explicitly messianic text just a few verses later:

> Why then the law? It was added because of transgressions, till the offspring should come to whom the promises had been made. (Gal. 3:19)

Paul paraphrases Gen. 49:10, a line from Jacob's blessing of Judah in his testament. The enigmatic Hebrew reads, *ad ki yabo Shiloh,* which the LXX renders, *heōs an elthē ta apokeimena autō.* The messianic interpretation of the blessing of Judah is apparent in Jewish sources.[34] This line is rendered:

4QPB:
> "Until the Messiah of Righteousness comes, the branch of David."

Fragmentary Targum Genesis 49:10:
> "Until the King Messiah comes, for the kingdom belongs to him."

Targum Neofiti Genesis 49:10:
> "Until the King Messiah comes, whose is the kingship; to him shall all the kingdoms be subject."

In each case, the Hebrew is read not to mean "until Shiloh comes" but "until he comes for whom it is" (i.e., until he comes to whom it [the promise] belongs).

In Galatians, "offspring" ("seed") has been inserted into the paraphrase of Gen. 49:10, confirming the link with more obvious messianic oracles like 2 Samuel 7 and Psalm 89, as well as with the preceding citation of Gen. 22:18. Paul interprets the Torah as an interim ordinance valid only "until the offspring should come to whom the promise had been made"—that is, the promise made "to Abraham and to his seed." What lies at the base of this construction is the identification of

---

34. Aberbach and Grossfeld, *Targum Onkelos on Genesis 49,* 14–15.

Jesus as Messiah. That identification makes possible the association of the various scriptural texts.

Summary

The establishment of a link with Genesis 22 was to bear considerable fruit—a case that has been argued by Vermes and by Nils Dahl, among others.[35] The clear allusion to Gen. 22:18 in Rom. 8:32, for example, suggests the possible shape of an interpretive tradition: as Abraham did not spare his only son, so God did not spare his—as the means of fulfilling his promise to Abraham that in his seed all the Gentiles would be blessed.[36] Paul could use the argument to defend his ministry to Gentiles or to prove that the death of the Messiah was a suitable climax to the ministry of the one whom God designated as the source of blessing promised Abraham in remembrance of the Akedah.[37]

The point is not that such arguments are demanded by the Scriptures but that they are understandable given certain ground rules and a basic assumption. The traditions depend upon an approach that is scholarly though not scholastic. The connections established among the various scriptural texts that underlie Paul's arguments in Galatians and Romans, and Luke's construction in Acts 3, depend upon analogy that is based on similar wording. They depend upon the identification of Jesus as the "seed." That identification, in turn, depends upon messianic oracles like 2 Sam. 7:10–14, which could be applied to Jesus because he was confessed as the Christ. The Scriptures were used not to prove that Jesus was the Christ but to explain what the confession means and what the implications are. The "proof" of Jesus' messiahship in Acts represents a further development.[38]

The brief commentary on 2 Samuel 7 from cave 4 at Qumran proves

---

35. An additional link between the "seed" in Genesis and messianic tradition may be provided by Psalm 2, a "messianic" psalm that says to the Lord's anointed, "Ask of me, and I will make the nations your heritage, and the ends of the earth your possession." The psalm not only provides the scriptural justification for a messianic interpretation of Abraham's "seed" but offers evidence of such an interpretation within the Bible itself.

36. Vermes, "Redemption and Genesis xxii: The Binding of Isaac and the Sacrifice of Jesus," in *Scripture and Tradition,* 193–227; and Dahl, "The Atonement: An Adequate Reward for the Akedah?" in *The Crucified Messiah,* 146–60.

37. For the logic of such arguments and a fascinating introduction into the lore of the Akedah, see Spiegel, *Last Trial.*

38. On christological proof in Acts, see Kurz, "The Function of Christological Proof from Prophecy in Luke and Justin" (diss., Yale Univ., 1976).

that Nathan's oracle was read as a messianic promise prior to the NT, and it serves as a useful comparison with Christian exegesis. The passage furnished the sectarian community with an opportunity to reflect on their future in terms of the "place" and the "rest" God promised David. Christian interpreters were more interested in the images used of the coming king, like "seed" and "son." The images provided links with other material that allowed reflection on Jesus' death, on the status of Gentiles within the believing communities, and on the relationship of the gospel of the crucified Christ to the law of Moses.

The paucity of allusions to 2 Samuel 7 suggests that its importance was located at a stage in the history of interpretation soon superseded, a stage to which we have only limited access. Enough traces remain, however, for us to identify Nathan's oracle as one of the foundational christological texts. The oracle provided a way into the Scriptures for those who confessed Jesus as the promised Messiah, and it generated interpretive traditions that led into the more developed reflection of the early church.

4

CHRIST
THE CRUCIFIED

Christian Interpretation
of the Psalms

THE ROLE OF THE PSALMS IN THE
PASSION TRADITION

The Psalter played a critical role in the development of the passion tradition. In all the Gospels, the story of Jesus' death is narrated with features taken from Psalms 22, 31, and 69, to name the most obvious. It is perhaps not difficult to understand why biblical language would have been employed to narrate this most solemn event in Jesus' career. The conviction that Jesus' ministry was "in accordance with the scriptures"—that is, in accordance with the will of God—was severely tested by Jesus' inglorious death at the hands of the Romans. The greater effort was thus required to demonstrate the "scriptural" character of his rejection and death. Nor is it surprising that Jesus' followers turned to the Psalter to understand his crucifixion. The suffering of the righteous was a matter of considerable interest to the religious community out of whose experience and for whom the psalms were composed. In numerous psalms, innocent sufferers bring their case before God in the form of complaints and petitions. The thesis I am arguing in this book, however, is that the starting point for interpretation of the OT was the confession of Jesus as the crucified and risen Messiah. The question is thus whether that proves true in the case of the psalms. Our task in this chapter is to understand why particular psalms were selected to speak about Jesus' death, and what their selection and interpretation contribute to our understanding of messianic exegesis.

A first step in answering such questions is to examine the place of the "passion psalms" in NT tradition. We began our study in the opening chapter with a brief examination of the confessional tradition to which Paul refers in 1 Cor. 15:3–7: ". . . that Christ died for our sins in accordance with the scriptures, that he was buried, that he was raised on the third day in accordance with the scriptures, and that he appeared to Cephas, then to the twelve." The psalms are enlisted to speak about Jesus' death, but they say nothing about atonement ("died for our sins"), and they provide little imagery with which to speak of Jesus' resurrection after three days. The psalms seem to have provided language and imagery not for the confessional tradition of the church but for narratives. In Mark, the narrative of which they are a part is only artificially connected to the Easter stories[1] and is virtually devoid of atonement imagery. The psalms are part of the narrative tradition, and there is good reason to follow the lead of form critics who have argued that the narrative tradition and the confessional tradition should be examined separately.

In view of the circuitous argumentation that follows, it might be helpful to summarize my thesis in advance. First, despite repeated attempts by source critics to isolate the OT allusions in the passion story from royal motifs (i.e., from Jesus' death as King of the Jews), the psalms were in all likelihood employed from the earliest stages of the tradition to recount the death of Jesus the King. Psalms 22, 31, and 69 were thus from the outset read as "messianic." No precedent exists in Jewish tradition for such a messianic reading of the psalms. The presupposition for such exegesis is the death of Jesus as a messianic pretender. The logic of such argumentation is midrashic. Precedent for reading these psalms as describing Jesus' death must thus be sought not in traditions about righteous sufferers but in the logic of messianic exegesis. Other biblical passages, like Psalm 89, which were read as messianic by Jewish interpreters, provided links in a chain of argumentation that can explain how these psalms came to be part of the passion tradition and why precisely Psalms 22, 31, and 69 should have been selected to tell the story of the death of the King of the Jews.

Our next step will be to locate the psalms in the story of the passion in the Synoptic Gospels.

---

1. I presume that Mark's Gospel in the earliest form available to us ended with 16:8.

THE PSALMS IN THE PASSION NARRATIVE

The passion narratives have received considerable attention since the advent of form criticism. It is particularly notable in Mark that the account of Jesus' trial and death is uncharacteristic of the tradition visible elsewhere in the Gospel. There is less unevenness. The narrator takes the trouble to mention special times and places ("It was two days before the Passover"; "And on the first day of Unleavened Bread . . ."; "And they went to a place which was called Gethsemane"; "And they brought him to the place called Golgotha"; "And it was the third hour, when they crucified him"; "And when the sixth hour had come . . ."; "And at the ninth hour . . ."). Following the lead of Martin Kähler, the great form critics Rudolf Bultmann, Martin Dibelius, and Karl Ludwig Schmidt insisted that the passion narrative and its history were something special, requiring a separate analysis of setting and development.

Proposals about the history of that tradition are almost as numerous as the scholars who have advanced them. Since the rise of redaction criticism in the late fifties, there has been increasing appreciation for Mark's own contributions to the passion narrative as it appears in his Gospel.[2] The growing conviction is reflected in a recent dissertation by Frank Matera.[3] There is still no consensus about the history of the Markan composition, however, much less a consensus about the history of the passion tradition itself.

One reason is the way the history of tradition is examined. Proposals usually begin with source analysis of one kind or another, a necessary enterprise in working back from the literature now available to us. In the Pauline letters, that involves identifying certain passages as remnants of earlier tradition—confessional fragments, hymns, liturgical material, and so on. The approach works well because there are clear indicators in the letters that Paul is working with traditional material. On occasions he says so (1 Cor. 15:3–7; 11:23–26). The structure of Rom. 1:2–4 and Phil. 2:5–11 is a reliable indicator of previous formulation, and we can understand why Paul would have made use of traditional material in both contexts.

The problem is more difficult in the Gospels, where narratives make no reference to sources. Where sources can be identified, as in the case

---

2. For various proposals about the history of the passion tradition, see the first chap. in my *Messiah and Temple,* and the brief introductory chap. and bibliography in Matera, *Kingship.*

3. See previous note.

of Matthew and Luke, separation of earlier and later layers in the tradition can be carried out with some conviction. With Mark, the case is different. Source analysis depends on the ability to break the narrative down into parts. Form critics have been able to show that in many cases those components were individual units of traditions—or perhaps collections of units—from which the evangelist fashioned his narrative. In the passion narrative, however, the contours of those units are more difficult to identify. Source analysis must rely on alleged unevenness in the narrative—breaks, contradictions, redundancies, or other signs of clumsy editing that betray sources. Arguments must then depend upon identification of Markan vocabulary and Markan compositional techniques that enable one to distinguish tradition from redaction.

The limitations of the method are obvious. What is "Markan" is associated primarily with disruptions and corrections obvious in the narrative. And what constitutes contradiction or redundancy is often determined without any attention to the flow of the story as a whole. If we begin studying the Gospels by searching for inconsistencies and disruptions, we shall surely find them. If we begin by examining the narrative itself, we may discover that the alleged disruptions and inconsistencies disappear. For those interested in questions about a pre-Markan narrative, studying Mark must surely be the first order of business. Training in form criticism produced a generation of scholars almost incapable of reading stories as stories. Though that has changed in recent decades, studies of Mark still appear that make use of a narrow range of techniques—developed by source critics—which are least capable of generating convincing arguments.[4]

---

4. Matera is a good example of a recent scholar who relies on "redactional techniques" as a way of identifying the work of the evangelist. Though he insists that he is not interested in sketching a history of the passion tradition and that he pursues compositional analysis (*Kingship,* 4–5), his identification of Mark's literary activity still depends upon the distinction between tradition and redaction. See my *Messiah and Temple* for a critique of such an approach, and the more recent works by Petersen *(Literary Criticism for New Testament Critics)* and Tannehill ("The Gospel of Mark as Narrative Christology," *Semeia* 16 [1979]: 57–95; "The Disciples in Mark: The Function of a Narrative Role," *JR* 57 [1977]: 386–405). There are exceptions to the trends. Harvey, in his *Jesus and the Constraints,* employs historical reconstruction as the way to interpret Mark. He tries to show what would have been possible for the evangelist to write in view of the historical situation; this is an approach similar in many respects to that of Schweitzer. As I shall argue below, it is often the case that Harvey chooses to interpret the clear by the obscure, ignoring directions suggested by the text. His hypothetical historical reconstruction of the first Christian century becomes more a liability than a useful interpretive tool.

THE PSALMS IN MARK'S GOSPEL

One of the impressive features of Mark's passion narrative is its thematic consistency: Jesus is tried and executed as Messiah. That thematic note is introduced in his trial before the Jewish court. Mark intends to portray a formal trial. Witnesses are introduced, charges made, and a verdict pronounced. At the climax of the trial, the crucial question is put to Jesus by the high priest: "Are you the Christ, the Son of the Blessed?" For the first and only time in the Gospel, Jesus provides an unambiguous answer about this identity: "I am." The "Son of man" saying that follows promises vindication in the eyes of his would-be judges when they see him enthroned at God's right hand and coming with the clouds.[5] The trial is a climax in the Gospel.

Students of the trial of Jesus frequently point to a discordancy in Mark 15:1. The account of the gathering of the Sanhedrin early in the morning makes no reference to the trial. Jesus is handed over to Pilate, to be tried as a political criminal on political charges. The omission of the trial before the Sanhedrin would make virtually no difference to the action in the story. That is certainly true. It is remarkable that there is no effort, as in John, to explain why the Jewish court did not stone Jesus if he was convicted of a religious crime (John 18:28–32). Important questions remain for the historian, and the apparent lack of connection between the trial in Mark 14 and the gathering of the Sanhedrin in Mark 15:1 may offer a clue regarding Mark's sources. The trial before the Jewish court is anything but superfluous in its present setting, however; it performs essential functions in Mark's story. It gathers up repeated references to the temple from Mark 11—13 and introduces them into the passion story; they are picked up in 15:29, 38. Further, it introduces the basis of Jesus' "rejection" by the Jewish religious leaders as well as of his condemnation by Pilate. Jesus is tried and executed for claiming to be King—a designation Jesus accepts. The basis of Jesus' rejection will also serve as the basis for his vindication by God at his resurrection.

The tone of the Markan passion story is also consistent, and it too is set by the account of Jesus' trial. The story is deeply ironic. On the one hand, we are shown an alleged king whose movement collapses and who is incapable of helping himself. On the other, we are offered glimpses of

---

5. As in Jesus' "Son of man" statement in Mark 13:24–27, emphasis falls on the "seeing." The point is not that Jesus is Son of man as opposed to something else but that his judges (and eventually everyone) will see his vindication. See below, pp. 142–46, 165–67.

one who is already establishing the foundations of a new movement and whose supposed inability to save himself is a necessary part of the planned salvation. Peter's denial is an important clue. The sketchy account ends with Peter's recalling Jesus' prophecy: "Before the cock crows twice, you will deny me three times" (14:30). Events unfold precisely as Jesus predicted: Peter's denial, Jesus' death, and his resurrection are all included in his forecasts (14:28–30). And we learn that Peter's denial takes place as Jesus is being mocked as a prophet by servants of the court (14:65) in response to his absurd prediction about a heavenly enthronement and glorious return (14:62). Yet as they taunt him—"Prophesy!"—one of his predictions is being fulfilled to the letter. The story is ironic throughout. Jesus' would-be judges play roles assigned to them which are very different from what they understand them to be. Their actions make possible what Jesus has predicted—"as it has been written" (14:21).

Royal imagery dominates the ensuing narrative. Jesus is arraigned, tried, condemned, mocked, and executed as King. The kingship is expressed differently by the Jewish court and the pagan Romans. For Israelites, Jesus' alleged kingship is religious as well as political. "You are the Christ, the Son of the Blessed, then?" asks the high priest (14:61). The chief priests hurl the claim at Jesus as he hangs on the cross: "Let the Christ, the King of Israel, come down now from the cross, in order that we might see and believe" (15:32). Israel's King is "anointed by God," that is, the Christ.

To the Romans, the royal claim is understood in political terms: Jesus is tried, mocked, and crucified as King of the Jews. Jew is what Gentiles called Israelites; "King of the Jews" and "Christ, the King of Israel" are appropriate to the speakers.

In both cases, the use of the terms by Jesus' enemies is ironic. They speak the truth, though they do not know it. Jesus is the Christ, the Son of God (1:1; 14:61). The major christological titles appear on the lips of enemies, who regard them as inappropriate, blasphemous, or seditious. The irony is that they speak the truth about Jesus every time they taunt him. It is the enemies of Jesus who provide for his investiture and enthronement, contrary to their intentions and beyond their understanding.

The irony in the passion story works because the reader possesses information not available to the characters in the story. The privileged information includes knowledge that "the Son of man goes as it is written of him" (Mark 14:21). A script is provided for the story, which provides the author both with a way of testifying that the events occurred in accordance with the will of God and with a way of making sense of raw data that require interpretation. As signals of this "scriptural" dimension of the story, biblical words and phrases are used. Jesus' words at his trial are a case in point: "You will see the Son of man seated at the right hand of Power and coming with the clouds of heaven" (Mark 14:62).

The words allude to Ps. 110:1 and Dan. 7:13, perhaps also to Zech. 12:10. From early times these OT passages had an important place in Christian reflection on Jesus' resurrection (see below, pp. 139–50).[6] The biblical phrases anticipate what the reader knows will happen to Jesus, and they do so in such a way as to underscore the scriptural dimensions of the events.

In the account of Jesus' crucifixion, it is words and phrases from the psalms that perform this function. Clear criteria for determining possible allusions are important here, for Jesus' plight seems to fit the plots of many laments, and scholars have suggested numerous parallels.[7] The proposals have included passages like Isaiah 53, to which there are no verbal links in Mark 15.[8] It seems wisest to begin with the clearest allusions before proceeding to the less sure, making verbal identity with the LXX the basic criterion. The clearest allusions are to Psalm 22 (LXX 21), the most obvious being Jesus' last words: "My God, my God, why hast thou forsaken me?" (Mark 15:34 = Ps. 22:1 [LXX 21:2]). Similarly clear is the allusion to Ps. 22:18 (LXX 21:19) in Mark 15:24: "And they crucified him, and divided his garments among them, casting lots for them, to decide what each should take." In the psalm, the words appear on the lips of the sufferer: "They divide my garments among them, and for my raiment they cast lots." Only slightly less certain is the reference to the passers-by: "And those who passed by derided him, wagging their heads" (Mark 15:29 = Ps. 22:7 [LXX 21:8]). The verb for "derided" in Mark is *eblasphēmoun* ("derided" is a poor translation; it really means "blasphemed," and the relationship to the charge against Jesus cannot be missed); the psalm used *ekmyktērizein*.

---

6. Perrin, "Mark 14:62: The End Product of a Christian Pesher Tradition?" *NTS* 12 (1966): 150–55; Juel, *Messiah and Temple*, 85–93; and Lindars, *Jesus Son of Man*, 110–12.

7. Such parallels to Jesus' passion from the psalms include Pss. 27:12; 35:11; 109:2 (Mark 14:56–57); 35:7 (Mark 15:32); 38:13–16 (Mark 14:61); 109:25 (Mark 15:29).

8. Maurer, "Knecht Gottes und Sohn Gottes im Passionsbericht," *ZTK* 50 (1953): 1–38. See below, chap. 5.

In the same category belongs the comment about a bystander giving Jesus vinegar to drink, a probable allusion to Ps. 69:21 (LXX 68:22): "And one ran and, filling a sponge full of vinegar, put it on a reed and gave it to him to drink" (Mark 15:36). Again, the third-person narrative alters the first-person of the psalm: "They gave me poison for food, and for my thirst they gave me vinegar to drink." (69:21 [LXX 68:22]).

The allusions employ words from the psalms, agreeing almost word for word with the LXX. They do not intrude into the story, introduced by a formula, for the sake of making an argument.[9] The first-person form has been altered to third-person to fit the narrative mode. The allusions are part of the narrative, so much a part that more than one scholar has proposed that the psalms gave birth to the narrative.[10]

What the allusions imply we have yet to determine. At the very least, the phrases from the psalms remind those who know the Scriptures that this is no ordinary story. Behind the grim reality stands the will of God; Jesus goes "as it has been written of him." C. H. Dodd believed that the allusions imply more. Arguing that reference to part of the psalm calls to mind the whole psalm, Dodd saw in the movement of Psalm 22 from complaint to vindication a fitting interpretation of the story Christians wanted to tell. Such an interpretation remains attractive even if Dodd's thesis regarding the contextual nature of early Christian exegesis cannot be sustained.

Such appreciation of the function of scriptural allusions does not depend upon the conscious intention of the author. Nor is it relevant here to know at what stage in the tradition the biblical material found its way into the narrative. The point is that words and phrases from the psalms were used to construct a framework within which to make sense of Jesus' death—and to offer testimony that his death was "in accordance with the scriptures."

The matter of determining at what stage the psalms were incorporated into the passion tradition is particularly difficult. Dibelius and

---

9. On the significance of the absence of introductory formulas in Mark's account, see Suhl, *Die Funktion der alttestamentlichen Zitate.*

10. Those who argue that the psalms gave rise to features of the narrative include Dibelius (*From Tradition to Gospel,* 186–87) and Lindars (*New Testament Apologetic,* 90–91). Among the more ambitious attempts to derive the passion narrative from Psalm 22 is that by Peddinghaus ("Die Entstehung der Leidensgeschichte" [diss., Univ. of Heidelberg, 1965]). See also von Oswald, "Die Beziehungen zwischen Psalm 22 und dem vormarkinischen Passionsbericht," *ZTK* 101 (1979): 53–66. These views are discussed in Matera, *Kingship,* 125–30.

others have argued that the biblical material generated the narrative. Writing a history of tradition requires criteria, however, by which to distinguish primary from secondary, early from late. The coherence of the trial and death scenes makes it difficult to explain one feature or the other as an addition to a prior narrative. The story is ironic throughout. Characters, whether Jewish or Roman, consistently play the role of witnesses whose statements of abuse are true in ways they cannot understand. Royal imagery dominates both trial and death scenes. Even the mention of Jesus' alleged threat against the temple has an important role in Mark:[11] the "prophecy" is recalled in the mockery at the foot of the cross (15:29), and it is in some measure fulfilled with the tearing of the temple curtain at the moment of Jesus' death (15:38). The three passages gather up various statements about the temple in the concluding chapters of Mark (11:15–19; 12:28–34; 13:1–2; etc.).[12] The destruction of the old temple and the building of a new may well relate to messianic traditions, spelling out Jesus' role as the Christ (see 2 Sam. 7:13; Zech. 6:12; *Targ. Isa.* 53:5).[13] Allusions to Psalms 22 and 69 have an established place in a coherent story. And the role they play is consistent with the narrative: they contribute to the irony. Unknown to the characters in the drama, the events "have been written." The biblical allusions are in no sense extraneous additions tacked on to the story to make a point. Nor are they separable from other features of the narrative.

The persistence of source-critical analyses of Mark 14–15 is surely evidence that there is justification for viewing Mark as an author who composed by working with traditional material. Writing a history of those pre-Markan traditions, however, is another matter. Matera, the latest to apply redactional criteria to these chapters, finds evidence of Mark's hand everywhere. His excessively broad view of "bracketing" and other supposed features of Mark's style are not convincing, but his arguments from a redactional perspective are as convincing as any others—and he is able to show that each alleged redundancy has a role to play in the story. His study undermines the logic of the various reconstructions of a pre-Markan narrative, as he points out:

---

11. I have argued that the same irony is present in the "confession" of the centurion, whose statement is at one level an acknowledgment of a mistake and the harmless character of Jesus ("He was . . .") and at another level testimony to him as the Son of God. The grammatical ambiguity makes the genuine ambiguity—and the irony—possible. See Juel, *Messiah and Temple,* 82–83.

12. Those who regard the placement of the temple charge in the trial narrative as Mark's work include Dibelius, Bultmann, Schreiber, Linnemann, and Donahue. See ibid., 20–35.

13. Ibid., 127–42.

Therefore, we suggest that instead of a primitive narrative or a present historic tradition, we have a series of loosely connected phrases which Mark has assembled. . . . In other words, we do not believe that Mark was working with a connected narrative but rather with a series of traditions and details which he has assembled.[14]

The conclusion may seem vague. A form critic might well ask what conceivable form these "traditions and details" might have had in pre-Markan tradition and what their setting could have been. Perhaps such questions cannot be answered. That seems to be Matera's point. It is quite possible to sift through Mark's narrative for verses and half-verses that can be isolated from their present setting and woven together into another aesthetically satisfying unit. Eta Linnemann's identification of two separate trial traditions is but one example. Her proposal, which requires altering verse order as well as breaking single verses into two, only underscores how completely such analysis is a matter of personal taste and incapable of proof.[15] In view of the consistency of Mark's passion narrative, sufficient criteria simply do not exist for isolating a pre-Markan narrative—even if the theoretical possibility of such a narrative be granted.

If source criticism provides an insubstantial basis upon which to construct theories about the development of the passion tradition, the use of the scriptural material may provide a more promising foundation. We know that two psalms have played a role in shaping the story (Psalms 22; 69). If we take Luke into account, we can include Psalm 31 as well (Ps. 31:5, quoted in Luke 23:46: "Father, into your hands I commit my spirit"). It is difficult to imagine a stage in the tradition that was not influenced by the psalms. Jesus' death was never a matter for disinterested narration, as its absence from non-Christian sources makes apparent. Those who believed that the one crucified as King of the Jews was raised from the dead by the God to whom he had committed his cause went to the Scriptures for language suitable to tell the story of the one whose career culminated a history of promise, since it was in the Scriptures that God's will had been disclosed. The major question has to do with the relation of those psalms to the image of Jesus as the crucified Messiah. It seems reasonable to argue that from the outset, the biblical material was understood as messianic—that is, as appropriate to the story of the crucified Christ. If we are able to show how such an interpretation of Psalms 22, 31, and 69 is possible, we will have made an important advance in reconstructing the history of the passion tradition.

---

14. Matera, *Kingship*, 45.

15. For Linnemann's reconstruction of alleged pre-Markan trial narratives, see her *Studien zur Passionsgeschichte*, 129–34. For a critique, see Juel, *Messiah and Temple*, 24–29.

MESSIANIC INTERPRETATION OF THE PSALMS

Most interpreters have proposed that Psalm 22 holds the key to the use of biblical material in the passion tradition, if not to the tradition itself. Several recent studies take as their point of departure the numerous relationships between Mark 15 and Psalm 22.[16] Dibelius believed the psalm provided the first passion story. Dodd argued that the isolated references arose from a more comprehensive interpretation of the psalm—so that allusions to the lament would likewise direct the reader to the second half of the psalm, where God's rule is celebrated in anticipation of deliverance. Whether or not such cases can be argued convincingly, it does seem that the psalm was important for more than a verse or two. Several interpretations in the NT outside the Gospels attest to its importance (e.g., Heb. 2:12), and the allusions in the Gospel presume that Jesus is the speaker, to whom the various complaints are appropriate. By the time of Clement and Justin, the psalm was read as a whole (see below, pp. 110–12) as a script for Jesus.

The most ambitious proposal about Christian use of Psalm 22 has been undertaken by Hartmut Gese.[17] He proposes to locate the origin of the passion narrative and of the Lord's Supper in Psalm 22. His proposal seeks to bridge form-critical studies of the psalms with the study of early Christianity and the NT. He begins with the customary form-critical analysis, classifying the psalm as an individual lament coupled with an individual thanksgiving (p. 5). The distinctiveness of the psalm, he insists, becomes clear only through an analysis of the movement of the whole. The psalm deals in a paradigmatic way with God's rescue of a petitioner from death. What is unique is the inclusion in the concluding worship of the ends of the earth—even the dead:

> Contrary to the entire tradition of the laments, according to which every remembrance of Yahweh is impossible in the underworld, v. 29 anticipates . . . the adoration of the dead, who thereby share life; and v. 30 allows the proclamation of Yahweh's saving deed (singular! thus precisely this redemption of the petitioner from death) to be continued throughout the future: "for he has wrought it."[18]

What is expressed here, Gese argues, is nothing short of an apocalyptic theology. Verbal links with the theme of God's kingship (vv. 3, 28) tie the rescue of the righteous sufferer from death to the eschatological theme of the kingdom of God. It is this apocalyptic motif that Mark seems to express by means of his use of Psalm 22 in narrating the story of Jesus' death. In so doing, he builds on an older motif, perhaps the most ancient interpretation of Jesus' death:

---

16. See n. 10 of the present chap.

17. Gese, "Psalm 22 und das Neue Testament: Der alteste Bericht vom Tode Jesu und die Entstehung des Herrenmahles," *ZTK* 65 (1968): 1–22.

18. Ibid., 12.

Here the reference is not to atonement, as in Isaiah 53, indeed at this point not even to the Messiah. Rather, death, elevated to the deepest experience of suffering, leads, by means of the activity of God that redeems from death, to the inbreaking of the eschatological *basileia tou theou.*[19]

Students of the OT may reflect on the appropriateness of Gese's form-critical analysis; they may also wish to dispute his contention that the psalm expresses an "apocalyptic theology," however that is to be defined. For understanding the use of Psalm 22 in the NT however, Gese's analysis is of little use. The point is worth making in view of other studies of the use of psalms in the NT which reflect little appreciation of first-century modes of scriptural interpretation. There is no evidence that first-century interpreters were concerned about formal issues. The wording and form provided certain constraints, but they were hardly determining factors in midrashic tradition. Gese's approach simply ignores the difference between the religion and cult of ancient Israel and the world of first-century midrash—or perhaps more accurately, it ignores the difference between first-century and twentieth-century exegesis.

A glimpse at the midrash on psalms provides ample evidence of the distance that separates midrashic exegesis from the original setting of the psalms and from the modern world. The collection of interpretive comments is late; additions to the growing collection continued into the thirteenth century.[20] Many of the comments are far earlier, however, and the logic of exposition is little different from that of other midrashim. The most common exposition of the psalm reads it as a reference to Esther. Here are examples:

"My God . . ." (The verse is applied to Esther in *b. Meg.* 15b)

"For dogs have compassed me" (Ps 22:17)—that is, Haman's sons have compassed me; "the assembly of the wicked have inclosed me" (ibid.)—that is, Haman's hosts have inclosed me."
    "My hands and my feet they made repulsive" (Ps 22:17) [word play on the Hebrew]. According to R. Judah, Esther said: Though Haman's sons practiced sorcery on me so that in the sight of Ahasuerus my hands and feet were repulsive, yet a miracle was wrought for me, and my hands and feet were made to shine like sapphires. (*Midr.* Psalm 22; see 26)[21]

The comments presume that the speaker in the psalm is Esther. Once the initial identification was made, the psalm could be applied line by line to her story. Here the unusual Hebrew in v. 17 is derived from a

---

19. Ibid., 17.
    20. See the short introduction to *The Midrash on Psalms* by its translator, Braude (1:xxi–xxxvi).
    21. The translations are taken from ibid. (here 1:320).

word meaning "ugly"; the presence of other comments on the term, based on other derivations, testifies both to the unusual character of the word and to common midrashic technique. There is nothing eschatological about this interpretation, and connections between the psalm and Esther's story are made not by reference to themes but by play on words and images.

It is even possible to suggest how the initial connection between Esther and Psalm 22 was made. In the Midrash on Psalms, the majority of comments are devoted to an exposition of a mysterious phrase in the preface, *ayeleth ha-Shachar* (RSV: "hind of the dawn"). The unusual phrase provides a possibility for imaginative interpretations. One meaning for the phrase is "the first rays of dawn." The midrashic comments play on the light imagery. Commenting on v. 1 of the psalm by citing a verse from Isaiah that refers to the "light of Israel" (Isa. 10:17), the midrashist says, "'Light of Israel' refers to Esther who shone like the light of morning for Israel."[22] Another comment says, "And so 'hind of the dawn' refers to Esther who brought forth the morning out of darkness."[23]

In the ancient world, the morning star was personified as Ishtar. It is likely that, reading *ayeleth ha-Shachar* as "morning star," the name Esther was suggested to imaginative interpreters because of its similarity to the name of the goddess Ishtar. The proposal is substantiated by the association of Esther and Ishtar in the Babylonian Talmud (*Meg.* 13a). The midrashic comments associating Esther with "light" and "morning" thus seem quite natural.

These rabbinic interpretations of Psalm 22 are probably to be located in Babylonian schools, where the association with Ishtar would be most familiar. The academic, playful tone of the comments is likewise typical of school tradition. It is thus unlikely that the identification of the speaker in Psalm 22 as Esther is early. The point, however, is that for the rabbis, form-critical considerations were of little importance. Their interpretations arose from linguistic possibilities in the actual wording of the text—even (or especially) the wording of the psalm titles. However compelling Gese's exposition of Psalm 22 might be for present-day students of the Bible, it sheds little light on first-century exegesis. Early Christian interpretation was far closer to that of the rabbis than to that of modern biblical scholars.

---

22. *Midr.* Ps. 22, sec. 3 (p. 298).
23. *Midr.* Ps. 22, sec. 5 (p. 302). I thank my student Glen Menzies and my colleague Jonathan Paradise for calling my attention to these passages and the possible link with Ishtar.

Gese's second major argument, that the psalm depicts a paradigmatic righteous sufferer and that application of the psalm to Jesus is "premessianic," is shared by a wider circle of scholars. A. E. Harvey, Klaus Berger, and L. Ruppert are among those who locate the application of Psalm 22 to Jesus in specific interpretive traditions within postbiblical Jewish circles.[24] What is crucial for such scholars is the familiar plot in the psalm: the righteous sufferer commits his cause to God, for which he is mocked and threatened even with death; God vindicates the righteous one. During the time of the Maccabees in particular, when Jews were persecuted for their fidelity to the tradition, events forced reflection upon the suffering and death of the righteous. Biblical texts like Psalm 22 and Isaiah 53 provided ways of thinking about righteous suffering, exemplified most clearly in the Wisdom of Solomon 2—5:

> The classic model of the innocent sufferer, mocked, abused, and persecuted for his piety was familiar from the OT; the fate of groups within Judaism—particularly Pharisaism in its formative period—whose convictions forced them to oppose the general trends of the society around them is vividly expressed in inter-testamental writings. But most significant for our purpose is the dramatic account in the Wisdom of Solomon of the righteous man who claims to have knowledge of God and who is mocked and hounded by the ungodly to the point of death, but finally vindicated by God. The echo of this in Matthew's passion narrative (27:43)—and indeed in one of the earliest Christian writings we possess (Phil 2:8-9)—shows that this paradigm of suffering and death inflicted on one who was wise and righteous, though it is fully developed only in writing which is characteristic of a deeply hellenized Judaism, must nevertheless have been familiar in Palestine.[25]

The existence of such traditions is beyond doubt; one cannot accuse Harvey of anachronism. One might still ask if Psalm 22 played a prominent role in the development of the wisdom tradition—and even if it did, why only Psalm 22 should be alluded to in Mark, and not Isaiah 53. The most serious objection to the proposal, however, is that Jesus is never depicted as a paradigmatic righteous sufferer. Harvey, Berger, and others have argued that in pre-Christian Jewish tradition the figure of the eschatological prophet and the righteous sufferer had been fused, providing Jesus and his followers with a conceptual model for a messenger of God who is rejected, suffers, and is vindicated. Again, however,

---

24. Harvey, *Jesus and the Constraints;* K. Berger, "Die königlichen Messiastraditionen des Neuen Testaments," *NTS* 20 (1973–74): 1–44; and Ruppert, *Jesus als der leidende Gerechte?*

25. Harvey, *Jesus and the Constraints,* 148.

the proposal relies heavily on conjecture, and it ignores the one solid fact noted in our study of the passion narratives: Jesus is executed as a king. Martin Hengel's objections to the "righteous sufferer" tradition are absolutely correct:

> The pattern of humiliation and exaltation of the righteous is far too general and imprecise to interpret the event which Mark narrates so skillfully and with such deep theological conviction. He is concerned with the utterly unique event of the passion and crucifixion of the Messiah of Israel which is without any parallel in the history of religion. For Mark, the few psalms of suffering which illuminate individual features of the suffering and death of Jesus, like Psalms 22 and 69, are exclusively *messianic* psalms, such as Ps 110 and 118. The "righteous" does not appear in connection with Jesus either in the two psalms or in Mark; it is only Matthew, with his rabbinic training who makes the Messiah Jesus into an exemplary saddiq. Where features from the suffering of the righteous man appear, for example in the mocking of Jesus, they are also in a messianic key. The suffering "of the righteous" is to be integrated completely into the suffering of the Messiah. The Messiah alone is the righteous and sinless one par excellence. His suffering therefore has irreplaceable and unique significance.[26]

The passion narratives remain our point of departure. In all four Gospels, at least one allusion to Psalm 22 is part of the story of the crucifixion of the King of the Jews. The irreducible historicity of the title renders unsatisfactory any explanations of the history of tradition that view the royal imagery as somehow derivative from earlier conceptions. It is difficult to understand how the story of a paradigmatic "righteous sufferer" could have been transformed into an account of the death of the King of the Jews and Christ, the King of Israel. It is conceivable, however, that material from the psalms could have been employed to tell the story of the King. We have observed in chapter 3 how biblical passages never read as messianic could be "adopted" as messianic by following the logic of midrash. A plausible explanation for the use of Psalms 22, 31, and 69 in the passion narratives is that in these psalms there is exegetical warrant for regarding the speaker as the Messiah. If they were not read as messianic in pre-Christian Judaism, they may well be among those adopted texts whose presence in the constellation of messianic passages is due both to some external factor (the prior confession of Jesus as Messiah) and to exegetical logic we should be able to reconstruct. The critical factor, then, is the reconstruction of a midrashic logic that can explain how these psalms came to narrate the story of the King of the Jews.

---

26. Hengel, *The Atonement*, 41.

Psalm 89

Our interest is the history of psalm exegesis and not simply the history of the passion tradition. The point is an important one. The obvious priority of Psalm 22 in the narrative tradition does not necessarily demonstrate its priority in the interpretation of the Psalter. As we have observed in the case of 2 Samuel 7, frequency of citation does not always provide a reliable indicator of exegetical priority.

I wish to propose Psalm 89 as one of the keys to the interpretive tradition. This psalm, which speaks of the Lord's "anointed," provides justification for regarding the "I" of certain psalms as the Messiah, and it employs a specific vocabulary to speak of the Messiah and his humiliation which is common to the three psalms in question (Psalms 22; 31; 69). We will briefly examine Jewish and Christian interpretation of this psalm, then ask what role it played in the formation of the passion tradition (where, however, Psalm 89 appears neither in allusions nor in direct quotations).

For students of royal traditions in the OT, Psalm 89 is of obvious importance. It provides perhaps the earliest version of Nathan's oracle, the promise of God's eternal support for the Davidic dynasty. For students of messianic tradition in postbiblical Judaism, the psalm is potentially important because it includes mention of God's "anointed":

> But now thou hast cast off and rejected,
>   thou art full of wrath against thy anointed.
> Thou hast renounced the covenant with thy servant;
>   thou hast defiled his crown in the dust.
>   (89:38–39)

The psalmist makes an appeal on behalf of the king by recalling God's promise to David. The plight of the king is similar to that of the righteous sufferer, but the appeal is made on his behalf not in terms of God's concern for the righteous in general but in terms of his covenant with David.

> Lord, where is thy steadfast love of old,
>   which by thy faithfulness thou didst swear to David?
>   (89:49)

The "anointed" himself makes a final appeal in the concluding verses:

> Remember, O Lord, how thy servant[27] is scorned;
>   how I bear in my bosom the insults of the peoples,

---

27. Note that the RSV text chooses the variant "servant" in 89:50. The Targumim, the NT, and rabbinic citations regularly treat the term as a singular, taking the

with which thy enemies taunt, O Lord,
with which they mock the footsteps of thy anointed.
(89:50-51)

Jewish Interpretation

There is no evidence from extant literature that Psalm 89 was interpreted as a messianic psalm prior to the Christian era. There are, however, several instances of such exegesis in midrashic literature. The
following are among the most important and interesting.

1. *b. Sanhedrin* 97a, on Psalm 89:52

("Blessed be the Lord for ever! Amen and Amen.").

> It has been taught, R. Judah said: "In the generation when the Son of
> David comes, the house of assembly will be for harlots, Galilee in
> ruins, Gablan lie desolate, the border inhabitants wander about from
> city to city, receiving no hospitality, the wisdom of scribes in disfa-
> vor, God-fearing men despised, people be dog-faced, and truth en-
> tirely lacking."

2. *Genesis Rabbah* on 49:8.[28]

In the lengthy comment on Jacob's promise to Judah, a listing
of the great descendants from this tribe is concluded with the
following:

> Furthermore, the royal Messiah will be descended from the tribe of
> Judah, as it says, "And it shall come to pass in that day, that the root
> of Jesse, that standeth for an ensign of the peoples, unto him shall the
> nations seek" (Isa 11:10). . . . Judah was the fourth of the tribal
> ancestors to be born, just as the daleth is the fourth letter of the
> alphabet and is the fourth letter of his name. On the fourth day
> the luminaries were created, while of the Messiah it is written, "And
> his throne [shall endure] as the sun before me" (Ps 89:37) . . . and so
> it says, "The sceptre shall not depart from Judah" (Gen 49:10); it is
> also written, "And thy house and thy kingdom shall be made sure
> forever" (II Sam 7:16); also, "For ever will I keep him for My mercy"
> (Ps 89:29).

Psalm 89 is included here among the more familiar messianic oracles (Gen. 49:8–12; Isa. 11:1ff.; 2 Sam. 7:10ff.).

"servant" as a reference to "your anointed [singular]" in 89:51. The textual evidence
does not support such a reading, however. Though there are Hebrew MSS. with the
singular "servant," the LXX MSS. read simply *douloi.*

28. *Genesis Rabbah* 2.901. The translation is from *Midrash Rabbah,* trans.
Freeman.

3. *Genesis Rabbah* on 22:11.[29]

The comment is made on the verse in which Abraham is told not to slay Isaac. Though there is no specific mention of "Messiah," a link is established between God's promise to Abraham and his promise to David.

> R. Acha said: ("Abraham wondered): Surely Thou too indulgest in prevarication. Yesterday Thou saidst, 'For in Isaac shall seed be called to thee' (Gen 21:12); Thou didst then retract and say, 'Take now thy son' (22:2); while now Thou biddest me, 'Lay not thy hand upon the lad!'" Said the Holy One, blessed be He, to him: "O Abraham, 'My covenant with Isaac' (Gen 22:21). When I bade thee, 'Take now thy son, etc.,' 'I will not alter that which is gone out of my lips' (Ps 89:35). Did I tell thee, slaughter him? No! but 'Take him up' [reading the verb in Gen 22:2 literally]. Thou hast taken him up. Now take him down."

4. *Exodus Rabbah* on 13:1.[30]

> "Sanctify to me all the first-born." R. Nathan said: The Holy One, blessed be He, told Moses: "Just as I have made Jacob a firstborn, for it says: 'Israel is My son, My firstborn' (Exod 4:22), so I will make the King Messiah a firstborn, as it says: 'I also will appoint him first-born'" (Ps 89:28).

5. *Song of Songs Rabbah*[31]

> R. Jannai said: If you see one generation after another cursing and blaspheming, look out for the coming of the Messiah, as it says, "with which thy enemies taunt, O Lord, with which they mock the footsteps of thy anointed" (Ps 89:52), and immediately afterwards it is written, "Blessed be the Lord for evermore. Amen and Amen" (Ps 89:53).

6. Targum on Psalm 89:51–52.[32]

> Remember, O Lord, the revilement of Thy servant;
>   I bore in my bosom all the blasphemies of many nations,
> With which Thy enemies have scoffed, O Lord,
>   with which they have scoffed at the delay of the footsteps of Thy Messiah, O Lord.

The evidence from Jewish tradition cannot prove that Psalm 89 was interpreted as messianic prior to the Christian era. It does demonstrate

---

29. *Genesis Rabbah* 1.1499.
30. *Exodus Rabbah* 237–38.
31. *Song of Songs Rabbah* 127.
32. Levey, *The Messiah*, 121.

that in Jewish tradition, even if of a later date, the "anointed" in vv. 38 and 52 was understood not as a reference to any king but to the Messiah King expected to come at the end of days. The midrashic comments likewise combine texts in a way familiar to NT exegetes: a link is established between Genesis 22 and Psalm 89 (also 2 Samuel 7), as well as with Isaiah 11 and Genesis 49. The use of "firstborn" as a name for the Messiah is also attested in the NT. The presence of the term "anointed" in the psalm, coupled with evidence from midrashic tradition, makes clear how the first Christians came to read Psalm 89 as messianic. It is to the NT evidence that we now turn.

Christian Interpretation

The influence of Psalm 89 is remarkably widespread in the NT. Nestle lists over twenty allusions to the psalm, to which a few others may be added. References are spread through the Pauline corpus, Luke-Acts, the Fourth Gospel, the Apocalypse, Hebrews, and 1 Peter.

In the Lukan corpus, Mary's Magnificat alludes (Luke 1:51) to Ps. 89:11; in Zechariah's song, the reference to a "horn of salvation in the house of his servant David" in Luke 1:69 may allude to Ps. 89:24 (as well as Ps. 18:1, etc.). The reference to the oath God swore to David in Acts 2:30 alludes to Ps. 89:4.

Revelation 1:5 contains several allusions to the psalm:

> . . . and from Jesus Christ, the faithful witness, the firstborn of the dead, and the ruler of kings on earth.

The phrase *ho martys ho pistos* is from 89:37 (LXX 88:38); *ho prōtotokos tōn nekrōn kai ho arxōn tōn basileōn tēs gēs* is from 89:27 (LXX 88:28). Colossians 1:15 alludes to the same verse when it calls Jesus *prōtotokos pasēs ktiseōs.*

The most striking illustration of a messianic reading of the expression "firstborn" comes from Hebrews 1:6. After the citation of Ps. 2:7 and 2 Sam. 7:14, the author says, "And again, when he brings the first-born into the world, he says. . ." The verse from Psalm 89 is not quoted, but it has clearly contributed to the messianic vocabulary. The following verse from Psalm 45 includes the phrase "has anointed thee with the oil of gladness," indicating how the exegesis in Hebrews 1 proceeds (see above, chap. 3).

John 12:34 is another example:

> The crowd answered him, "We have heard from the law that the Christ remains forever."

The comment is a paraphrase of 89:36: "His seed shall endure for ever, his throne as long as the sun before me." In John 12, "the Christ" is substituted for "his seed"—precisely the interpretation we observed in chapter 3 (and that seems to underlie the exegesis of Rabbi Acha in *Genesis Rabbah* on Gen. 22:11).

Probably the most important exegetical comments for our purposes are found in Hebrews 11:26 and 1 Peter 4:14. Both are bound up with the term *oneidos* or the verb *oneidizein* from Ps. 89:50–51:

> Remember, O Lord, how thy servant is *scorned;*
> how I bear in my bosom the insults of the peoples,
> with which thy enemies taunt, O Lord,
> with which they mock the footsteps of thy anointed.

The first interpretation borrows a single expression:

> He [Moses] considered the abuse suffered for the Christ *[ton oneidismon tou Christou]* greater wealth than the treasures of Egypt, for he looked to the reward. (Heb. 11:26)

The phrase "abuse of the Christ" sounds conventional and in all likelihood presumes an interpretation of 89:50—reading "servant" as a singular (with the targumic tradition on Psalm 89).[33]

The second interpretation is more complex:

> But rejoice in so far as you share in Christ's sufferings, that you may also rejoice and be glad when his glory is revealed. If you are reproached *[oneidizesthe]* for the name of Christ, you are blessed, because the spirit of glory and of God rests upon you; . . . yet if one suffers as a Christian, let him not be ashamed. (1 Peter 4:13–16)

The use of the verb instead of the noun in 1 Peter, and the parallel drawn between the faithful (Christians) and the Christ, may presuppose a reading of "servants" in v. 50 as a plural—so that in this instance, "servants" is taken as a reference to those who "bear the name of Christ" and not to the Messiah. Notice also that the phrase "the spirit of God rests upon you" is a paraphrase of Isa. 11:2 ("And the Spirit of the Lord shall rest upon him"), another messianic text that has been "democratized" here to apply to "Christians" as well as to the Christ.[34] The association of Isaiah 11 and Psalm 89 is attested in *Genesis Rabbah* on 49:10, as we have already noted.

---

33. Ibid.

34. Cf. *Targ. Isa.* 11:2. A similar "democratization" of messianic promises can be observed in the interpretation of 2 Sam. 7:14, both within the OT and in the NT (2 Cor. 6:18).

The exegesis in 1 Peter is a significant contrast to a more common way of providing exhortation to those who suffer for the faith, as, for example, in 2 and 4 Maccabees. The theme of humiliation and vindication is present, but the one whose story provides hope to the suffering is not a paradigmatic righteous sufferer but the Messiah. Psalm 89 is important because it speaks of the reproach and humiliation of the Christ of God. The basis for hope lies in God's oath to David—in the case of the early Christian interpreter, in God's having fulfilled that promise to David. Those who suffer in the name of Christ can view God as a "faithful creator" (1 Peter 4:19) because they are confident that the "glory of Christ" will be revealed (4:13)—once again, because God has already kept his word (1 Peter 1:3–12). It is not general laments or the familiar plot of the vindicated righteous sufferer that provides a foundation for such exhortation but the story of the crucified and risen Messiah. Psalm 89 provides a scriptural foundation for speaking about the pattern of humiliation and vindication in the case of the expected Messiah from the line of David.

Psalm 89 provides a link between humiliation and messiahship. It offers a specific way of speaking about Jesus' vindication as a testimony to God's fidelity to his word: in delivering Jesus from Sheol (89:48), God keeps his word to David about an everlasting dynasty (the exegesis in Acts 2; 13).[35] The psalm says little about the nature of the suffering and humiliation, however. It cannot provide any basis for reflection on the meaning of a death. Other scriptural passages provide more striking images for a narrative tradition. Perhaps that is why Psalm 89 does not appear in allusions in Mark 15. Probably its major significance is that it provided links with other biblical material and images with which to speak of the Messiah. The Messiah is called "servant" in 89:39 (and 89:50, where "servant" is read as singular). That can provide justification for viewing "servant" as a messianic designation, extending potentially messianic texts to include those that speak of an otherwise-unidentified servant (see below, pp. 127–33). Similarly, the anointed is identified as David's "seed," also permitting analogical extension of messianic passages (e.g., Genesis 22; see above). The Christ speaks of his own sufferings in vv. 50–51, which may suggest that the "I" in other laments is likewise the Christ. The issue is not whether such interpretive moves are demanded by the Scriptures, nor even whether we would regard such analogies as justifiable by our standards. Given first-century rules of argument, such interpretive

---

35. See above, chap. 3, n. 28, on the book and the article by Loevestam.

moves were justifiable. More important, they represent a reasonable way of moving into the Scriptures, even for those to whom new things had been revealed. The point is that a messianic exegesis of Psalm 89 can help explain the messianic reading of other psalms, specifically Psalms 22, 31, and 69.

Psalms 31 and 69

The two psalms may be classified as laments. Neither is interpreted messianically in known pre-Christian tradition or in extant midrashic literature. There are numerous connections with Psalm 89, however, that provide ample justification for reading the psalms as messianic.

1. Both psalms are attributed to David and can thus be understood as royal.
2. Both psalms are among the handful in which the speaker identifies himself as God's "servant."
3. The psalms share a specific vocabulary with Psalm 89, most important of which is the frequent use of *oneidismos* and *oneidizein* (31:12 [LXX 30:12]; 69:8, 10, 11, 20, 21 [LXX 68:8, 10, 11, 20, 21]).

What these psalms share with Psalm 89 and with each other is not simply a common plot but a *distinctive vocabulary* that sets them apart from other laments. The verbal analogies, far more than similarities in form, would have suggested some association with the royal "servant" of Psalm 89 who begs God to remember his plight and the promises made to David.

In themselves, such potential links are not sufficient evidence that the earliest exegesis of the psalms actually proceeded in this way. The evidence does show *that* the two psalms could be read as messianic and *how* that could occur given the constraints of the texts and the interpretive milieu of the first century. It explains why these two psalms are singled out of the many other laments in which the speaker does not identify himself as God's "servant" and in which his plight is described by means of other imagery. The primary evidence that such exegetical constructions occurred is the use of the psalms in the passion narratives, which tell the story of the King of the Jews, who suffered and died "in accordance with the scriptures."

Psalm 22

One widely offered explanation for the place of Psalm 22 in the passion tradition is that Jesus actually spoke the words from the opening verse: "My God, my God, why have you forsaken me?" The explanation encounters several serious objections. First, there is some plausibility in the views of several redaction critics that the words from Psalm 22 have been offered as an interpretation of Jesus' "great cry."[36] More important, the verse is cited only in Matthew and Mark, whereas all four Gospels include at least an allusion to the casting of lots for Jesus' robe (in John it is an actual quotation with a formal introduction). It is more likely that Jesus' words are derived from the reference to casting lots than the reverse; the omission from Luke and John would otherwise be highly unusual. The use of the citation from Psalm 31 in Luke, finally, shows how biblical material continued to enrich the narrative even after it had been fixed in one form.

Most scholars, typified by Matera, Gese, Harvey, and others, argue that the psalm was important principally because of its plot: the lot of the righteous sufferer, which during the intertestamental period had become a "dogma,"[37] was applied to Jesus, the paradigmatic righteous one who was vindicated by God at his resurrection. The question remains: Why precisely was this psalm selected and how is it related to the royal motifs that lay claim to historical priority?

Links with messianic tradition are more difficult to identify in Psalm 22 than in Psalms 69 and 31. The speaker does not identify himself as "your servant" or as "seed." Nevertheless, the vocabulary of suffering is remarkably close to that of Psalms 89 and 69, and the psalm is ascribed to David in the title. Such loose analogies with Psalm 89 are perhaps not convincing in light of the infrequent use of 89:51–52 (cited only twice—in Hebrews and 1 Peter, which are not particularly "early"). There are other indications, however, that such analogies may be sufficient.

Jewish-Christian Interpretation

As we have noted, Psalm 22 was applied to the story of Esther from an early date. It is highly unlikely that the psalm was ever read as messianic in earlier tradition, though it is likely that it was understood as Davidic. There is some indirect evidence how such royal overtones could be understood, in Justin Martyr's *Dialogue with Trypho*. Justin's exegesis is highly developed, the result of more than a century of Christian reading of the scriptural texts. We can see in his writings further stages of the

---

36. The thesis, proposed by von Oswald and Peddinghaus (see n. 10 of the present chap.) is considered in Matera, *Kingship,* 128–31. His conclusion, with which I agree, is that the thesis is unprovable.

37. Matera (*Kingship,* 130) simply states the opinion.

construction of a Messiah from the OT based on the image of Jesus. His portrait of Jewish views may well be his own construction as well. His arguments with Trypho presume that they have common ground, in this case in believing that the psalm refers to the experience of a king:

> And again David said in another passage, in the twenty-first Psalm [LXX] with reference to the cross in mystical parable, "They dug through my hands and my feet. . . ." And ye say that this very Psalm was not spoken of Christ, blind as you are to everything and without understanding that no one in your race who was called king ever had his feet and hands dug through . . . save this Jesus only.[38]

Justin takes for granted that Trypho and his friends will agree that the speaker in the psalm is a king. That is perhaps obvious, since the psalm is attributed to David.[39] Justin's argument, encountered first in Peter's speech in Acts 2, is that the statement does not fit David. The question is only to which king it refers. Justin's answer is that it must be Jesus, whose hands and feet were dug through—and who is the Messiah-King. That this interpretation is not totally inconceivable within the realm of Jewish exegesis is demonstrated by the *Yalkut* on Isa. 60:1, where the psalm is expounded homiletically with respect to the sufferings of the Messiah.

Justin is aware that his interpretation requires justification. The move from David to the Messiah is not automatic. How can we know that the psalm is about the coming Messiah, apart from its application to Jesus the Messiah? Commenting on v. 3, Justin offers his reason:

> "But Thou dwellest in the sanctuary, O Praise of Israel" signified that he [the Christ] was to do something worthy of praise and admiration, being about to rise on the third day after being crucified, which he received from His Father. For I have shown that Christ is called both Jacob and Israel. . . .[40]

Justin reads Israel as a name for the Messiah, which he proves in rabbinic fashion from such passages as Ps. 72:18 (LXX Ps. 71) or perhaps Isa. 42:1 LXX. Finding names for the Messiah was a common midrashic exercise.[41] The exercise provided one means of forging links with new texts. Justin's rather impressive list of names for the Christ

---

38. Justin *Dialogue with Trypho* 97.

39. The psalm titles were of particular interest to rabbinic interpreters, perhaps mainly because of their enigmatic character. On the topic, see Childs, "Psalm Titles and Midrashic Exegesis," *JSS* 16 (1971): 137–50.

40. Justin *Dialogue with Trypho* 100.2.

41. Examples of such speculation on the names of the Messiah are found in passages such as *b. Sanh.* 96b–97a; *Lam. Rab.* 1.51–52; *Num. Rab.* 18, 21; *Pirke R. El.* 48.

includes King, Priest, God, Lord, Man, Chief Captain, Stone, Child-Born, Lord of Hosts, Jacob, and Israel.[42] Speculation on the names of God likewise has precedent.[43] Passages that use any of these names can be read as references to the Messiah and thus to Jesus. Analogy was the key to the construction, as it was in rabbinic exegesis.

Justin's exegesis, like that of earlier generations of Christians, began with the acknowledgment that Jesus was the Messiah. For him, the significance of that title is tied almost exclusively to scriptural interpretation. Other christological terms more adequately expressed Justin's views of Jesus and the significance of the gospel. The confession of Jesus as Messiah was foundational, a presupposition for the rest, as is the case in earlier stages of Christian tradition.

His exegetical reflections on Psalm 22 likewise began with the NT use of the psalm to tell of the death of the King of the Jews. The psalm was perceived as royal from the first. We cannot learn from Justin where that messianic reading began. From Psalm 89 Christians learned that one could speak of the scorn and humiliation endured by the Messiah in scriptural terms. They learned from the psalm that the Messiah, as well as David, could speak in psalms. They encountered a fairly specific vocabulary with which to speak of that suffering. Perhaps that is a sufficient explanation for the identification of Psalm 22 as a "royal" psalm. It was attributed to King David, after all. Such analogies provide a better explanation for its selection, in any case, than the appropriateness of the plot by itself. Such interpretation was "inspired," but that does not mean it was without logic. Extension from known messianic tradition to newly discovered biblical passages *by means of analogy* was one way in which the Spirit could work within the community of exegetes.

If there is a pre-Markan passion tradition that can be isolated, the psalms surely form the basis of the tradition. It is unlikely that Jesus' story was ever told as a recitation of facts. And from the outset, psalms were employed to tell the story not of a paradigmatic righteous one or a prophetic martyr, but of the King of the Jews, "the Christ, the Son of the Blessed," whose resurrection proved that he was indeed the Christ, the Stone, rejected by the builders, which became the head of the corner.

---

42. Justin *Dialogue with Trypho* 34.

43. On such speculation, see Segal, *Two Powers in Heaven,* and Dahl and Segal, "Philo and the Rabbis on the Names of God," *JSJ* 9 (1979): 1–28.

"My God, My God, Why Have You Forsaken Me?"

Certainly the most striking reference to Psalm 22 is Jesus' anguished cry from the cross. And the most striking feature of that cry is that it is quoted in Aramaic. Any theory about the use of Psalm 22 in the passion tradition should have to account for the Aramaic in Mark 15.

Unlike the inscription of the charge against Jesus formulated by Pilate, Jesus' last words do not invite historical analysis. They are not part of the public record. No one understands what Jesus says—except the narrator and the reader. Part of the narrative function of Jesus' last words is to generate one final misunderstanding in a career that has been consistently misunderstood: even his last, anguished cry is misheard by the crowd who believe he is calling for Elijah.

As we have come to expect in Mark, however, even the misunderstanding makes some ironic sense. As readers, we know about Elijah—that he has already come in the person of John, and "they did to him whatever they pleased" (Mark 9:13). Like John's (Elijah's) commission, Jesus' comes from heaven (Mark 11:27–33); and like John (Elijah), Jesus is rejected. The misunderstanding points us to features of the story far beyond the comprehension of the audience which only readers and the all-knowing narrator comprehend.

The reference to Psalm 22 in Jesus' last cry is for the reader, not the audience in the story. It is drawn from a great treasury of information from which the anonymous narrator can draw. He knows, for example, that in Jesus' dramatic appearance before the high court he promised vindication in the eyes of his would-be judges, using expressions from Ps. 110:1 and Dan. 7:13. Such biblical allusions are not different in kind from those hidden in the narrative itself. The author makes no effort to explain who could have reported what Jesus said at his trial, just as he provides no suggestion who could have understood Jesus' last words properly and recorded them, whether the women watching from a distance or the lone centurion of whom we hear nothing further. The reason is that it is beside the point. The narrator and the reader know what those present could not possibly know. That Jesus' words, like his death, correspond to some biblical script has already been stated earlier in the story. The presence of scriptural allusions is to be expected.

What we discover in Luke and John is not that the situation is different for them but only that the biblical script is conceived differently. In Luke, Jesus' last words are likewise scriptural: "Father, into your hands I commit my spirit" (Luke 23:46, alluding to Ps. 31:5). The tone of this scriptural passage better suits Luke's passion narrative, which depicts Jesus' death as a noble act. His final cry bespeaks that nobility, radiating a sense of confidence in God's power. In view of the scriptural allusion in Luke, it seems almost comical to argue that Jesus chose the opening line from Psalm 22 as his last cry to express his confidence in the God who vindicates the sufferer at the end of the psalm.[44] Other scriptural texts would have been far more suitable for such purposes.

---

44. Examples of commentators who argue that Jesus chose Psalm 22 to express confidence in God include Klostermann (*Das Markusevangelium,* 166), Schmid (*The Gospel according to Mark,* 295–96), and with some qualification, Taylor (*The*

The last words of Jesus in John, "It is finished," are likewise more appropriate to the narrative in the Fourth Gospel. Their irony is pronounced, and they provide a more fitting expression of Jesus' "exaltation," which is now completed.

It is possible, of course, that Mark wove the thread from Psalm 22 into the fabric of his narrative because Jesus actually spoke the words at his death. A theory would have to be proposed to explain how the misunderstood words could have been properly heard by someone and transmitted as part of the tradition. This would explain why the saying is employed in the Aramaic. There are too many other complications, however, for the theory to be plausible. We would have to explain, for example, why Luke and John made use of the allusion to casting lots for Jesus' clothing—a bit of information significant only because of its relationship to the psalm verse—yet failed to include his last word, the most striking allusion to the psalm.

The use of the Aramaic is significant, but probably not as an indication of what Jesus did or did not say. There are other Aramaic words or sentences in Mark—three, in fact (5:41; 7:34; 14:34). Two occur in miracle stories and add a touch of mystery to the accounts—though Mark translates the phrases, thus preventing their being regarded as magical words. The use of "Abba" is probably to be traced to Jesus himself. The Aramaic in 15:34 also lends a certain flavor to the narrative, but it is different, since it is a biblical allusion. The words correspond to the targumic rendering of the Hebrew in known traditions. The priority of the Aramaic is underscored by Matthew's alterations. He has tried to make a clearer connection between the "Eloi" and Elijah's name by changing the opening words to Hebrew ("Eli, Eli . . ."), but the rest of the saying is preserved in Aramaic.

In their present setting, the last words of Jesus are intimately tied to the story via the misunderstanding, which is in turn linked closely to the rest of Mark's Gospel. Determining at what stage in the passion tradition the saying became incorporated into the story is perhaps not possible in light of the evidence we possess. One tempting explanation is that it became part of tradition as a proverbial expression of distress. Arguments for such a view would be difficult to muster. We know virtually nothing about the place of Psalm 22 in the liturgical life of postbiblical Judaism, and in extant literature there is no evidence that the psalm or any part of it was a familiar expression of distress. Rabbinic interpreters applied the words to various figures, from David to Esther. Such historicizing exegesis does not rule out alternative explanations or wider use, however, and the proverbial character of the opening line of the psalm might explain the persistence of the Aramaic even after it had to be translated to be understood.[45]

Jesus' last words presume, for Mark's readers, that the speaker in the psalm is Jesus—or as Luke argues with regard to other psalms, the Messiah. The

Gospel according to St. Mark, 593–94). Schweizer (_The Good News according to Mark_, 353) ignores the historical argument and moves directly to preaching: "This passage presents the search for faith which knows that God is real even in times when the believer feels forsaken."

45. The suggestion that the Aramaic words from the psalm had become a proverbial expression of lament was made to me by Geza Vermes.

allusions to Psalm 22 in the narrative reflect the same assumption. Details from the psalm have generated narrative—or to put it less boldly, they may have been responsible for the preservation of certain bits of history. The words themselves are bound up with the narrative and cannot easily be disengaged. The Elijah misunderstanding depends upon the opening line from the psalm and cannot be accorded a separate history. John's mention of the casting of lots for Jesus' clothing gives evidence of the widespread influence and fundamental significance of the psalm in the passion tradition. It is difficult to conceive the passion narratives without allusions to Psalm 22. It is as difficult to explain allusions to the psalm as secondary.

Yet the question persists: Why was this particular psalm considered an appropriate vehicle for narrating Jesus' death? Even if the opening lines or the whole psalm is regarded as a proverbial expression of distress, Jesus' death is not thereby understood as proverbial or paradigmatic because verses from the psalm have been used to tell of his death. The rabbis read the psalm as the story of Esther, not a paradigmatic sufferer but a great queen who saved her people by risking her life. The opening line attributes the psalm to David, who is the king. The use of the psalm to speak about Jesus tells us only that the events that concluded his ministry were "scriptural." His identity is provided by the rest of the narrative. It seems likely that the use of the psalm is also bound to Jesus' identity as King of the Jews, though the derivation of this royal exegesis remains elusive.

CONCLUSIONS

1. The so-called passion psalms—Psalms 22, 69, and possibly 31—were from an early date employed to tell the story of Jesus' death. The interpretive tradition has left traces in the nonnarrative portions of the NT (Epistles) as well as in the narrative portions (Gospels, Acts, Revelation).

2. From the outset the psalms were part of a tradition that narrated the death of the King of the Jews. The psalms were read as messianic—that is, as referring to the anointed King from the line of David expected at the end of days. Justification for such a reading of the psalms cannot be derived from pre-Christian Jewish exegesis, from which we have no examples of messianic interpretation. The creative interpretation, which must be ascribed to early Christian exegetes, derives rather from the unique events that climaxed the career of Jesus of Nazareth—his death as a messianic pretender and his vindication by God. In light of the history of the King of the Jews, Christian practitioners of midrash discovered new possibilities within ancient psalms—possibilities that were justifiable in terms of current modes of scriptural interpretation.

3. Psalm 89 and its interpretation provide one key to the use of the passion psalms. In this psalm, understood in Jewish tradition as

messianic in the narrow sense, it is the Messiah who is mocked, reviled, and threatened. The prayer for vindication is made by means of an appeal to God's oath to David. The psalm identifies the Messiah as servant and seed, making possible associations with other biblical passages by means of analogy. The language of reviling, for example, provides a link with a small number of laments. Psalm 89 shows that the speaker in a psalm may be the Messiah, and that the Messiah can complain about maltreatment. Christian exegetes took advantage of the interpretive potential in other psalms as they sought to tell their story of the King who died on a cross.

4. There is ample evidence in the NT that Psalm 89 played an important role in the evolution of christological tradition. The evidence is found principally in nonnarrative portions of the NT—in various Epistles or in earlier creedal or hymnic material embedded in them. The priority of Psalm 89 in the tradition can be demonstrated logically if not chronologically. The psalm was cited not to prove Jesus was the Christ but to make sense of that confession—largely by providing links with other biblical passages that could further develop the kerygma "in accordance with the scriptures." The confession of Jesus as Messiah is not a goal toward which scriptural interpretation moves but the presupposition for the interpretive tradition. It is not the solution to some problem generated by earlier exegesis but in large measure the generative problem itself.

5. The lack of atonement imagery in the narrative tradition should be viewed not principally in chronological but in formal terms. Narratives had a different function from confessions or hymns. The function of different types of christological language deserves further study, and in that context greater clarity about the place of various exegetical traditions can be achieved.

5

THE
SERVANT-CHRIST

Christian Interpretation
of Second Isaiah

As we attempt to determine the sources of christological language, we are obliged to keep in mind that biblical language employed by early Christians was not drawn from Scriptures that existed in a vacuum. The Bible was available to those in the first century only through the medium of tradition. We may easily forget, however, that the Bible is not directly available to us. It is mediated by an even longer tradition of interpretation, ranging from the variety of translations, to scholarly monographs, to popular notions of "what the Bible says." The power of these conventions to determine what we see can scarcely be overestimated. The appropriateness or inappropriateness of such conventions may become apparent only when new data or new questions force a reappraisal of our tradition of interpretation. In the last decades, for instance, scholars of early Christianity have reconsidered and offered a new appraisal of the servant poems from Isaiah.

SUFFERING SERVANT

Without a doubt the image of the Suffering Servant, and the relevant texts from Isaiah, have been central to recent descriptions of NT Christology. The following are representative views:

The teaching concerning Messianic suffering and death is bound up in the mind of Jesus with His sense of vocation. . . . The teaching is based on a unique combination of the idea of the Suffering Servant of Isa liii with that of the Son of Man.[1]

Although actual quotations from this famous chapter are not especially numerous in the NT, allusions to it are embedded so deeply in the work of all the principal writers that it is certain that it belongs to the earliest thought of the primitive church. . . . The original position, closely connected with the rudimentary Atonement doctrine, had been that Jesus, who is the Messiah, had in his atoning death fulfilled the mission of the Servant of the Lord.[2]

The purpose of the schematization of the disciples' misunderstanding of Jesus in Mark's gospel is to press for acceptance of a suffering servant Christology in the church for which Mark is writing.[3]

Joachim Jeremias is perhaps the best-known advocate of servant traditions. His collection of relevant material from Jewish and Christian sources provides a suitable basis for reflection on the use of the famous passages.[4]

There have been periodic challenges to the alleged importance of the so-called servant poems. Henry Cadbury, for instance, advised caution about hasty generalizations regarding the Suffering Servant.[5] The most sustained attack on the interpretation of Jeremias, Vincent Taylor, and others was made by Morna Hooker in her book *Jesus and the Servant.*[6] In the opening chapters, she reviews the arguments of several scholars who assign servant passages fundamental significance in early Christianity, particularly in the development of doctrines of atonement. By meticulous analysis of alleged allusions to the servant poems, she has demonstrated the degree to which arguments depend upon prior assumptions about the status of the Suffering Servant and the servant poems in pre-Christian Judaism. Even the most ardent proponents of influence from Isaiah must admit the paucity of actual quotations from the texts and the infrequency of the term *pais* in the NT. Arguments for the importance of the passages are based largely on implied allusions or even similarities of ideas. Advocates must likewise admit that most of the few actual quotations (Matt. 8:17; 12:18–21; Acts 8:32–33) make little out of the vicarious suffering that seems so basic to the vocation of

---

1. Taylor, *The Gospel according to St. Mark,* 378.
2. Lindars, *New Testament Apologetic,* 77, 80.
3. Perrin, *What Is Redaction Criticism?* 56.
4. J. Jeremias, "pais theou," *TDNT* 5 (1972): 677–717.
5. Cadbury, "The Titles of Jesus in Acts," in *Beginnings of Christianity,* ed. Foakes-Jackson and Lake, 1:354–74.
6. Hooker, *Jesus and the Servant.*

the servant. If it could be demonstrated that the Suffering Servant was a distinct personality, well known in Jewish tradition, the argument might be plausible that no more than vague allusions were needed to conjure up the whole servant tradition among Jesus' followers or in later Christian circles. Evidence from Jewish sources is thus crucial to the whole debate.

About one thing there can be no doubt: material from various passages in Isaiah now termed "servant poems" was applied to Jesus. But on what grounds and for what purpose? Although the evidence has been examined before, we need to review it again in view of altered conceptions of Jewish eschatological and exegetical tradition. Precisely because the history of Christian interpretation makes the connection between Jesus and the servant of Isaiah so obvious, and for the very reason that Christ's death "for our sins, in accordance with the scriptures" seems so clearly to point to Isaiah 53, we should take time to ask about the state of affairs in the first century of the Common Era. Did Jesus and his contemporaries understand the servant poems to belong to one constellation of images, referring to the career of one figure known as the servant of the Lord? Would they have understood that figure to be the Suffering Servant? And if so, what relationship could have existed with traditions about eschatological deliverers?

Jewish Interpretations

I have collected examples of interpretations from a variety of Jewish sources, some pre–first-century, many from post–first-century sources. The selection is by no means exhaustive but, I hope, representative.

Septuagint
Isa. 42:1:
> Jacob my servant, I shall take his part;
> Israel my chosen, my soul received him gladly.

Cf. RSV:
> Behold my servant, whom I uphold,
> my chosen, in whom my soul delights.

The LXX translator has applied the passage to Israel, reading "my servant" as a collective, by inserting the words "Jacob" and "Israel" into the text.

Jesus Ben Sirach
11:12–13:
> There is another who is slow and needs help,
> who lacks strength and abounds in poverty;

but the eyes of the Lord look upon him for his good;
  he lifts him out of his low estate
and raises up his head,
  so that many are amazed at him.

Isa. 52:15 RSV:
So shall he startle many nations.

LXX:
Thus many nations shall be amazed at him.

The passage speaks about the typical righteous one, using imagery from the poem in 52:13—53:12.

48:9-10:
  You who were taken up by a whirlwind of fire,
    in a chariot with horses of fire;
  you who are ready at the appointed time, it is written,
    to calm the wrath of God before it breaks out in fury,
  to turn the heart of the father to the son
    and to restore the tribes of Jacob.

Isa. 49:6:
  It is too light a thing that you should be my
    servant
  to raise up the tribes of Jacob
  and to restore the preserved of Israel.

The passage refers clearly to Elijah whose return is prophesied in Mal. 4:5-6. Malachi 4:6 has been supplemented with a line from Isaiah.

Wisdom of Solomon
  2:13:
  He professes to have knowledge of God,
  and calls himself a child [*pais*] of the Lord.

The words occur as part of a taunt directed at the righteous one. In the description of his plight as a *pais* of God, there are numerous reminiscences of Isa. 52:13—53:12, though few explicit verbal links. The associations are particularly apparent in 2:13-20 and 5:3-6.

Daniel
  12:3:
  And those who are wise shall shine like the brightness of the firma-
  ment; and those who turn many to righteousness, like the stars for ever
  and ever.

Isa. 53:11:
  By his knowledge shall the righteous one, my servant, make many to
  be accounted righteous.

Talmud[7]

b. Sotah 14a:

R. Simlai expounded: Why did Moses our teacher yearn to enter the land of Israel? Did he want to eat of its fruits or satisfy himself from its bounty? But thus spake Moses, "Many precepts were commanded to Israel which can only be fulfilled in the land of Israel. I wish to enter the land so that they may all be fulfilled by me." The Holy One, blessed be He, said to him, "Is it only to receive the reward (for obeying the commandments) that thou seekest? I ascribe it to thee as if thou didst perform them"; as it is said "Therefore will I divide him a portion with the great, and he shall divide the spoil with the strong; because he poured out his soul unto death, and was numbered with the transgresors; yet he bare the sins of many, and made intercession for the transgresors." "Therefore will I divide him a portion with the great"—it is possible (to think that his portion will be) with the (great of) later generations and not former generations; therefore there is a text to declare, "And he shall divide the strong," i.e., with Abraham, Isaac, and Jacob who were strong in Torah and the commandments. "Because he poured out his soul unto death"—because he surrendered himself to die, as it is said, "And if not, blot me, I pray thee, etc." "And was numbered with the transgresors"—because he was numbered with them who were condemned to die in the wilderness. "Yet he bare the sins of many"—because he secured atonement for the making of the Golden Calf. "And made intercession for the transgressors"—because he begged for mercy on behalf of the sinners in Israel that they should turn in penitence; and the word pegiah ("intercession") means nothing else than prayer, as it is said, "Therefore pray not thou for this people, neither lift up cry nor prayer for them, neither make intercession to Me."

Targum[8]

Targ. Isa. 42:19:

If the wicked return, shall they not be called "my servants"? . . .

Cf. RSV:

Who is blind but my servant,
    or deaf as my messengers whom I send?

Targ. Isa. 50:10:

Who is there among you of them that fear the Lord that obeyeth the voice of his servants the prophets? . . .

Cf. RSV:

Who among you fears the Lord
    and obeys the voice of his servant?

---

7. The translation is from the Soncino edition of the Babylonian Talmud, ed. Epstein.

8. The translations are from *The Targum of Isaiah,* trans. Stenning.

Targ. Isa. 52:13:
> Behold, my servant, the Messiah, shall prosper; he shall be exalted, and increase, and be very strong.

Cf. RSV:
> Behold, my servant shall prosper,
> he shall be exalted and lifted up,
> and shall be very high.

The entire song in 52:13—53:12 is interpreted by the targumist as a reference to the Messiah. The interpretation, however, removes virtually every suggestion that the servant will suffer and, by ingenious readings and shifts of words, applies the suffering to the Messiah's enemies or to Israel, whom the Servant-Messiah rescues. Verses 4–5, for example, are paraphrased,

> Then he shall pray on behalf of our transgressions, and our iniquities shall be pardoned for his sake, though we were accounted smitten, stricken from before the Lord, and afflicted. But he shall build the sanctuary that was polluted because of our transgressions and given up because of our iniquities.

In v. 5, the verb *mecholal* is read as "polluted," and the pronoun subject is taken to refer not to the servant but to the temple. The passage then reads, "It [= the temple] was polluted because of our transgressions." In light of Zech. 6:12 and 2 Sam. 7:13, the Servant-Messiah is then identified as the builder of the destroyed sanctuary. The preoccupation with the temple is typical of the Isaiah Targum.

To an extent unparalleled in the Targum, the famous Servant Song is drastically reinterpreted. The reason for this striking revision and the messianic reading has been discussed elsewhere.[9]

Results

On the basis of the selection above, the following observations may be made:

1. "Servant of God," whether in Greek or Hebrew, is never treated as a title like Christ. It does not appear in Jewish literature in statements like, "So and so is the servant of the Lord." The term can be used of various biblical figures, like Moses or Elijah, following biblical precedent, but it always occurs with some modifier (commonly "my"). Usage does not

---

9. Two of the most important discussions of the Targum on Isaiah 53 are Hegermann, *Jesaia 53 in Hexapla, Targum, und Peschitta,* and Seidelin, "Der 'Ebed Jahwe' und die Messiasgestalt im Jesajatargum," *ZNW* 35 (1936): 194–231. See also my *Messiah and Temple,* 192–95.

justify speaking of "the servant of the Lord" as though the designation referred to some known figure or distinct personality other than the "servants of the Lord" identified elsewhere in Scripture (Moses, David, the prophets, the righteous, etc.).[10] The expression "the Suffering Servant" never appears. To use the phrase when speaking of postbiblical tradition is thus anachronistic and misleading.

2. The servant poems are not treated as a unity in Jewish tradition; reference to one poem does not imply reference to another.[11] The passages are not isolated and dealt with as units apart from their setting. It is thus misleading to speak of the Servant Songs to describe these texts as they were viewed by Jews in the early part of the Common Era. Isolating the poems and analyzing them as units is a modern phenomenon. Cadbury's warning is still appropriate:

> In their atomistic use of Scripture the early Christians were very different from the modern theologian who, gathering together the four "servant passages" of Isaiah, derives from them a complete concept, treating them as a whole, and then assumes that this Christological concept underlies the passages mentioned, and even such passages as have no more echo of Isaiah than the simple *pais*. [12]

3. Extant Jewish literature includes a wide range of quotations from servant poems in which a few words, or a line or two, are applied to a known figure like Moses or Elijah. Jeremias is aware of the references but discounts them as evidence of Jewish interpretive tradition:

> The recurrent applications of individual servant passages to individual figures are without significance. For such references . . . are all without exception references to individual verses which do not tell us how the rabbis concerned expounded the passages in context.[13]

The comment is a strange one, for the frequent applications of small pieces of the so-called Servant Songs provide the most striking demonstration of Cadbury's point: atomistic exegesis was widely practiced by both Christians and Jews. The rabbis felt free to interpret these verses from Isaiah as they did others in the Bible, without regard for context. The evidence suggests that there was no "standard" interpretation of the servant poems. Nor do the passages cited from Jewish literature indicate that application of any feature of a unit implies application of the

---

10. Hooker, *Jesus and the Servant,* 156–57.
11. This conclusion had been reached some time ago by H. A. Fischel, whose study J. Jeremias cites with approval in his article "pais theou."
12. Cadbury, "The Titles of Jesus in Acts," 369–70.
13. J. Jeremias, "pais theou," 686.

unit as a whole. It is thus misleading to speak even of the "mission of the Servant of the Lord," as Lindars does, as if any one view of the servant or any overall pattern of interpretation was shared by Jewish exegetes.

4. In every passage cited above, verses or portions of verses from Isaiah which speak about an otherwise unidentified "servant of the Lord" are applied to known figures who elsewhere in Scripture are called servants of God: Moses (Josh. 1:7, 13; Dan. 9:11; etc.); Elijah (1 Kings 18:36; etc.—LXX *doulos*); Jacob/Israel (Isa. 41:8; 48:20; etc.); the righteous (Proverbs and Psalms, regularly); the prophets (2 Chron. 36:5 LXX; Jer. 35:15; etc.); the Messiah (Zech. 3:8; Psalm 89:39—LXX *doulos*). The antiquity of this method of employing Scripture to interpret Scripture is attested by the Septuagint translator's insertion of "Jacob" and "Israel" in Isa. 42:1. He simply identified this unknown "servant" by referring to another servant mentioned in the Bible—in this case, in Isa. 41:8, among other passages.

This method of verbal association is basic to all Jewish exegesis. The potential for identifying the "servant" in each Isaiah passage by referring to other "servants" in the biblical story is, of course, virtually limitless, as a glance at a concordance confirms. As befits the whole spirit of midrash, the appropriateness of a particular interpretation to the original setting in Isaiah is not a criterion for exegetes. Jewish interpreters obviously exercised their freedom to apply any portions of the servant passages they chose to various "servants of the Lord."

5. The Isaiah Targum provides the clearest illustration of this approach. In the passages cited from the Targum, "servant" is in one instance taken as a reference to penitents, in another to the prophets, in a third to the Messiah. In each case, the identification of the servant can be supported by use of the term in other biblical passages. The targumist can identify the servant in 52:13—53:12 as the Messiah because in Zech. 3:8 and in Ps. 89:39 the Messiah is called God's servant ("Branch" in Zech. 3 is a designation for the Davidic Messiah, as in Jer. 23:5; 33:15). Not every reference to an unidentified "servant" in the servant poems is taken as a reference to the Messiah, however. And there is nothing to suggest that the messianic reading of Isa. 52:13—53:12 was standard among Jews or even that it predates the Christian era. What the Targum does demonstrate is that "servant" in Isa. 52:13—and elsewhere in Isaiah—could be read as a messianic designation. It was an option for Christian exegetes.

The messianic reading of Isaiah 53 in the Targum does not support the thesis that there existed a pre-Christian concept of a suffering

Messiah whose career was understood in light of the chapter. In the Targum, virtually every element of suffering is eliminated from the career of the Servant-Messiah. The resulting portrait, though purchased at the expense of the obvious meaning of the text, accords in every respect with the portrait of the Messiah elsewhere in the Targum and in other Jewish literature. It is thus difficult to argue, as Jeremias does, that the striking interpretation by the targumist represents an effort to conceal an earlier tradition of a suffering Messiah that Christians found too useful. Were that the case, the image of a suffering Messiah would represent a complete anomaly in the Targum as a whole.[14] The painstaking redoing of the passage by the targumist required by the initial identification of the servant as the Messiah need not obscure the usefulness of the passage to the targumist even apart from anti-Christian polemics. The initial description of the servant as exalted and glorified is perhaps sufficient cause for the messianic "translation."

Summary

Our brief survey should render two separate assumptions insupportable. First, there is no evidence of an overall interpretation of the servant passages in Isaiah. We encounter a variety of exegetical traditions none of which views the poems as a unity and none of which appears to be standard. We should not speak of "the Suffering Servant" or "the servant of the Lord" as if the phrases represent a distinct conception in postbiblical Judaism. Second, Jews apparently did not customarily understand the servant passages in Isaiah to refer to the Messiah. And even where examples of such interpretation can be found, there is no indication that prior to Christianity the Messiah was expected to suffer after installation to office or that his suffering was viewed as atoning in light of Isaiah 53. Notions about the vicarious suffering of the Messiah do appear in Jewish tradition, but only later, and probably in response to the careers of such figures as Simon bar Kokhba.[15]

CHRISTIAN INTERPRETATION:
THE SERVANT-CHRIST

The servant poems from Isaiah played an important role in the development of Christology. Precisely what role they played will be assessed

---

14. This is the argument of Seidelin in "Der 'Ebed Jahwe.'"

15. On the traditions regarding the Messiah ben Joseph, who dies in war, see Vermes, *Jesus the Jew,* 139; *b. Sukk.* 52a; and Segal, *Rebecca's Children,* 64–67, 86.

differently if we cannot assume a uniform interpretation of the passages and if there existed no servant figure in postbiblical Jewish tradition. Cadbury's observation is still a sound place to begin:

> Even where parts of Isaiah 53 are plainly quoted by early Christians, it is important not to assume that the whole chapter is in the quoter's mind. The Christian use of Old Testament passages usually called attention to the actual part quoted, or even less than the whole quotation, in a quite verbal and literal sense.[16]

Perhaps the most striking illustration of Cadbury's point is the citation of Isa. 53:7–8 in Acts 8:32–33:

> As a sheep led to the slaughter or a lamb before its
>   shearer is dumb, so he opens not his mouth.
> In his humiliation justice was denied him.
> Who can describe his generation?
> For his life is taken up from the earth.

The citation avoids any mention of vicarious suffering so prominent in the passage. Barnabas Lindars does not regard that as a problem, arguing that the "precise words quoted are not intrinsically necessary to the argument, but stand for the whole prophecy."[17] Striking, however, is the omission even of the parallel line from v. 8b (*apo tōn anomiōn tou laou mou ēxthē eis thanaton*). The citation, in fact, says precisely what the narrator wants it to say. It speaks of one who did not speak in his defense, was unjustly killed, whose progeny (understood perhaps as successors: here, the circle of those gathered around the apostles)[18] will be beyond imagination, and whose life is "taken up from the earth" (the verb *airō* means literally "lift up"). The allusion to Jesus' ascension as recorded in Acts seems obvious. Each feature of the citation is important, and nothing is said of vicarious suffering. There is no reason to import such a notion from the rest of the famous poem, for it is not quoted—and in Luke-Acts, virtually nothing is said about the atoning value of Jesus' death. According to Acts 8, Isaiah 53 speaks about Jesus' rejection and his vindication by way of ascension.

An equally striking example of such specific exegesis is found in Matt. 8:16–17, where phrases from Isa. 53:4 are retranslated so as to apply not to vicarious sufferings but to healings and exorcisms:

> That evening they brought to him many who were possessed with demons; and he cast out the spirits with a word, and healed all who were sick. This

---

16. Cadbury, "Titles of Jesus in Acts," 369.
17. Lindars, *New Testament Apologetic,* 83.
18. On this passage, see Haenchen, *Acts of the Apostles.*

was to fulfill what was spoken by the prophet Isaiah, "He took our infirmities and bore our diseases."

In similar fashion Isa. 42:1–4 is quoted in Matt. 12:18–21 to explain why Jesus wishes not to be made known (Matthew's explanation for the injunctions to silence in Mark). Isaiah 53:12 is quoted in Luke 22:37 (not part of the passion narrative!) to prove that Jesus' treatment as a criminal (*kakourgos*) was in accord with the Scripture.

The various citations show that Jesus could be identified with the servant mentioned in various biblical texts. The citations, however, do not reflect an overall appraisal of Jesus' career. They shed light on various aspects of his ministry, demonstrating that he acted in accordance with the Scriptures. Verses could be enlisted to speak of Jesus' death, though they have no claim to centrality. Only in 1 Peter are verses from Isaiah 53 which speak about vicarious suffering systematically applied to Jesus. The evidence suggests a gradual application of so-called servant poems to Jesus, with full appropriation of the material encountered only in later stages of christological development (e.g., Justin Martyr's *Dialogue with Trypho*).

Noteworthy is the absence of unambiguous terms from servant poems in passages that speak of Jesus' death. Traditional arguments that Isaiah 53 is one of the texts behind the "in accordance with the scriptures" in 1 Cor. 15:3 must rely on overall theories about the use of Isaiah rather than specific details. The phrase *hyper tōn hamartiōn hēmōn* cannot be derived from the Hebrew or the Greek. The same may be said of language in passages like Mark 10:45 and 14:24, passages that scholars like Jeremias view as having fundamental christological significance, perhaps deriving from Jesus' own teaching about his death. Hooker has examined the passages in detail and has shown how little evidence of verbal links exists. It is unnecessary to recapitulate her detailed arguments here.[19] Her contention seems justified: arguments advanced by those who view servant texts as basic to Jesus' and early Christians' understanding of Jesus' death depend ultimately upon general assumptions about the Suffering Servant in Jewish and Christian tradition that are untenable. The greatest interest in the passages as sources of atonement language must be located in later stages of biblical tradition and in the era after the composition of the NT (110 C.E.).

In her strenuous rejection of influence from servant texts, however, Hooker has underplayed the importance of such passages even within the NT. Her overriding interest in "doctrinal" interpretation that

---

19. Hooker, *Jesus and the Servant*, esp. 74–79, 80–83.

relates to the "meaning" of events, notably Jesus' death, unnecessarily restricts her view of the role of biblical exegesis in early Christian groups. The evangelists' use of the material seems to her little more than typological exegesis or proof from prophecy. And Hooker has little to offer by way of explaining how the initial link between Jesus and the servant poems occurred:

> In spite of this increased use of the Servant Songs in Matthew and Luke, as compared with Mark, there is no indication that they have in any way distorted the primitive tradition, or have done more than draw in clearer detail, as they do continually, the parallel between the events of Jesus' life and passages from the Old Testament.[20]

> Matthew's partiality for Old Testament prophecies suggests that the significance of these quotations lies in his desire to find passages which foreshadow particular events, and not in any intention to identify Jesus with the Servant of the Songs.[21]

Such explanations are unsatisfying. Christians did not search the whole of the Scriptures for passages that struck them as parallels to Jesus' career or as possible foreshadowings. There was more logic and order in their movement through the Bible! It is likely that some train of logic led Christian interpreters to these texts, and that something suggested that application to Jesus was appropriate or justified.

One possible explanation is that Jesus understood his career in light of the servant poems and shared that view with his disciples. Such an interpretation would have been quite unprecedented, since there seems to have existed no Suffering Servant or servant of the Lord as a distinct figure or even vocation in Jewish tradition which would serve as a paradigm. The explanation is not impossible, but in view of the evidence it is improbable. We have no more than possible allusions to Isaiah in the sayings tradition which cannot bear the weight of such a hypothesis. The evidence is even more insubstantial in light of Hooker's critique. It is conceivable, as T. W. Manson argued, that Jesus restricted such creative biblical interpretation to private instruction intended only for his disciples, which might explain the absence of explicit references to servant texts in the tradition of Jesus' public pronouncements.[22] If so, however, we will probably never know those esoteric teachings, and the

---

20. Ibid., 150.
21. Ibid., 149.
22. See J. Jeremias, "pais theou," 717, with reference to the views of Taylor and Manson.

theoretical possibility of their existence cannot serve as the foundation for a major hypothesis.

It is more likely that servant passages were applied to Jesus by his followers because they believed him to be the Messiah. The hypothesis is simpler, requires no support from secret teachings of Jesus, and accords with the evidence from Jewish sources. Believing Jesus to be the promised Messiah and following accepted principles of interpretation, his followers were led to the servant poems as potentially messianic texts, since the Messiah is called God's servant in Zech. 3:8 and Ps. 89:39, passages traditionally understood as messianic in postbiblical Jewish circles. The Isaiah material, according to this view, was not used to prove that Jesus was the Servant, since there existed no such figure in the interpretive tradition. Rather, the texts were read as messianic, as verses that could legitimately be used to describe the career of "my servant the Messiah."

Such an exegetical move is paralleled in the Targum. "My servant" in Isa. 52:13 is taken to mean "my servant the Messiah," and the passage is consistently read as a reference to God's Christ. The striking difference between the NT and the targumic readings of Isaiah 53 derive from prior conceptions. The targumist reads the Isaiah passage in light of traditional Jewish conceptions of the Messiah; Christians came to the text with a very different messianic conception, modeled after Jesus the Messiah. Christians were no less careful in their exegesis, no less concerned about words and verbal associations than their contemporaries in the Jewish community. What permitted them to find in the servant poems useful christological material was the verbal link between "servant" and "Messiah." What motivated them to make use of the passage was the need to rethink traditional conceptions of messiahship in light of Jesus' death and resurrection.[23]

Confirmation of the link between "servant" imagery and royal ideology is provided by Acts. In Acts 4, the term *pais* is used twice to speak of Jesus, a rare occurrence in the NT (4:27, 30). David is also called God's *pais* (v. 25). The prayer that Peter prays includes a quotation of Ps. 2:1–2, which speaks of the "Lord and his anointed." The term *pais* in this context is royal language, appropriate to David the king and to the Messiah-King.

---

23. Chilton (*A Galilean Rabbi,* 200) comes to a similar conclusion: "servant" material was applied to Jesus because the term could be used to speak of the Messiah, as demonstrated in the Targum on Isaiah.

Results

It is unnecessary to examine all of the real and alleged citations of and allusions to the servant material in the NT. Our particular interest is starting points and initial connections. If my analysis is correct, however, there are some important implications about sketching a history of interpretation of passages from Isaiah.

1. There is no basis for speaking of a "paidology," as if there existed in early Christian circles a distinct constellation of images revolving around Isaiah's servant or a distinct area of reflection about Jesus in terms of servant texts. Material from Isaiah was used as part of the larger interpretive projects within early Christian circles.[24]

2. Arguments, such as those offered by Jeremias and Lindars, which seek to accord a priority to servant material over messianic imagery cannot be sustained. If imagery from Isaiah 42 was used to speak of Jesus only because he was confessed as Messiah, there is little reason to argue that in the account of Jesus' baptism in Mark, the basic text alluded to in the voice from heaven (Mark 1:11) is Isa. 42:1, and that Ps. 2:7 is only subsidiary. It is rather the messianic imagery that is primary—or in the case of the Markan baptismal account, we should say that there is no cause to separate Psalm 2 and Isaiah 42 into distinct branches of interpretive tradition.

3. The remarkable paucity of references to Isaiah in the passion narratives and in passion tradition as a whole makes it difficult to support arguments that Isaiah 53 provided the foundation for Christian reflection on Jesus' death. The passage was important, but mainly at later stages of the tradition and in the times after the NT. A glimpse at the passage's history within postbiblical Jewish tradition lends little credibility to the notion that the vocation of the Suffering Servant was available to Christians as a way of making sense of Jesus' death. Christological reflection on the meaning of the cross seems to have been far more creative than often assumed, and what Paul and the earlier tradition had in mind when they said, "Christ died for our sins in accordance with the scriptures," is still far from clear.

4. Allusions to Isaiah seem more likely to have provided Jesus' followers with a way of speaking of Jesus' death and vindication. The citation in Acts 8 is a prime example. The verses from Isaiah are important because they speak of one who is humiliated and vindicated. In the Christ hymn in Philippians 2, the one who "assumes the form of a slave

---

24. Chilton, *A Galilean Rabbi*, 129–35.

[*doulos*, not *pais*; the question of an allusion to Isaiah is difficult]" is "highly exalted," *hyperhypsōsen*. That characterization is perhaps derived from the *hypsōthēsetai* in Isa. 52:13 (cf. Acts 2:33 and 5:31 in reference to exaltation to God's right hand; and John 3:14, which speaks about Jesus' "lifting up" by way of analogy with the brass serpent in the wilderness). In Acts 3:13, *doxazō*, the other term from Isa. 52:13, is employed to speak of Jesus' resurrection and vindication ("God glorified his servant, Jesus whom you handed over"). The regular use of the term *hypsoun* to speak of Jesus' resurrection in John (7:39; 8:54; 11:4; 12:16, 23; 14:13; 16:14; 17:5) may likewise testify to the use of Isa. 52:13.

Perhaps, therefore, we should speak not of the Suffering Servant but of the "rejected and vindicated servant," acknowledging that Isaiah 52—53 was important primarily as a way of speaking about Jesus' humiliation and exaltation. To put it more accurately, it was a way of speaking about the death and vindication of Jesus the Servant-Christ, the King of the Jews.

6

CHRIST
AT THE RIGHT HAND

The Use of Psalm 110
in the New Testament

It is generally acknowledged that Psalm 110 played an important role in the development of christological tradition. Its precise role has been carefully detailed by David Hay in *Glory at the Right Hand*.[1] Much of this chapter will assume the results of Hay's study. I will focus on questions of the function and the origin of Psalm 110.

OVERVIEW OF INFLUENCE

Psalm 110 is an important OT text in early Christianity, though the number of actual quotations from it is small. The opening verse is quoted by Jesus in a discussion about the Son of David recorded in each of the Synoptic Gospels (Matt. 22:41–46; Mark 12:35–37a; Luke 20:41–44). The wording of the verse is identical in the three versions. The verse is quoted in Peter's Pentecost speech (Acts 2:34); the wording in Acts is identical with the citation in the Gospels. Finally, the opening verse of Psalm 110 is included among the string of biblical verses cited in Hebrews 1. Hebrews also quotes Ps. 110:4 three times (Heb. 5:6; 7:17, 21). Note that the actual quotations of the opening psalm verse are identical, and all agree word for word with the LXX (the sole divergence lying in the consistent omission of the definite article that appears before the

---

1. Hay, *Glory at the Right Hand*.

initial "Lord" in Ps. 110:1a LXX).[2] The number of allusions is significantly higher. Nestle's chart lists eight NT allusions to v. 1 (not counting
Synoptic pars.) and six allusions to v. 4. Hay lists thirteen allusions to v.
1 and eight to v. 4.[3] The precise wording of the NT allusions tends to
differ significantly from that in quotations, even within the same book.
Allusions feature several different constructions with *dexia,* as Hay
points out,[4] employing *en,* or the simple dative. The allusions often
employ *hypokatō* instead of *hypopodion.* The differences may be due to
variant forms of the Greek OT available to NT authors or direct translations from the Hebrew. More likely, the source of many allusions is
traditional material in which the language of Psalm 110 has been fixed
in distinctive ways, sometimes perhaps because of the influence of
other biblical passages with which it is associated. Hay considers it
likely that several references to imagery from Psalm 110 were drawn
directly from traditional material without knowledge of the OT source.
The NT data suggest that Psalm 110, at least the first verse, became an
important feature of Christian exegetical tradition at an early date and
decisively shaped hymnic and confessional language.

Judging from the NT references to Ps. 110:1, the primary importance
of the verse lay in the imagery it provided: Jesus is enthroned at God's
right hand. The verse was also significant because it provided language
with which to speak about the exalted Jesus. He is "lord," the one addressed as such by the Lord God. The verse is important in Peter's
Pentecost speech precisely because it "proves" that Jesus can be called
Lord. Finally, Hay argues that the verse of the psalm was important as a
way of speaking about the subjection of powers to Jesus in a variety of
ways (see, e.g., 1 Cor. 15:25–26; Eph. 1:20), and of his heavenly intercession (see, e.g., Rom. 8:34). The singular employment of the reference to
Melchizedek in Hebrews represents a distinctive contribution to the
interpretive tradition, though the author surely drew on earlier exegesis.[5]

It is significant that there was no other interest in the rest of the psalm
until after NT times. Justin Martyr interprets the whole of the psalm as
a reference to Jesus, as he does with Psalm 22. Unlike Psalm 22, however, Psalm 110 does not appear to have been of interest as a whole to
exegetes of the first century; interest was confined to the opening verse
and v. 4.

---

2. Ibid., 35.
3. Ibid., 163–66.
4. Ibid., 35–36.
5. On Melchizedek, see ibid., 135–43, and the literature cited there.

JEWISH BACKGROUND

To understand early Christian use of this psalm, it is helpful to know something about the place of the psalm in postbiblical Jewish tradition. Once again, Hay has done a careful job of surveying the literature. His chapter on Jewish interpretation is short.[6] The psalm is not widely quoted in intertestamental or rabbinic sources. As significant references Hay mentions

1. *Testament of Job* 33.3 (Job's response to Elihu).

   Be silent. Now I will point out to you my throne, its glory and splendor. My throne is in the heavenly world and its glory and splendor are at the right hand of God (*ek dexiōn tou theou*).

   The passage has been employed to speak about the vindication of a righteous sufferer—a motif not uncommon in martyrologies.[7] Nothing further is made of Job's future status in the heavenly court as king.

2. Possible use of the psalm by Hasmonean rulers. Hay identifies phrases in the *Testament of Levi* that may contain language from the psalm. Though the allusions are not uniformly convincing, they may suggest that the psalm, particularly its linking of kingship and priesthood in the figure of Melchizedek, was appropriated for court propaganda during the time of the Hasmoneans.

3. Daniel 7:9–14. Hay proposes that the seer who composed Daniel constructed his vision of the divine throne room, which includes a place for a humanlike figure enthroned in God's presence, with an eye to Ps. 110:1, the "only scriptural text which explicitly speaks of someone enthroned beside God" (p. 26).[8] Whether this is the case, it is clear that later interpreters found an association between the two passages. It is possible that the association lies behind a comment attributed to Rabbi Akiba that will be considered in the next chapter. The passage from *b. Sanh.* 38b reads,

   . . . but how explain "Till thrones were placed?" [Dan. 7:9]—One [throne] was for Himself and one for David. Even as it has been taught: One was for Himself and one for David: this is R. Akiba's view. R. Jose protested to him: Akiba, how long wilt thou profane the Sheckinah? Rather, one [throne] for justice, and the other for mercy.

---

6. Ibid., 19–33.
7. See Nickelsburg, *Resurrection, Immortality, and Eternal Life.* For connections between such traditions and the binding of Isaac, see Spiegel, *Last Trial.*
8. Hay, *Glory at the Right Hand,* 26.

Did he accept [this answer] from him or not?—Come and hear! For it has been taught: One is for justice and the other for charity; this is R. Akiba's view. Said R. Eleazar b. Azariah to him: Akiba, what hast thou to do with *Aggada*? Confine thyself to [the study of] *Nega'im* and *Ohaloth*. But one was a throne, the other a footstool: a throne for a seat and a footstool in support of His feet.

The comments of Eleazar are undoubtedly later, reflecting discomfort even with the standard way of interpreting Daniel 7 in terms of God's attributes of justice and mercy. What is of interest is that his comments presume that the scene in Daniel is to be understood from Ps. 110:1, though the passage is not even quoted. Whether or not the association can be assumed for earlier interpretations of Daniel 7 outside Christian circles is difficult to determine.

4. Rabbinic interpretation.[9] The rabbis most frequently identify the second "lord" in v. 1 as the Messiah,[10] though that is by no means the only reading of the verse. Rabbi Ishmael, for example, applies the verse to Abraham (*b. Ned.* 32b):

R. Zechariah said on R. Ishmael's authority: The Holy One, blessed be He, intended to bring forth the priesthood from Shem, as it is written, "And he [Melchizedek] was the priest of the most high God." But because he gave precedence in his blessing to Abraham over God, He brought it forth from Abraham; as it is written, "And he blessed him and said, Blessed be Abram of the most high God, possessor of heaven and earth, and blessed be the most high God." Said Abraham to him, "Is the blessing of a servant to be given precedence over that of his master?" Straightway it [the priesthood] was given to Abraham, as it is written, "The Lord said unto my Lord, Sit thou at my right hand, until I make thine enemies thy footstool"; which is followed by, "The Lord hath sworn, and will not repent, Thou are a priest for ever, after the order of Melchizedek." (See also *b. Sanh.* 108b and *Midr.* Ps. 110, sec. 4.)

The importance of the strange figure Melchizedek in Gen. 14:18–20 provides an obvious link with the psalm. Justin Martyr suggests that Jews in his day interpret the opening verse as a reference to

---

9. Hay suggests possible references to Ps. 110:1 in Enoch traditions and in 11QMelch, but the evidence he cites is not convincing.

10. There is little direct evidence in extant texts for a messianic interpretation of Ps. 110:1. One example is found in *Midr.* Ps. 18, sec. 29: "R. Yudan said in the name of R. Hama: In the time-to-come, when the Holy One, blessed be He, seats the lord Messiah at His right hand, as it is said, 'The Lord saith unto my lord: "Sit thou at My right hand"' (Ps. 110:1) . . ." (*The Midrash on Psalms*, trans. Braude, 1:261). The passage in Mark 12, however, seems to presume widespread agreement that the psalm speaks of the Davidic Messiah. For Hay's assessment of the evidence, see his *Glory at the Right Hand*, 29–30.

Hezekiah, though this interpretation is not corroborated in extant rabbinic tradition (Justin *Dial.* 33, 83). The targumic rendering of the verse understands it as a reference to David, taking the "Sit at my right hand" to mean "Sit (wait) for the Benjaminite (Saul)."[11] Many have taken this as a reference to the Messiah, though it seems more likely that Samson Levey is correct that the targumic rendering arises from historicizing exegesis, relating the psalm to David's past reign.[12] The interpretation is thus of the same sort mentioned by Justin.

Hay's survey of postbiblical literature suggests there is no single interpretive tradition that can be regarded as normative. The verses were applied in at least one instance to a pious individual (Job) who was rewarded by exaltation to God's presence. The verses could be applied to historical figures (David, Abraham, Hezekiah, the Hasmonean rulers) as well as to eschatological deliverers, like the Messiah. We may speak at best of interpretive possibilities available to Christian exegetes. Though the opening verse clearly suggests enthronement in God's presence, the verse did not attract as much attention from Jewish commentators as Dan. 7:9, which mentions that "thrones" are placed and that the Ancient of Days sits on one. Daniel 7 was viewed as a dangerous passage, liable to misunderstanding among heretics.[13] We have no such warning about Ps. 110:1.

THE ORIGIN OF CHRISTIAN EXEGESIS

What led to the initial interest in Ps. 110:1, and on what basis did it become part of christological tradition? Jewish tradition offers at least two possibilities: the verse might have been applied to Jesus as a pious sufferer who was vindicated by God, or it might have been applied to him as Messiah. Barnabas Lindars opts for a version of the second suggestion: the psalm verse was first used in early Christian apologetic, he argues, to demonstrate that Jesus was the Messiah because he was raised from the dead.[14] In the case of this psalm, Lindars believes, Christians based their case on a literal interpretation of the opening verse. "Right hand" was taken as a reference to a place in heaven at

---

11. The translation is from Levey, *The Messiah.*
12. Ibid.
13. See Segal, *Two Powers in Heaven.*
14. Lindars, *New Testament Apologetic.*

God's side, not as a figurative way of speaking about a place of honor for the king in an earthly setting. Because Jesus was actually exalted to the right hand of God at his resurrection, he fulfills the psalm and is shown to be the Christ.

There are several difficulties with Lindars's arguments, some of which have been cited above. One is his conviction that the speeches in Acts represent an early stage in exegetical tradition. In fact, Acts represents a rather developed stage of sophisticated scriptural argumentation.[15] Lindars's conviction that scriptural exegesis was important for Christians first as a missionary tool to convince Jews of the truth of the kerygma suffers from the same one-sidedness as Martin Dibelius's emphasis on preaching as the sole *Sitz im Leben* of Christian tradition. The earliest use of Scripture was internal, though this does not exclude the need to formulate arguments. The Bible provided the data for reflection on the gospel and its implications, as well as the language of prayer and praise. Exegesis was the matrix for theologizing. Carefully structured arguments, particularly of the sort found in Acts, are subsequent developments.

The proposal about literal fulfillment is likewise unconvincing. Even if the mode of argument in Peter's speech were regarded as primitive ("David did not ascend into the heavens . . . but Jesus. . . ."), the conclusion the speech draws—that because he was exalted to God's right hand, Jesus is shown to be lord and Christ—depends upon an assumption that Ps. 110:1 would have been taken unquestionably as a messianic reference, that is, that anyone exalted to the right hand of God would be understood to be the Messiah. The application of the passage to Job and Abraham in postbiblical Jewish tradition, as well as to historical figures like the Hasmoneans or even Hezekiah, makes it unlikely that such a text could provide the basis for confessing Jesus as Messiah. It is likely the text came to be of interest to Christians as a potentially messianic passage—but only because Jesus was already confessed as the vindicated Christ. Luke's use of the verse presupposes a prior history of interpretation within Christian circles.

Hay has done a masterly job of analyzing the various strands of NT exegesis concerning the psalm verses. He has also offered suggestions about the reason for the psalm's popularity among Christian exegetes.

---

15. Juel, "Social Dimensions of Exegesis: The Use of Psalm 16 in Acts 2," *CBQ* 43 (1981): 543–56; Kurz, "The Function of Christological Proof from Prophecy in Luke and Justin" (diss., Yale Univ., 1976); and Haenchen, *Acts of the Apostles,* 177–89.

He is tentative, however, about what led exegetes to the passage in the first place, and about the basis for its becoming part of Christian tradition. There is a logic within the development of christological tradition—at least to the degree that we can understand why particular passages came to be regarded as fruitful for reflection and appropriate as descriptions of Jesus and his career. Jesus' followers did not simply leaf through the Scriptures randomly, landing fortuitously upon verses that seemed of interest.

It would appear that the verses from Psalm 110 were important, like 2 Samuel 7, Psalm 89, and Isaiah 11, as messianic texts. It is not necessarily relevant that the original psalm functioned in a royal setting; what is crucial is that in the first century the verses in question could be read as part of the constellation of biblical passages referring to the coming King from the line of David. Extant Jewish tradition permits us to say at least that much. The "son of David" passage in the Synoptics presumes that the "scribes" understood the psalm verse as a reference to the Messiah. If Jesus was confessed as the crucified and vindicated Christ, the image of enthronement at God's right hand would have seemed quite appropriate as royal language. The presence of rabbinic applications of the verse to the Messiah suggests that Psalm 110 could be—and perhaps prior to the Christian era actually was—understood as messianic. The rather consistent NT use of Ps. 110:1 to speak of the heavenly session of Jesus as a vindication of his messianic office supports such a suggestion.

Once applied to the risen Christ, the psalm offered additional possibilities for Christian interpreters. Paul could make something of the "until" in Ps. 110:1c to speak of the time between the present and the consummation of God's victory over his enemies, reading the reference to "subjection" in terms of Psalm 8:7. The author of Hebrews could develop the priestly notions in v. 4 as a way of explicating the work of Christ. Whatever the developments, however, the initial connection between the psalm verse and Christian tradition seems to be the confession of Jesus as Christ. The second "lord" in the opening verse was taken to be the Christ.

The Gospel of Mark

Two passages of particular importance in establishing that claim are found in Mark. One is the debate about the son of David in Mark 12:35–37; the other is Jesus' response to the question of the high priest at his trial in 14:62.

Mark 12:35-37

And as Jesus taught in the temple, he said, "How can the scribes say that the
Christ is the son of David? David himself, inspired by the Holy Spirit,
declared, 'The Lord said to my Lord, Sit at my right hand, till I put thy
enemies under thy feet.' David himself calls him Lord; so how is he his
son?" And the great throng heard him gladly.

The verses have been included in Mark within a section of controversies
that precedes Jesus' arrest, trial, and execution. Throughout this portion of Mark, Jesus' opponents are the religious officials—the scribes,
the elders, and the chief priests, those in charge of the temple. The issues
that are the subject of controversy here—the authority of Jesus and
John (11:27–33), the status of those in charge of the vineyard (12:1–12),
the sensitive issue of tribute to Caesar (12:13–17), the compatibility
of the resurrection and scriptural tradition (12:18–27), and the relationship of temple worship to Torah piety (12:28–34)—turn out to be matters of considerable import for the Jewish community in the latter
decades of the first century. The messianic discussion may be regarded
as an appropriate issue in this context and need not be discarded as
something Mark included here without thought simply to show that
Jesus was capable of "beating the rabbis with their own stick."[16] We can
presume that the discussions were relevant to Mark's audience.

If we assume that the verses make sense in Mark, we should begin by
noting that there is nothing elsewhere in the Gospel to suggest Mark
intends to prove that Jesus is not the "son of David." The "confession"
of blind Bartimaeus in 10:47 suggests rather that the title "son of David"
is appropriate for Jesus: the blind man sees what Jesus' disciples (and
the authorities) cannot. To argue that Jesus could accept the designation
"Christ, the Son of the Blessed" from the high priest (Mark 14:61–62)
while insisting two chapters earlier that the Christ is not "son of David"
is improbable, whether we are considering the actual words of Jesus or
Mark's story world. The little evidence that Jewish tradition knew of a
non-Davidic Messiah is relatively late, and the conception of a Messiah
ben Joseph would do little to clarify Jesus' comments in Mark 12. Attempts to prove that "the Christ" could refer to a prophetic or priestly
figure are unconvincing, and in any case the substitution of such a
Christ figure would do nothing to solve the problem Jesus poses for his
opponents by quoting Ps. 110:1.

The comments are enigmatic, but it is best to view the juxtaposition
of "son of David" and "lord" in Jesus' comments within the category of

---

16. Lindars, *New Testament Apologetic,* 46–47.

alleged scriptural contradictions familiar from rabbinic tradition.[17] Chapter 7 will provide several highly formalized examples of the genre. In the developed form, two scriptural verses are cited that appear to be contradictory. The interpreter then solves the apparent contradiction, often by identifying spheres within which each verse can be understood as true.[18]

In this case, the view of the scribes that "the Christ is David's son" may be a shorthand substitution for the actual citation of a passage like 2 Sam. 7:12–14. With this scriptural view is juxtaposed another, from Ps. 110:1, that seems to call into question what the Bible says elsewhere. Though the form of the pericope differs from that of the surrounding controversies, we are to assume that Jesus' concluding question implies an answer to the question he poses.[19] Some point has been scored that would have made sense to the audience. Assuming that the verses represent an authentic logion, some argue Jesus' point was a rejection of Davidic messianology.[20] That would make totally inexplicable, then, the account of Jesus' trial and death as "the Christ, the Son of the Blessed" and the King of the Jews, and the readiness of his followers to confess him as Messiah. Others who regard the verses as the product of Christian exegetical reflection view the alleged attack on Davidic descent as intended to head off explicit criticism of Jesus' credentials.[21] Such accusations are not a major issue anywhere in the NT, however; one of the earliest confessional pieces, attested by Paul in Rom. 1:2–4, asserts Jesus' descent from David *kata sarka*. And given what we know of Jewish tradition, it makes no sense to suggest that one could use "the

---

17. This interpretation is argued eloquently and convincingly by Loevestam ("Die Davidssohnsfrage," *SEA* 27 [1972]: 72–82). See also the comments on Mark 12:35–37 in Lane, *The Gospel according to Mark.* And see Dahl, "Contradictions in Scripture," in *Studies in Paul,* 159–77.

18. The widespread practice of working with alleged contradictions in the Scriptures resulted in the development of formal ways of dealing with them, and eventually to specific exegetical principles. The famous thirteenth rule of Rabbi Ishmael reads, "Two passages opposing one another and conflicting with one another stand as they are, until a third passage comes to decide between them" (*Mekilta* Pischa 4; the translation is from *Mekilta de Rabbi Ishmael,* ed. Lauterbach, 1:32). The rule was developed primarily for determining matters of law, but the presence of conflicting passages was not restricted to legal material. See Dahl, "Contradictions."

19. On the form of the pericope, see Bultmann, *History of the Synoptic Tradition,* 51, 136–37.

20. The various alternatives are discussed by Bultmann (*History of the Synoptic Tradition,* 136–37).

21. For representative views, see Loevestam, "Die Davidssohnsfrage," 74–75.

Messiah" as a reference to a general eschatological deliverer. Language about the Christ derives from royal ideology associated with David. That is certainly true in Mark.

It seems more likely, as Evald Loevestam has argued, that the implied solution to the problem Jesus has posed—a possible contradiction within the Scriptures—is provided by events the readers know will soon follow. Jesus, the son of David, rejected by the temple authorities, was raised from the dead and enthroned at God's right hand. It is appropriate for David to call his messianic son "lord" in view of Jesus' installation at God's right hand. Only if Jesus, the son of David, has been elevated to that position at God's side does the alleged contradiction in the Scriptures disappear. As in rabbinic tradition, the apparent contradiction provides an occasion to score some point—here, that death and resurrection are not incompatible with what the Scriptures have to say about the Christ. Since tradition knew nothing of a crucified Messiah, it could hardly have any conceptions of a resurrected King. The use of Psalm 110:1 to construct a scriptural image of a dying and rising Messiah is an example of creative Christian exegesis.

The advantage of this interpretation is that it is compatible with what we know of postbiblical messianic tradition and does not result in a contradiction within Mark. The comment in Mark 13:26 that all will see the "Son of man coming in clouds" presumes that the humanlike figure was already in heaven (see below, pp. 160–62, on the interpretation of Daniel 7). In this context, the promised return of the Son of man in the clouds points to the final public vindication of the true Christ—as opposed to the false Christs mentioned in v. 21. As I have argued elsewhere, the point is not that Jesus is the Son of man instead of the Christ, but that his return will offer vindication of those who have remained faithful to the true Messiah.[22]

The passage presumes no distinction between an earthly and a heavenly deliverer. As in Acts, Psalm 110:1 becomes part of an argument according to which God's promise to David of a seed to sit on his throne forever (2 Sam. 7:12–14; Ps. 89:3–4) is fulfilled only with the installation of the risen Christ in heaven. It is as the enthroned "lord" that Jesus is son of David.

Mark 14:61–62

But he was silent and made no answer. Again the high priest asked him, "Are you the Christ, the Son of the Blessed?" and Jesus said, "I am; and you

---

22. See Juel, *Messiah and Temple,* 85–95.

will see the Son of man seated at the right hand of Power, and coming with the clouds of heaven."

Jesus' response to the high priest at his trial, like the question about David's son, shows signs of considerable exegetical activity. Norman Perrin has suggested that Jesus' response alludes to no less than three biblical texts, the "you will see" coming from Zech. 12:10.[23] His argument depends in part on the tradition, attested in Matt. 24:30 and in Rev. 1:7, combining Zech. 12:10 and Dan. 7:13 in a promise that at the return of the Son of man, "all the tribes of the earth will wail on account of him" (for a similar use of Zech. 12:10, see *b. Sukk.* 52a). Though Perrin's arguments may not be convincing, they do point to a rich interpretive activity that underlies the present allusions to the verses from Psalm 110 and Daniel 7.

What may be noted about the statement at Jesus' trial, in addition, is its relationship to the "confession" of Jesus as "the Christ, the Son of the Blessed." For the first and only time in Mark's Gospel, the two titles with which the Gospel begins are put together. In keeping with the ironic tone of Mark's narrative, it is Jesus' would-be judges who formulate the "confessions" and speak the truth.[24] Jesus' unambiguous acceptance of the designations is likewise unparalleled in Mark. Through the remainder of the passion story, Jesus is tried, mocked, and finally executed as King. The high priest's formulation is a central moment in the narrative; it introduces the theme of the ensuing conflict and provides the basis upon which Jesus will be rejected—and subsequently vindicated. Jesus' response is not intended as a redefinition or qualification of his acceptance of the designation as Christ and Son of the Blessed. Rather, his response points to the vindication that can be expected: his judges "will see." Jesus' statement is probably a reference both to the resurrection, understood here as Jesus' installation at God's right hand, and to Jesus' return with the clouds.[25] The return with the clouds is promised in Mark 13:24–25 as the climax of the events leading to the end, the moment when the elect will be gathered and all "will see" that their faith in Jesus has not been misplaced.

The allusion to Psalm 110 is important here not as proof that the risen Jesus will be called Lord, but as promised vindication for the one condemned as Christ and Son of God. The psalm furnishes language to

---

23. Perrin, "Mark 14:62: The End Product of a Christian Pesher Tradition?" *NTS* 12 (1965): 150–55.

24. Juel, *Messiah and Temple,* 47–48.

25. Ibid., 93–95.

speak of Jesus as enthroned at God's side, from whence he will return with the clouds. Likewise the reference to Daniel 7 is important not because Jesus is shown to be the Son of man as opposed to the Messiah and Son of God but because his return as the Son of man will prove true the claims made that he is Christ. The concept of the Messiah is of course redefined, but it is the whole context that demands some radical reinterpretation of traditional conceptions—while not denying that Jesus is the Christ.[26]

The combination of allusions presumes a developed stage of reflection. In Mark (and Matthew and Luke), references to Daniel depict Jesus' return to earth. They imply that he is in heaven. Such a reading of Daniel seems to presuppose, then, an interpretation of Jesus' exaltation in terms like those expressed in Ps. 110:1. The absence of Daniel 7 from the Pauline corpus and the presence of Psalm 110 suggest that the exegesis of the psalm predates that of Daniel.

The placement of the quotation in Mark 14:62, as the citation of Ps. 110:1 in Mark 12:35–37, makes it clear that the psalm verse was understood as a messianic text. The "Lord" is here understood as the Messiah, as is explicitly stated in 12:35–37. The combination with Daniel 7 opens the possibility of wider speculation about the one who is enthroned at God's right hand. The verse from Daniel was among texts that nurtured speculation about principal angels and heavenly intermediaries. The link between Psalm 110 and Daniel 7 is not, however, intended to qualify Jesus' identity as Christ. It opens the possibility of creative "messianic exegesis" in which Jesus' special relationship to God as Son can be explored.

One direction in which this exploration moved involves the language of the psalm verse: the use of "Lord" as a designation for Jesus. The place of Ps. 110:1 in this highly significant christological development merits some comment.

The Confession of Jesus as Kyrios

One place where the language of the psalm figures in christological discussions is in Peter's Pentecost speech.[27] In Acts 2:34–35, Ps. 110:1 is quoted as a comment on the concluding line in Psalm 16, which speaks

---

26. The irony of Mark's narrative works only if Jesus both is the Christ and differs from expectations.

27. Haenchen, *Acts of the Apostles,* 177–89, and the literature cited there; Lindars, *New Testament Apologetic,* 36–59; and Juel, "Social Dimensions of Exegesis."

of "pleasures at your right hand." In the speech's argument, Jesus' resurrection proves that he is the holy one in the psalm—hence (according to Acts) the Messiah. The quotation from Ps. 110:1 with its comment on the "right hand" in Psalm 16, supplies the information necessary to make the argument in the speech: Jesus can be called Lord. The point is crucial to Peter's argument, for that means the Lord in whose name salvation is offered, according to Joel ("Whoever calls on the name of the Lord will be saved," 2:32) is the Lord Jesus.

Several things should be said about the speech. First, it represents a developed, sophisticated midrashic argument that cannot be classified as early or typical.[28] As in the case of rabbinic midrash, what appears in the final form often presupposes several interpretive steps that are unexpressed. The audience is expected to supply what is lacking. One indication is the failure to quote the last line from Psalm 16. The apparent introduction of the "right hand" in Acts 2:33 makes perfect sense if the author is commenting on the last line of Psalm 16, which is for some reason not quoted. Second, the use of Psalm 16 cannot be considered early or typical of early Christian exegesis, contrary to the view of Lindars. The psalm is important nowhere else in the NT, and the "messianic" reading of the psalm seems to be Lukan.[29] Finally, the importance of the LXX is central. Peter's argument that Jesus is the Lord referred to in Joel 3 works only if the author is reading *kyrios* in the LXX text and not some substitute for the ineffable name, YHWH, which appears in the Hebrew.

There is considerable uncertainty among scholars about the treatment of God's name in LXX manuscripts; several have been discovered in which the name is not translated but represented by letters in archaic Hebrew script or with transcriptions like IAO.[30] On the other hand, the

---

28. Juel, "Social Dimensions of Exegesis," 550–56; and Kurz, "The Function of Christological Proof."

29. On the distinctive features of Luke's two-stage christological argument, see Kurz, "The Function of Christological Proof," and Dahl, "The Story of Abraham in Luke-Acts," in *Jesus in the Memory of the Early Church,* 66–86.

30. Hahn (*Titles of Jesus*) is typical of the group of scholars who argue that the use of "Lord" for Jesus is largely the result of the LXX's use of *kyrios* in translating the sacred name of God. For more recent views, see Howard, "The Tetragram and the New Testament," *JBL* 96 (1977): 63–83; Fitzmyer, "Der semitische Hintergrund des neutestamentlichen Kyriostitels" (1975), now in English in Fitzmyer, *A Wandering Aramean,* 115–42; and for evidence that Philo read Greek OT mss. that employed *kyrios* for the tetragram, Dahl and Segal, "Philo and the Rabbis on the Names of God," *JSJ* 10 (1979): 5–6.

quotation from Joel, as it appears in Acts 2, uses *kyrios*—and it seems reasonable that Luke, like Philo, knew manuscripts in which *kyrios* was employed as a translation for the sacred name. In fact, only if the Greek OT text from which Acts quotes used *kyrios* to translate YHWH in Joel 2:32 (Heb. 3:5) is it possible to distinguish between the "Lord" here and the "Lord" at the conclusion of the verse (designated as "the Lord our God" in Acts 2:39).

The issue is important because it might suggest *kyrios* entered Christian tradition as a name for Jesus through the application of Psalm 110:1 to him. Having proved that Jesus could be called Lord, Christian interpreters would then have reread the Scriptures to determine on which occasions the term could appropriately be referred to Jesus.

This argument is unlikely for several reasons. First, the argument in Acts is hardly ancient. No reference to Psalm 16 can be found outside Acts, but references to Psalm 110 are spread broadly through the tradition. The use of Psalm 110 predates that of Psalm 16. Second, in view of the Greek manuscripts in which God's name is not translated, we can no longer assume an unreflective application of the title *kyrios* to Jesus. There is unambiguous evidence in Philippians 2 that *kyrios* was used as an appellation for Jesus with awareness that the term was used for God (see the use of Isa. 45:23: the "name that is above every name" in Isaiah is God's special name).[31] The full range of meanings in the title Lord would be most apparent in the Greek world, making it likely that the confession "Jesus is Lord" occurred first in Greek-speaking Christianity. The linguistic evidence, however, is insufficient to argue that it was in a Greek-speaking environment that Christians first began using Lord as a divine title to speak of Jesus and first understood scriptural passages using the divine name to refer to him. Speculation in Jewish circles focusing on the identity of a principal angel who bears the name of God makes it quite likely that the term "Lord" was used of Jesus even in Aramaic-speaking circles with full awareness of possible relations to the name of God.[32] Such speculation, at least in some Jewish circles, was not understood to compromise the oneness of God. It became increasingly problematic, however, as Alan Segal has demonstrated in his study of "two powers" controversies, and was eventually proscribed by the rabbis.

---

31. On the use of Isaiah 45 in Philippians 2, see Nagata, "Phil. 2:5–11: A Case Study in the Contextual Shaping of Early Christology" (diss., Princeton Theol. Sem., 1981).

32. Segal, *Two Powers in Heaven,* 205–19.

In summary, it seems unlikely that the use of "Lord" to speak of Jesus was the sole result of interpreting Ps. 110:1, though the verse certainly furnished important support for the practice at least at certain stages in the tradition. And as Acts 2 demonstrates, the psalm could be used for scriptural argument long after it had become established practice to speak of Jesus as the one on whom God's own name had been conferred.

CONCLUSIONS

Psalm 110:1 provided imagery that was to be of considerable importance in the evolution of christological tradition. It also provided connections with other biblical texts. The reference to the lifting-up of Jesus to God's right hand in Acts 2:33 and 5:31 may signal a link with Isa. 52:13; this is made more likely by the use of *pais* in 4:27, 30 as a reference to the anointed one of Psalm 2. Several passages in the NT indicate a connection between Ps. 110:1 and Psalm 8 (e.g., 1 Cor. 15:25–28).[33] The connection with Dan. 7:9–14 proved particularly fruitful (see chap. 7).

The occurrences of Ps. 110:1 in the NT derive from early Christian scriptural interpretation; there is little evidence that they derive from Jesus' own exegesis of the verse. The interpretations presuppose that Jesus is confessed as the Christ and that he was raised from the dead by God. The psalm verse most likely suggested its appropriateness not simply because the psalm is inherently royal but because it could be referred to the coming Christ. It entered Christian tradition as a messianic text that provided ways of speaking about Jesus' exaltation. Once the identification was made, interpretations could move in a variety of directions. Hay is correct that the reference to a session at the right hand soon became an established feature of Christian tradition and could be employed without reference to its scriptural origin.

Questions remain. To what degree, for example, did the psalm provide a basis for Christian reflection on Jesus' exaltation? Philipp Vielhauer has argued vigorously that Philippians 2 and Rom. 1:2–4, among the earliest christological traditions known to us, speak about exaltation without reference to Psalm 110—suggesting that the origin of the concept of exaltation (and thus of a fundamental christological category) must be sought elsewhere.[34] But where? Evidence for the existence

---

33. Hay, *Glory at the Right Hand,* 42.

34. Vielhauer, "Ein Weg zur neutestamentlichen Christologie?" in *Aufsätze zum Neuen Testament,* 162–75.

of mythic figures like the Son of man on the basis of which Jesus' ministry could be explicated has virtually disappeared. What we find instead, at least within Jewish communities, are exegetical traditions about heroes and martyrs and heavenly intermediaries. Where else might we look for scriptural ways of expressing exaltation and vindication? The question must be left for another occasion.

7

THE RISEN CHRIST AND THE SON OF MAN

Christian Use of Daniel 7

Here I will examine the use of Daniel 7 in Christian tradition, especially the imagery in 7:9–14. The famous judgment scene figures prominently in the Apocalypse of John, which is perhaps not surprising given the similarity of the visions attributed to John the seer and to Daniel. The number of allusions to the familiar verses from Daniel elsewhere in the NT, however, is remarkably small, particularly in light of the inordinate attention the passage has received in the history of biblical scholarship. There is not a single quotation of Dan. 7:9–14 in the NT, and there are only a handful of clear allusions. The attention these verses have received must be explained by factors other than the frequency of their use in early Christian tradition.

THE SON OF MAN

The explanation is not difficult to find: the reference in Dan. 7:13 to "one like a son of man" may be related to the enigmatic self-designation used by Jesus in all the Gospels, *ho huios tou anthrōpou*. The "title" has received considerable attention both because of its frequency and because of its tantalizingly enigmatic character.

1. The "title" is used only by Jesus, except in Acts 7:56, where Stephen sees "the Son of man standing at the right hand of God" (nowhere else is there reference to the Son of man standing), and in John 12:34.

2. There are places where the expression is clearly a self-designation,

sometimes even interchangeable in the tradition with "I" (cf. Matt. 16:13 with Mark 8:27, and Matt. 16:21 with Mark 8:31). On other occasions, Jesus' statements leave open the possibility that he is referring to the Son of man as another figure (e.g., in Luke 12:8; Mark 8:38).

3. In several instances (Mark 13:26; Matt. 24:30; 25:31; Luke 21:27; Mark 14:62 par.), the phrase "the Son of man" is used in a context where allusions to the vision in Daniel are obvious. In a few instances, there are allusions to the imagery from Daniel without the use of "the Son of man" (Matt. 28:18 and Rev. 1:7; in Rev. 1:13 and 14:14 we read about one *homoion huion anthrōpou*, which is not equivalent to the common *ho huios tou anthrōpou* but comes directly from Daniel).

4. There is not a single use of "the Son of man" nor a clear allusion to Daniel 7 in Paul's letters.

Several important questions arise from the data:

1. How is the expression "the Son of man" to be understood in the present NT? Should it be understood as a title with specific content or as some form of unusual self-designation with unspecified content? Does each use of the expression "the Son of man" imply some relationship with the vision in Daniel 7?

2. What light does the history of interpreting Daniel 7 shed on the use of the expression "the Son of man" in the NT, and what light does NT usage shed on the history of Daniel 7 in early Christianity?

The library of scholarship on the use of "the Son of man" in the NT testifies that the questions can be answered in more than one way.[1] The evidence is susceptible of several interpretations. Particularly when the goal of interpretation is to account for the origin of a particular phrase in the tradition or for the use of a particular biblical passage, exegesis involves an intricate relationship between available historical data, specific texts, and hypothetical models employed by the exegete.

Various examples of past proposals make the point clear. Surveying the use of "the Son of man" in Mark, for example, Albert Schweitzer determined that the only way to understand how the various uses of the term were related was to trace the expression back to Jesus and his

---

1. Among the most recent works, which provide an ample review of previous scholarship, are Casey, *Son of Man,* and Lindars, *Jesus Son of Man.* See Vermes's *Jesus and the World of Judaism,* 89–99, for the most recent review of his own specific proposals about the linguistic background of "the Son of man" and a response to critics. The important contributions of Fitzmyer should also be noted, esp. "The New Testament Title 'Son of Man' Philologically Considered," in *A Wandering Aramean,* 143–60.

self-conception. That self-conception, he insisted, had to be reconstructed within Jesus' own world, which Schweitzer—together with
many of his contemporaries—took to be one dominated by apocalyptic
dreams of the future. His interpretation of the "Son of man" sayings in
Mark thus required attention to specific passages in the Gospels, attention to postbiblical Jewish literature, and arguments arising from an
imaginative view of early Christianity that Schweitzer sketched.

Rudolf Bultmann, although sharing some of Schweitzer's views of
early Christian history and the significance of apocalyptic in the first-
century environment, was far more skeptical about using the Gospels to
reconstruct Jesus' own beliefs. A full interpretation of "the Son of man"
required attention to the history of Christian tradition in addition to
Jesus' own words. Only a tradition that made the object of its preaching
the one who pointed to a redeemer figure other than himself—to the
Son of man—could unify the various "Son of man" sayings that Bultmann argued were otherwise nonharmonious. His conviction that only
Jesus' references to the Son of man as someone else were authentic, and
that the remaining sayings must be attributed to the early church, is
based on a reconstruction of postbiblical tradition according to which
there existed an interpretation of Daniel 7 as referring to a mythic
figure known as the "apocalyptic Son of man," which Bultmann and
others related in a complex way to theories of the primal man and to a
"gnostic Redeemer." The NT was read in light of historical arguments
about Jewish tradition as well as of Bultmann's own reconstruction of
early Christian tradition.

The point of these comments is not to demonstrate that previous
generations of exegetes were biased whereas we can now read the texts of
the NT "as they are." It is rather to point up how involved the interpretive questions are, how much is invested in historical information about
postbiblical Judaism and in hypothetical historical models within
which the literature of the NT is located. Advances in recent decades
have resulted both from the availability of new historical information
(Qumran, Nag Hammadi, and the like) and new imaginative models for
reconstructing the history of Christian tradition.

Daniel 7 in the New Testament

We first need to determine to what extent questions about the history
of Daniel 7 in early Christianity are bound up with the phrase "the
Son of man."

1. The phrase "the Son of man" is unusual in Greek, corresponding
to no known idiom. It is not derived from the Greek OT. Its form must

be derived from a Semitic phrase, with determinative form (definite article).[2]

2. With two exceptions (Acts 7:56; John 12:34), the phrase appears on the lips of Jesus. It is what he calls himself.[3]

3. The phrase is never used as a title similar to Christ or Son of God or Lord. It never appears as a predicate in a sentence like "Jesus is the Son of man." The expression can thus be termed a title only in a limited sense.

4. The phrase is more than a simple replacement of "I." Some special significance must be assumed in expressions like "the days of the Son of man" (Luke 17:22–30), "the hour of the Son of man" (Matt. 24:44), and "the Parousia of the Son of man" (Matt. 24:37, 39). The same is true when Daniel 7 is clearly in mind (Mark 13:26; 14:62).

5. In the NT, "the Son of man" is understood as a reference to Jesus, even where the statements themselves are capable of another interpretation (e.g., Mark 8:38).

The Approach

The many and varied attempts to understand the "Son of man" statements in the NT and to account for their presence in the Gospels seek to locate the Gospels in a larger context that will provide some basis for evaluating various interpretive possibilities. The contexts include early Christian tradition as a whole and postbiblical Judaism. In most cases, Daniel 7 is understood to have played a critical role in the development and use of the expression "the Son of man" in the NT. Also in most cases, the importance of Daniel is understood to have been as part of a tradition of interpretation that produced the mythic construct known as the "apocalyptic Son of man," a heavenly redeemer alleged to have

---

2. Colpe, "ho huios tou anthrōpou," *TDNT* 8 (1972): 404; and Vermes, *Jesus and the World of Judaism,* 90.

3. In Acts 7:56, the reference to "the Son of man" seems clearly to presuppose an interpretation of Daniel 7. The usage in John is more difficult. In 12:32, Jesus says, "When I am lifted up . . ."; the crowd, responding to Jesus' comment, uses *ho huios tou anthrōpou* and *houtos ho huios tou anthrōpou* in reference to him: "How do you now say that the Son of man must be lifted up?" Since Jesus simply speaks in the first-person singular and does not use "the Son of man" at all, the narrator seems to presuppose that "I" and "the Son of man" are interchangeable. The issue is further complicated by the crowd's use of "the Messiah" in their response to Jesus. Whatever the prehistory of the Johannine text, in its present form the passage suggests that the final redactor understood "the Son of man" to be interchangeable with Jesus' "I," and that both are somehow related to "the Messiah."

been an important feature of Jewish apocalyptic tradition. Scholars as different as Bultmann and Morna Hooker presuppose the existence of such a figure, the critical question being whether Jesus believed himself to be the "coming Son of man" or whether he referred to such a redeemer as another than himself.

In the last decade and a half, there has been developing a conviction that the "apocalyptic Son of man" is a construct of late-nineteenth- and early-twentieth-century scholars and cannot be used as a way of understanding NT data. There are two basic reasons for the shift: one has to do with information about postbiblical Judaism gleaned from the Qumran literature and other sources; the other has to do with a fresh explanation of the linguistic background of "the Son of man" in Aramaic. We will summarize each briefly.

1. The data from the Qumran scrolls do not permit such neat distinctions between otherworldly and earthly salvation figures as proposed, for example, by Sigmund Mowinckel and, more recently, Ferdinand Hahn.[4] Sectarians at Qumran spoke of eschatological redeemers who would play crucial roles in the events of the last days. Among those figures, however, there is no single heavenly redeemer and no one identified as "the Son of man." Neither is there a neat distinction between otherworldly and political redemption. Dualistic conceptions receive concrete expression in the community itself, where coming deliverers like the anointed prince and priest play a role in the expected affairs of the sectarians, and where the historical conflict between the sectarians and their enemies is pictured as part of the cosmic struggle between the powers of light and darkness.

The finds have also provided negative evidence that militates against the "Son of man" construct. One of the major pieces of evidence for the existence of such a redeemer figure has been the so-called Parables of Enoch (chaps. 37–71). Although fragments from the remaining portions of *Enoch* have been discovered in the caves at Qumran, no portion of the parables has been found—suggesting to most scholars that the parables cannot be assumed any longer to be pre-Christian.[5] That does not rule

---

4. Hahn, *Titles of Jesus*. For an assessment of the Qumran material, see Dahl, "Eschatology and History in Light of the Qumran Texts," in *The Crucified Messiah*, 129–45.

5. Among recent commentators there is a tendency to date the Similitudes toward the end of the 1st or at the beginning of the 2d cent. See the comment by Holladay (*Semeia* 30 [1984]: 79) regarding the dating of *Enoch* and the matter of chronology in general.

out their significance in reconstructing the development of eschatological tradition and the history of Daniel 7, but it does make arguments for the existence of an "apocalyptic Son of man" less impressive.[6]

Literature from Nag Hammadi has confirmed the view of Carston Colpe that there is no evidence of a comprehensive mythic construct linking "Son of man" concepts to some gnostic redeemer myth or a myth of the primal man. Though there may be some relationships among such later traditions, it cannot be presumed that the title "the Son of man" served as a focal point for any overall mythic construct.

2. A second reason for reassessing the evidence is the forceful proposal made by Geza Vermes with respect to the linguistic background of the Greek *ho huios tou anthrōpou,* first in 1965 and more recently in his collected studies.[7] Others had acknowledged that behind the definite Greek *ho huios tou anthrōpou* must have been an Aramaic phrase also in the definite form. No real evidence had been advanced, however, for regarding the definite *bar [e]nasha* as a possible self-designation. A generic use of the phrase is attested, but that could explain only a very few of the "Son of man" sayings in the Gospels. Vermes has advanced evidence that, though scanty, suggests that the definite form *bar [e]nasha* could be used as a self-designation (a "circumlocutional use," with an indirect reference to the speaker).[8] "Son of man" was never understood as a title in Judaism, he insists. Rather, behind the unusual Greek lies an Aramaic idiom, which may be used to refer to "a man" in general or to a speaker, whether as a representative of humankind ("I, who am a man") or as an individual in a context where awe, reserve, or modesty is called for.[9] The precise nuances of the expression as a self-reference may be disputed by experts.

That fact would explain why the expression "the Son of man" appears almost exclusively in the sayings tradition: it was actually used by Jesus as a way of referring to himself. The "authentic" usage would thus be traced back to Jesus, but no longer with the notion that Jesus used the expression to refer to an eschatological redeemer. The places in the

---

6. For a review of the evidence, see Lindars, *Jesus Son of Man,* 1–28.

7. Vermes's lecture, "The Use of BAR NASH/BAR NASHA in Jewish Aramaic," was delivered in 1965 and published as an appendix to Black, *An Aramaic Approach to the Gospels and Acts*; it is now reprinted in Vermes's *Post-Biblical Jewish Studies,* 147–68. See more recently his *Jesus the Jew,* 163–68, 188–91; and *Jesus and the World of Judaism,* 89–99.

8. Vermes, *Jesus and the World of Judaism,* 90–95.

9. Ibid., 90.

tradition where the phrase clearly serves as a self-designation (the "present activity" and "suffering" groups of "Son of man" sayings; see below, pp. 158–60) would have to be explained as in some sense secondary or derivative.[10]

The focus of this chapter is the use of Daniel 7. There is sufficient doubt about the existence of a mythic "Son of man" to question the approach to the phrase as a title in the NT. At some points it is little more than a self-reference (e.g., in Matthew 16). We shall examine the NT data to ask where clear references to Daniel 7 are present. The wisdom of Barnabas Lindars seems apparent at this point:

> Seeing that ke-bar enash in Dan 7:13 was not recognized as a title even in such works as refer to the passage (Rev., 2 Esd., Similitudes of Enoch ["that son of man"]) . . . it is altogether improbable that the Son of Man always carried an allusion to this passage. The phrase by itself could not do this. Only when other features of a saying connect it with Dan 7:13–14 does the phrase necessarily presuppose identification with the Danielic figure. Such features are lacking in the majority of Son of Man sayings, particularly in those which are found to have the best claim to authenticity when examined critically. It is thus most likely that the phrase did not refer to the Daniel passage to begin with. The original meaning of the Son of Man on the lips of Jesus must be found elsewhere.[11]

NEW TESTAMENT ALLUSIONS TO DANIEL 7

The standard classification of "Son of man" sayings into three groups ("present activity," "suffering," and "future coming") was useful particularly for those who presupposed that the phrase "the Son of man" represented a distinct personality whenever it was used. The three-way classification was important for Bultmann, for example, as a way of demonstrating that Jesus did not speak of himself as an apocalyptic deliverer but referred to the coming Son of man as someone other than he. For Bultmann, the sayings about the coming Son of man were authentic (spoken by Jesus himself).

If, however, we may no longer assume that outside the NT "the Son of

---

10. Bowker ("The Son of Man," *JTS* 28 [1977]: 19–48) makes a similar argument, drawing attention to data from targumic traditions. He seeks to establish a basis for understanding "the Son of man" as denoting "man subject to death" (as well as the object of divine vindication).

11. Lindars, *Jesus Son of Man*, 15–16.

man" would have been understood as a title referring to a distinct personality, and if, furthermore, there is even a question as to what extent "the Son of man" is a title within the NT, there may be more helpful ways to group the sayings. Lindars, for example, convinced by Vermes about the existence of an idiomatic Aramaic self-designation, seeks to identify NT sayings that clearly presuppose the idiom and may thus be regarded as possible words of Jesus himself (other criteria must be applied before making a final decision, of course).

For our purposes, the relevant question is whether or not a "Son of man" saying alludes to Daniel. Since it cannot be assumed that every occurrence of the phrase conjures up the biblical imagery, we will have to confine ourselves to those passages where there is good reason to suspect an allusion. And since we are concerned about tracing traditions back to their origin, it will be significant to note whether material appears in Mark or in Q.[12]

Seemingly Indisputable Allusions

1. Matthew 16:27–28. Matthew supplements the allusions to Daniel 7 ("coming in glory . . . with his angels") with imagery from Ps. 62:13 (God as judge). Mark's "kingdom of God" in 9:1 (Luke 9:27) is replaced by the coming of the Son of man in his kingdom.

2. Matthew 19:28 (par. Luke 22:28–30). Matthew has combined material from Mark and Q, to which he has apparently added "the Son of man" and "his glorious throne."

3. Matthew 24:27, 37, 39: "the Parousia of the Son of man." Cf. Luke 17:22, 24, 26, 30: "the day(s) of the Son of man." The eschatological setting of the verses, with explicit reference to imagery from Daniel, makes an allusion to Daniel almost certain.

4. Matthew 24:30. The imagery from Daniel is supplemented by Zech. 12:10 (see also Rev. 1:7).

5. Matthew 24:31. The passage is paralleled in Mark 13:24 and Luke 21:27, with the difference that in Matthew the allusion to Daniel is linked with Zech. 12:10 ("They shall look on him whom they have pierced, and they shall mourn") (par. Rev. 1:7, where more of Zechariah is quoted). Matthew also refers to the "sign of the Son of man in heaven." In all three versions, the point of the saying is the promised vindication of the faithful at the return of the Son of man.

---

12. The Johannine tradition poses special problems.

6. Matthew 24:44: "the Son of man is coming."

7. Matthew 25:31. The judgment scene seems to take place on earth where the Son of man is enthroned. The enthroned Son of man, who pronounces judgment, is a royal figure (v. 34: "Then the king will say . . ."). The scene is described in imagery reminiscent of Zech. 14:5 (see 1 Thess. 4:16 and *Didache* 16.7–8, where the Zechariah passage seems to have provided a basis for eschatological speculation). It is possible that at an earlier stage the parable understood "the King" as God.[13]

8. Matthew 26:64 (par. Mark 14:62). Once again, the point is "you will see." Jesus' statement also includes an allusion to Ps. 110:1.[14] Jesus' response in Luke 22:69 includes the allusion to Ps. 110:1 and "the Son of man" but omits reference to "coming with [upon] the clouds of heaven" from Daniel 7 and "you will see."

9. Luke 21:36: ". . . stand before the Son of man" (included in Luke's account of the Synoptic apocalypse).

10. Revelation 1:7. See above; Zech. 12:10 with Dan. 7:13.

11. Revelation 1:13–14. Here the only feature from Daniel's vision of the humanlike creature is the white hair ("white as white wool," v. 9), which in the original vision refers to the Ancient of Days. John identifies the Ancient of Days with the humanlike figure, thus presupposing the reading *hōs* in the Old Greek instead of *heōs* in Theodotian's translation.

12. Revelation 14:14–15. One like a Son of man is "seated upon a white cloud." Here the scated figure is depicted as royalty—crowned. The similarity between the crowned figure, who reaps, and the angels—who do the same—is striking. The scene in Daniel is taken to refer to enthronement and judgment. The one like a Son of man does not come or go.[15]

Likely Allusions

1. Matthew 10:23: "The Son of man comes."

2. Matthew 24:44 (par. Luke 12:40). Both include references to the coming of the Son of man in Q material, which has been combined

---

13. Lindars, *Jesus Son of Man*, 126–27.

14. Perrin argued that the verb "will see" derives from an interpretation of Zech. 12:10 ("Mark 14:62: The End Product of a Christian Pesher Tradition?" *NTS* 12 [1966]: 150–55).

15. Casey (*Son of Man*, 148–49) argues that Daniel 7 is not in view here, but his interpretation of *homoion huion anthrōpou* seems forced and highly unlikely.

differently in each Gospel. Note that Matthew equates "your Lord" in 24:42 with "the Son of man" in 24:44.

3. Matthew 28:18. The reference to "all authority in heaven and on earth" may well represent an allusion to Daniel 7. The expression "the Son of man" is not present.

4. Mark 2:10 (par.): "But that you may know that the Son of man has authority on earth to forgive sins." In both the Old Greek and Theodotian, the word *exousia* is used to speak of "one like a son of man" in Dan. 7:14. Given the allusion to the vision elsewhere in Mark, this is a likely reference to the verse.

5. Mark 8:38 (par. Luke 9:26). The reference to the "coming" of the Son of man, with the term "glory," makes an allusion to Daniel likely. In the related saying in Matt. 10:33, however, Jesus uses the first person in place of "the Son of man," which suggests that Matthew did not understand the reference as an allusion to Daniel.

6. John 5:27: "And he gave to him the authority to judge, because he is *huios anthrōpou.*"[16]

Questionable Allusions

1. Matthew 10:32 (par. Luke 12:8). The court imagery and the apparent eschatological thrust make an allusion to Daniel 7 possible. Only Luke, however, uses "the Son of man"; Matthew uses "I."

2. Luke 18:8. The parable ends with reference to the coming of the Son of man; no other imagery from Daniel is included.

Interpretation of NT Data

1. Even in the NT, "the Son of man" is not consistently understood as a title (see esp. the use in Matt. 16:13 compared with Mark 8:27, and in Matt. 10:33 compared with Mark 8:38). Where it is employed as a title, it is used to refer to Jesus, even if specific verses considered in isolation would not demand such an interpretation.

2. Among "Son of man" sayings, some relationship to Daniel 7 seems most apparent in settings where the future is in view (the third group of "Son of man" sayings). Imagery from Daniel is understood as royal (cf. Matthew: throne, kingship); it is typically regarded as depicting the coming of a humanlike figure to earth; less frequently, and with less certainty, it is read as describing a court scene. The Son of man can

---

16. The grammatical singularity of the expression and its place in Johannine tradition require special explanation.

appear as advocate or judge. The imagery is not employed in such a way as to require that the various interpretations all derive from a uniform conception.

3. Some sayings in non-future-oriented passages seem to presume allusions to Daniel 7—especially Mark 2:10 and Matt. 28:18. This would suggest that the one identified as the humanlike figure is already acting with authority that in the vision is conferred at the end. The allusion in Matthew 28 suggests that Daniel 7 could be used even without the title "the Son of man," though that is the exception.

4. In many of the "Son of man" sayings, the language provides little evidence that an allusion to Daniel 7 is intended. This is the case in most of the "Son of man" sayings in the "present activity" and "suffering" groups.

5. Though John's Apocalypse contains clear allusions to Daniel's vision, "the Son of man" (with the definite article) does not appear. Where reference to the humanlike figure is made, the biblical "one like a son of man" appears (1:13; 14:14). Material from the vision can be appropriated without even using the phrase (see, e.g., 1:7).

6. Sayings from Q pose a special problem. If there were extrabiblical evidence for a distinct personality known as the "apocalyptic Son of man," some sayings from Q might be read to suggest that Jesus looked for the coming of a redeemer other than himself (see also Mark 8:38). Such extrabiblical evidence has now been called into question, which means that even in Q we are to read "the Son of man" as a reference to Jesus. The question is to what extent there is evidence of any influence from Daniel 7. It does seem that Q presupposes Jesus' resurrection; the Son of man who has nowhere to lay his head is the same one who will return (in the Parousia or "days of the Son of man"). Where does such a conception arise? Daniel 7 is probably not the only possibility, though the references to "coming" must presume an interpretation of Daniel.[17] It is possible that the notions of exaltation presupposed by Q may arise from traditions about heavenly ascents and enthronement, like those

---

17. Lindars, *Jesus Son of Man*, 95–96 (commenting on Matthew 24 and Luke 17, material from Q): "Thus there can be no doubt that, in this sequence at any rate, the titular use of the Son of Man to denote the Danielic figure is already found in Q. This causes no difficulty, because consciousness of the allusion may have been a factor in the Greek translation of bar enasha anyway. Nothing is gained by trying to maintain that he who was proclaimed as exalted Messiah in terms of Ps 110:1 was not also recognized as the Danielic figure, even if identifiable allusions to Daniel in the New Testament are rare."

reflected in the Similitudes of Enoch.[18] Such speculation need not have achieved any mythic unity by the Christian era. In this case as well, Q may presuppose exegetical traditions arising from reflection on other biblical texts (i.e., Psalm 80 or 8), though the importance of Daniel 7 cannot be excluded.

JEWISH INTERPRETATION

Messianic[19]

1. *1 Enoch* 45–71. In the visions of Enoch, the influence of Daniel 7 is apparent throughout in the depiction of the enthroned Son of man, who is identified as the Elect One (49.3) and as the Messiah (48.10). Influence from Isaiah 11 is similarly pronounced (e.g., 46.3 and 49.3), indicating that Daniel has been integrated with other traditional messianic passages.[20]

2. *4 Ezra* 13:1–53. In the vision of the man from the sea, the influence of Daniel 7 is apparent. The redeemer figure who appears as a lion in the previous vision (11:37) is identified as the Messiah (12:32), probably reflecting the influence of the oracle of Judah in Gen. 49:9. The reference to the flaming breath of the man from the sea perhaps also reveals the influence of Isa. 11:4. Once again Daniel has been combined with traditional messianic passages.

3. *b. Hagiga* (cf. *b. Sanhedrin* 38a).

One passage says: "His throne was fiery flames" (Dan 7:9) and another passage says: "until thrones were placed; and One that was ancient of days did sit"—there is no contradiction: One (throne) for Him, and one for David: this is the view of R. Akiba. Said R. Yosi the Galilean to him: Akiba, how long will you treat the divine presence as profane! Rather, one for justice and one for grace. Did he accept (this explanation) from him, or did

---

18. One of the most important traditions of heavenly ascents and enthronements is in the account of Moses' enthronement, in the extant fragments of Ezekiel the Tragedian. See Jacobson, ed., *The Exagogue of Ezekiel,* and van der Horst, "Moses' Throne Vision in Ezekiel the Dramatist," *JJS* 34 (1983): 21–29.

19. Horbury ("The Messianic Associations of 'the Son of Man'" *JTS* 36 [1985]: 34–55) provides an intelligent discussion of the evidence from Jewish tradition, arguing that "the Son of man" had messianic associations in pre-Christian Judaism. Even if his arguments for pre-Christian dating are not all convincing, his observations about the association of Daniel 7 with other royal texts and about the link between "the Son of man" and the possibly messianic term "man" provide insight into the logic of Christian exegesis.

20. Ibid., 44–45; and J. Theisohn, *Der Auserwählte Richter,* 98.

he not accept it?—come and hear: One for justice and one for grace; this is the view of R. Akiba.

4. *Sibylline Oracles* 5.414–33.

For there has come from the plains of heaven a blessed man with the sceptre in his hand which God has committed to his clasp: and he has won fair dominion over all, and has restored to all the good the wealth which the former men took. And he has destroyed every city from its foundations with sheets of fire, and burnt up the families of the men who before wrought evil, and the city which God loved he made more radiant than the stars and the sun and the moon; and he set it as the jewel of the world, and made a temple exceedingly fair in its fair sanctuary, and fashioned it in size of many furlongs, with a giant tower touching the very clouds and seen of all, so that all the faithful and all the righteous may see the glory of the invisible God, the vision of delight. East and West have hymned forth the glory of God: for no longer are wretched mortals beset with deeds of shame, adulteries and unnatural passions for boys, murder and tumult, but rivalry is fair among all. It is the last time of the saints, when God accomplishes these things, God the sender of thunder, the Creator of the great Temple.

The reference to Daniel is not obvious, but the figure of a man who comes from the "plain of heaven" in the "last time of the saints" may well be drawn from Dan. 7:13, 22. William Horbury suggests allusions to Ps. 2:9 (the scepter; perhaps also Ps. 110:2); Isa. 1:4 and Num. 24:18 (the burning of the cities); and 2 Sam. 7:13 (the rebuilding of the temple).[21]

5. Justin *Dialogue with Trypho* 31–32. After Justin quotes Daniel 7, Trypho says,

Sir, these and suchlike passages of scripture compel us to await One who is great and glorious, and takes over the everlasting kingdom from the Ancient of Days as Son of man. But this your so-called Christ is without honour and glory, so that He has even fallen into the uttermost curse that is in the Law of God, for he was crucified.

Representing the "Jewish" opinion, Trypho does not dispute the messianic interpretation of Daniel 7. He insists rather that Jesus, as one who was crucified, cannot be the one about whom the prophecy speaks.

6. *b. Sanhedrin* 98a.

R. Alexandri said: R. Joshua opposed two verses: it is written, "And behold, one like the son of man came with the clouds of heaven," whilst [elsewhere] it is written, "[behold, thy king cometh unto thee . . .] lowly, and riding on an ass."—If they are meritorious, [he will come] "with the clouds of heaven"; if not, "lowly and riding upon an ass."

---

21. Horbury, "Messianic Associations," 44–45.

The problem is allegedly contradictory scriptural passages. Important is that both Daniel 7 and Zechariah 12 are assumed to refer to the coming Messiah.

7. *Midr.* Ps. 21:5.

R. Berechiah said in the name of R. Samuel: One verse reads of the king Messiah that "One, like the son of man . . . came to the Ancient of days, and they brought him near before Him" (Dan 7:13), but in another verse God says, "I will cause him to draw near, and he shall approach unto Me" (Jer 30:21). How reconcile the two? Angels will bring the king Messiah to the outer edge of their encampment, and then the Holy One, blessed be He, will reach out His hand and bring the king Messiah near to Him. Hence it is said, "I will cause him to draw near."

The point is the apparent contradiction: in one passage, the angels bring the Messiah near, in another God speaks of that as his task. The interpretation reconciles apparently contradictory passages. Significant for our purposes is that Daniel 7, with its "one like a son of man," is regarded as a reference to the Messiah. Though this passage is obviously later than NT times and appears in a late collection of midrashim, the interpretation of Daniel 7 and the form of the midrash are considerably earlier, as attested by the tradition noted above.

8. *b. Sanhedrin* 96b–97a.

R. Nahman said to R. Isaac: Have you heard when Bar Nafle [from Greek *huios nephelon,* transliterated back into Aramaic, which means "son of the fallen"] will come? "Who is Bar Nafle?" he asked. "Messiah," he answered. "Do you call the Messiah Bar Nafle?" "Even so," he rejoined, "as it is written, 'In that day I will raise up the tabernacle of David ha-nofeleth [the fallen one].'"

Angels and Other Heavenly Figures

1. *Mekilta of Rabbi Ishmael* Bahodesh 5, Shirta 4.

"I am YHWH your God": Why is this said? Because when He was revealed at the sea, He appeared to them as a mighty hero making war. As it is said, "YHWH is a man of war." He appeared at Sinai like an old man, full of mercy, as it is said, "And they saw the God of Israel" (Exod 24:10). And of the time after they had been redeemed what does it say? "And the like of the very heaven for clearness" (Exod 24:10). Again, it says, "I beheld 'til thrones were set down" (Dan 7:9). And it also says, "A fiery stream issued and came forth from him, etc." Scriptures would not give an opportunity to the nations of the world to say, "There are 'two powers,'" but declares, "I am YHWH your God" (Exod 20:2). I was in Egypt. I was at the Sea. I was in the past, I will be in the future to come. I am in this world, I am in the world to come.[22]

---

22. Quoted and interpreted in Segal, *Two Powers in Heaven,* 33–34.

Daniel 7 is included among dangerous passages that might be taken to imply more than one God. The "solution" to the problem focuses on the use of two names for God, which are understood to refer to his different aspects or attributes.

2. *b. Sanhedrin* 38b.

R. Yohanan said: in all the passages which the minim have taken (as grounds) for their heresy, their refutation is found near at hand. Thus: let us make man in our image (Gen 1:26)—and God created (singular) man in His own image (1:27) . . . " 'Til thrones were placed and [one that was] the ancient of days did sit" (Dan 7:9).

The point is made that passages which might suggest a plurality of gods are followed by the use of singular pronouns which disprove the dangerous interpretation. In Daniel, "Ancient of Days" is singular, despite the plural "thrones."[23]

INTERPRETATION AND CONCLUSIONS

It need scarcely be said that the evidence is complicated and yields no easy explanation. The following observations bear on the question under examination, namely, how Daniel 7 entered Christian tradition and what its importance was.

1. The NT contains no explicit quotations of Daniel 7, and the number of clear-cut allusions is limited.

2. The verses from Daniel are absent from the Pauline tradition, though Paul can certainly speak of Jesus' exaltation and his return for judgment (Romans 2). It is possible that interpretations of the human-like figure in Daniel 7 had already become part of traditions about the primal man prior to Paul—but a consideration of this issue is too complex to be examined in detail here.

3. Allusions to Daniel 7 usually, though not always, make use of the phrase "the Son of man." The exception is John's Apocalypse, which in at least one instance uses no title at all, and in other cases uses the biblical "one like a son of man."

4. The use of "the Son of man" as an equivalent for "human being" or as a self-reference with no apocalyptic traces suggests that the epithet "the Son of man" cannot be derived from Christian exegesis of Daniel 7 (contra Philipp Vielhauer and Norman Perrin). It is more likely that use

---

23. Segal (*Two Powers in Heaven*, 60–73) offers a glimpse of the varied speculation that focused on Daniel 7, among other texts. On the possible relationship between Metatron and Dan. 7:9, see p. 67 n. 24, inter alia.

of Daniel 7 in the NT is partly derived from a previous use of the
designation "the son of man." This would explain why allusions to
Daniel are confined almost exclusively to "Son of man" passages—and
thus to the sayings tradition.

5. The character of allusions to Daniel 7 renders unlikely one uniform
exegesis of the passage. Most frequently, the text is read as a description
of the coming of the humanlike figure to earth. The same interpretation
is encountered among the rabbis, where the figure is presumed to be the
Messiah. Some references, however, do not speak of a movement but
view the scene as a description of a throne room in which the humanlike
figure is seated like a king. In a few instances, traits of that son of man
are predicated of Jesus in the present. In at least one instance, the court
scene is retained but the son of man is pictured as an advocate.

The variety of interpretations is encountered within Jewish tradition
as well, where the verses can be read to describe the coming of the
messianic king or as portraying some angelic being enthroned in God's
presence. It is the latter in particular that provided the basis of serious
exegetical reflection in the post-NT period (and perhaps earlier, if Alan
Segal is correct).

6. There is no contrast in the NT between the Messiah, a mundane
eschatological figure, and the Son of man, an apocalyptic redeemer. In
most cases, sayings about the coming Son of man serve as promises of
vindication—either for Jesus or for those who place their confidence in
him. In Mark 13 and 14, promises of the coming Son of man serve as
validation of Jesus' claim to be the true Christ, the Son of God. The
point of the sayings is not that Jesus is Son of man, as opposed to
something else, but that everyone will witness his public vindication.[24]
Even in Mark 8:31, Jesus' prediction of the suffering and resurrection of
the Son of man is in no sense a replacement for Peter's "Christ." Jesus'
prediction of what must happen to the Son of man is fulfilled in the
account of his death as Christ, Son of the Blessed, King of the Jews, and
Christ, the King of Israel.

What is said of the Son of man, in other words, is entirely compatible
with royal imagery such as that located particularly in the passion material. The verses from Daniel seem to have provided Christians with a
way of speaking about the destiny of the crucified and risen Messiah,
whether in terms of enthronement and the receiving of an everlasting
kingship (7:14) or in terms of a return in power.

---

24. Juel, *Messiah and Temple,* 77–95.

Daniel 7 does not, however, provide the basis for confessing Jesus as Messiah, contrary to Hahn and Reginald Fuller. As we have noted above, Jesus is not regularly depicted as the one who will return to reign as Christ. The title, with the attendant royal imagery, appears principally in the passion narratives and in the confessional tradition (in the latter, the Son of man has no role at all). The portrait of the Christ in Acts 3:20–21 ("and that he may send the Christ appointed for you, Jesus, whom heaven must receive until the time for establishing all that God spoke by the mouth of his holy prophets") cannot be regarded as the basis for messianic reflection but must be viewed as only a later development. "Son of man" traditions drawing on Daniel 7 serve primarily to promise the final vindication in the eyes of the world of the one who was crucified as King of the Jews and raised from the dead on the third day. Daniel 7 is not the origin of the confession of Jesus as Messiah. It must presuppose the confession.

Because Daniel 7 occurs most frequently in conjunction with other biblical passages, notably Ps. 110:1 and Zech. 12:10, it likely represents a secondary stage in tradition which presupposes the resurrection of Jesus and some reflection on it in terms of other biblical imagery (esp. Ps. 110:1). The absence of the title "the Son of man" and references to Daniel 7 in Paul's letters tends to confirm the hypothesis. This may be the case even in Q, where, however, royal imagery is notably lacking.

7. How could the initial connection have come about? It is not necessary to presuppose the existence of an "apocalyptic Son of man" to understand the use of Daniel 7. First, there is evidence of a tradition of interpretation of the verses in postbiblical Judaism. One set of traditions understands the humanlike figure to be one of the manifestations of God or to be a principal angel; another regards the verses as messianic prophecies. It is possible to date both types of interpretation close to the Christian era, if not prior to it.[25]

It seems most likely that Daniel 7 could serve as an important passage only on the basis of some prior interpretation—particularly of Psalm 110, according to which the king had taken his place at a throne in God's presence. Nils Dahl has suggested that Daniel 7 might even represent an early interpretation of the Psalm verse, since Ps. 110:1 is the only verse in the Bible which depicts another figure enthroned in God's presence. The royal imagery in Daniel 7 is a sufficient explanation of the

---

25. Horbury, "Messianic Associations."

use of the verse even without having to presume a pre-Christian messianic reading of the verse.

There may even be a particular mechanism to explain the link. Psalm 80:14–16 reads,

Turn again, O God of hosts!
  Look down from heaven, and see;
  have regard for this vine,
    the stock which thy right hand planted [Heb.: "and upon
    the son whom thou hast reared for thyself"].
They have burned it with fire, they have cut it down;
  may they perish at the rebuke of thy countenance!
But let thy hand be upon the man of thy right hand,
  the son of man whom thou hast made strong for thyself!

The verse makes possible a link between the one seated at God's right hand in Ps. 110:1 and the one like a son of man in Dan. 7:13. The link becomes somewhat more plausible in light of the later targumic rendering of the verses from the psalm. The Targum on Ps. 80:16 reads *malcha mashiach* for *ben,* thus taking the reference to the "man of thy right hand" and the "son of man whom thou hast made strong for thyself" as references to the Messiah. The interpretation accords with messianic readings of Ps. 110:1 and Dan. 7:13 noted elsewhere in Jewish tradition. The targumic rendering of the psalm verses cannot be traced directly back to the first century, but it at least provides evidence that a particular set of exegetical inferences not only is possible but became a reality.[26]

Another factor must be taken into account in our determination of a starting point for Christian use of Daniel 7: the almost total confinement of allusions to Daniel to sayings of Jesus in which the title "the Son of man" is used. Christian exegesis of Daniel 7 cannot account for all the occurrences of *ho huios tou anthrōpou* in the gospel tradition, as we have seen. On the other hand, use of the unusual Greek phrase seems to lie at the foundation of exegetical traditions focusing on Daniel 7. Had exegesis of Daniel 7 developed independently of the title, we would expect to find some allusions to the verses in Paul or in the narrative tradition. The Apocalypse of John provides the only unambiguous example of employment of Danielic material without reference to the title "the Son of man" and in other than sayings of Jesus (though see Matt. 28:18;

---

26. On the interpretation of the psalm and Daniel 7, see Dodd, *According to the Scriptures,* 101–2; Gelston, "A Sidelight on the 'Son of Man,'" *SJT* 22 (1969): 189–96; and Hill, "'Son of Man' in Psalm 80 v. 17," *NovT* 15 (1973): 261–69.

Mark 2:10). The usage, however, cannot be regarded as the basis for all NT interpretation.

It seems most likely, therefore, that Christians came to view the visions of Daniel 7 as significant both because Jesus' sayings contained the enigmatic *ho huios tou anthrōpou* and because the verses provided royal imagery with which to speak of the enthronement and the final vindication of the crucified Messiah.

8. In his study of rabbinic controversies regarding two powers in heaven, Segal has shown the degree to which postbiblical Jewish exegesis was interested in (and concerned about) the possibilities provided by Daniel 7 for speculating on angelic powers in heaven and angelic intermediaries. The use of the verses by Jesus' followers provides a link with a rich tradition of exegetical reflection that becomes important in the later christological and trinitarian reflection within Christian circles—leading to controversies that were to have an important bearing on the relationship among many marginal Jewish groups and the parent community in coming decades and centuries.

The initial interest in Daniel 7 may have more than one component; Christian exegetes cannot have been unaware of the background of the verses in postbiblical tradition. The connection with their own experience, however, seems to be the royal imagery implicit in the Daniel verses—mediated through Ps. 110:1 and perhaps Psalm 80; their exegesis may be related to the use of "man" as a messianic title.[27] That is not to say that early Christian interpreters could think of Jesus in no way other than as Christ. It is to say that what distinguished their exegesis from that of other Jewish sectarian groups was the link with a specific historical figure, Jesus of Nazareth, who was crucified as a royal pretender and vindicated by God at his resurrection. It is still the confession of Jesus as the vindicated King that provides the connection point and controls the shape of the tradition. Later generations would spend more time probing the relationship of Jesus to other heavenly intermediaries like Wisdom or the Logos, or to principal angels; the relationships between the heavenly beings would be worked out in considerable detail during the later trinitarian controversies. The title "the Son of man" would become important as a designation not of a heavenly figure but of the humanity of the Son of God.

Throughout, however, the connection with the earthly Jesus re-

---

27. Horbury, "Messianic Associations," 48–52; and Vermes, *Scripture and Tradition,* 153–54.

mained crucial—and it was as the crucified and vindicated King that Jesus was identified with the humanlike figure in Daniel whose appearance at the end of days would prove to the world the truth of the Christian confession.

Problems still remain, particularly for understanding the place of Daniel 7 in traditions underlying Q. Neither the title *Christos* nor references to Jesus' passion appear in Q. Yet "Son of man" sayings in the "future coming" group seem to presuppose Christian exegesis of Daniel 7. Does this suggest an alternative route to Daniel? It is conceivable that "the Son of man" may presuppose traditions of the exaltation of human beings to heaven, understood perhaps in light of Psalm 8 or 80 or other biblical verses. It seems likely that the usage in Q presumes an interpretation of Jesus' resurrection—though perhaps more in terms of an exaltation like that of *Enoch*. As the literature testifies, the question is a difficult one.

CONCLUSIONS

I have attempted to examine christological exegesis in early Christian tradition. The work has involved attention to specific passages as well as to the character of scriptural interpretation in the first century of the Christian era, comparison with postbiblical scriptural exegesis in Jewish sources, and the testing of a hypothetical model for the development of the tradition. Of particular concern has been identifying a starting point for the historical development of the tradition to which the NT writings bear witness. I have argued that the confession of Jesus as the crucified and risen King of the Jews stands *at the beginning* of christological reflection and interpretation of the Scriptures—at least the reflection and interpretation that form the substructure of NT Christianity. Beginning with the historical realities of Jesus' passion as King of the Jews, we can understand the process by which a variety of biblical passages came to be enlisted in the task of making sense of Jesus and his career, and how they were combined. The exegetical data, I have argued, confirm the hypothesis regarding a starting point.

Here at the end I will review the argument briefly. One component in the argument is data from postbiblical Judaism. What resources were available to those who sought to speak about Jesus and the implications of his ministry? Among the considerable variety within Jewish eschatological traditions, to the degree that they can be reconstructed, are certain discernible patterns. One of those patterns may be termed messianic, indicating that an important figure in the coming deliverance will be a king from the line of David. Though the Messiah was not prominent in every eschatological vision, the royal offspring of David is common enough to permit a delineation of certain prominent features.

The Messiah in postbiblical Jewish tradition is a royal figure expected to play the role of king. The variety in portraits arises from the range of functions appropriate to a king. There is no evidence of traditions about the suffering and death of the Messiah prior to the Christian era.

What guarantees the consistency of messianic tradition is the constellation of biblical passages accepted as messianic by a wide spectrum of Jewish interpreters, from the Qumran sectarians to early Christians to the rabbis. Such passages include 2 Sam. 7:10–14; Isaiah 11; Num. 24:17; Gen. 49:8–10, Zechariah 6; Psalm 2; and perhaps Daniel 7 and Psalm 110. A sketch of messianic expectations is possible, though there is greater clarity with regard to the core than to the periphery. The precise interrelationship of these messianic oracles and other passages from the Scriptures is dependent upon many factors in the setting of each literary expression, including social and historical forces and the influence of prominent individuals (e.g., Jesus, the Teacher of Righteousness, and Simon bar Kokhba).

A second factor in the argument is the way the NT uses language about Jesus. "Christ," we have noted, is the most frequent christological designation, often appearing as a second name. When the term is employed as a title, its royal connotations are apparent. There is a striking concentration of occurrences in the passion tradition, where in view of Jewish tradition it would seem least appropriate. In the Gospels, Jesus is called Messiah and King as the one who died and was vindicated by God—the crucified Messiah. The most reasonable explanation is that Jesus was executed as a messianic pretender, to be subsequently vindicated by God.

Christians employed a wide variety of scriptural imagery in speaking about Jesus. All the christological titles are derived from the Scriptures. To understand the evolution of christological language, we must reconstruct the interpretive process by which biblical imagery came to be employed. Given the constraints of interpretive method and interpretive tradition, how are we to understand the process of exegetical reflection?

Beginning with accepted messianic texts like 2 Samuel 7, Psalms 89 and 2, and Isaiah 11, we can see how interpretive traditions developed. On the one hand, early Christians made little explicit use of traditional messianic oracles. That is not surprising, since the imagery from Isaiah 11 about slaying the wicked with the breath of his mouth, or from Psalm 2 about triumphing over enemies, or from Num. 24:17 about smashing the forehead of Moab, hardly fit Jesus' career. On the other hand, features of these texts provided Christian interpreters with important language to speak about Jesus—as God's Son, as the "seed" of David, as the "Shoot." Perhaps even more crucial to the whole process is the link these passages provided with other more apt biblical texts. Christians came to "adopt" as messianic passages those which may well have had no prior history as part of messianic tradition (e.g., Psalms 22; 31; 69; or Isaiah 53 and Genesis 22). What we can substantiate is not that such passages were read as messianic prior to the Christian era but that, given the mode of scriptural interpretation in the first century of our era, there is justification for such "adoption" of texts, notably verbal links. Thus as "seed" of David, Jesus can be understood as the "seed" promised Abraham in Gen. 22:18; as the "servant" in Zech. 6:12 or in Psalm 89, he can be understood as the enigmatic "servant" of Isaiah. As King, he can be identified with the humanlike figure in Daniel's vision or as the second "lord" of Ps. 110:1. Once the links were established, imagery could become part of christological tradition, providing a basis for further reflection and additional scriptural connections.

The point of the argument is that the presupposition for the development is the confession of Jesus as the Messiah. It is a confession that, given the biblical data, cannot be derived from Jesus' teachings or from an explicit self-consciousness but can be derived only from the events of Good Friday and Easter as they are reported in the Gospels.

At stake is more than a historical reconstruction of early Christian tradition. The burgeoning interest in biblical studies among Roman Catholic scholars since Vatican II has resulted not simply in the production of first-class scholarly work on the Bible and early Christian history but in a revitalized conversation between biblical scholars and systematic theologians, more familiar in Protestant circles. Edward Schillebeeckx, as a prime example, intends in his massive christological project to make the historical Jesus a major criterion for systematic constructions.[1] His first volume, *Jesus,* includes a painstaking analysis of recent exegetical and historical work as an essential component of his systematic project. Echoing the views of scholars like Ernst Käsemann,[2] he insists that Christian theology cannot dispense with the historical Jesus:

---

1. Best known are Schillebeeckx's two major works, *Jesus: An Experiment in Christology* and *Christ: The Experience of Jesus as Lord.* For an indication of the impact made by Schillebeeckx and of the current state of christological discussion, see *Semeia* 30, entitled "Christology and Exegesis: New Approaches."

2. Käsemann, "The Problem of the Historical Jesus" (1954), in *Essays on New Testament Themes,* 15–47.

That is why for me the Christian faith entails not only the personal living presence of the glorified Jesus, but also a link with his life on earth; for it is precisely that earthly life that has been acknowledged and empowered by God through the Resurrection. For me, therefore, a Christianity or *kerygma* minus the historical Jesus is ultimately vacuous—not Christianity at all, in fact. If the very heart of the Christian faith consists of an affirmation, in faith, of God's saving action in history—and that decisively in the life-history of Jesus of Nazareth . . . then the personal history of this Jesus cannot be lost sight of, nor our speaking of it in the language of faith degenerate into ideology.[3]

In such a setting, it is the task of biblical scholars to make available the results of historical and exegetical work as well as evidence to substantiate such proposals, in order to hold theology accountable to history and the biblical witness. I understand my historical analysis of christological exegesis to be part of a larger proposal with particular consequences for systematic theologians. Though Christian exegesis probed such areas as incarnation and the relationship of Jesus to God the Father, such reflection does not provide a point of departure for the tradition. Those who confessed Jesus to be the crucified and risen Messiah went to the Scriptures to understand the relationship between the Messiah and the Father, whether in an earthly or a heavenly setting. The interpretation of the Scriptures is far more a response to the shocking events of Good Friday than to Jesus' teaching or healing ministry. It is, as Schillebeeckx notes, Jesus who is executed and vindicated, not John the Baptist or Barabbas. But it is the Jesus who is executed as King of the Jews to whom the exegetical tradition is a response.

Schillebeeckx is concerned to provide a criterion for Christology in the ministry of Jesus, a critical moment on the basis of which speech about Jesus may be tested. He finds the critical moment in Jesus' unique God-consciousness.[4] Though there is evidence that Jesus spoke of God in unprecedented ways that are reflected in his actions and in the views of those who witnessed his ministry, his God-consciousness hardly represents a substantial foundation on which to build a Christology. Historically we can say that it was not the point of departure for the early church. More central were the events that climaxed Jesus' ministry. In the church's creeds, it is Jesus' death at the hands of

---

3. Schillebeeckx, *Jesus,* 76.
4. Ibid., 256–69.

Pontius Pilate and his resurrection on the third day that provide the center.[5] For those interested in the history of Jesus of Nazareth, the events of the last week of his ministry have a public character and are accessible to the historian. Although they do not disclose a great deal about Jesus' self-understanding, they do provide a substantial basis for making a connection between the Jesus of history and the Christ of faith. All the Gospels agree that when asked if he was the Messiah, Jesus did not deny it. That he was executed as King of the Jews tells us something about Jesus' views as well as about his contemporaries' perception of him. That may not be all we would like to know about Jesus' reflections during the climactic days of his ministry, but it is at least a solid basis from which to look back at Jesus' career and forward to what can be expected of the future.[6]

The confession of Jesus as Messiah is the presupposition for NT Christology, but not its content. Those who confessed Jesus as Israel's Messiah were faced with a formidable interpretive agenda as they turned to their Scriptures for enlightenment. What we see are the results of their creative reflection: their response to the historical ministry of Jesus, in particular his death on the cross and his vindication on the third day. The relationship of Jesus' messianic death to his non-messianic ministry was as problematic for the first generation of believers as it remains for us. Those who insist upon anchoring Christian tradition in Jesus' teaching or healing ministry or in his self-consciousness will find the cross as troublesome as did Jesus' own disciples. The weakness of Schillebeeckx's study of Jesus is his failure to wrestle with the historical particularity of Jesus' trial and death as King of the Jews.[7] Though there is surely an "implicit Christology" in Jesus' ministry of teaching and healing, revealing perhaps some unique sense of relatedness to God,

---

5. The centrality of the resurrection is reflected even in language used to speak of God. Küng (*On Being a Christian*, 361) notes that "'He who raised Jesus from the dead' becomes practically the designation of the Christian God." This is particularly true in the Pauline corpus, where "who raised him from the dead" occurs in 1 Thess. 1:9–10; Gal. 1:1; 2 Cor. 4:14; Rom. 4:23; 6:4; 8:11; 10:9; Eph. 1:15; Col. 2:12. It also occurs in 1 Peter 1:21 and at other places.

6. Dahl, "The Crucified Messiah," in *The Crucified Messiah*, 10–36.

7. Particularly notable are Schillebeeckx's reliance on K. Berger (see above, chap. 1) and his inadequate analysis of Jesus' trial (*Jesus*, 312–18). His discussion of the trial focuses almost exclusively on Jesus' confrontation with the Jewish authorities and on possible religious grounds for the conflict. He takes little account of the political dimensions of the trial and execution of Jesus as King of the Jews.

the confession of Jesus as Messiah is not its predictable outcome. On the contrary, the final chapters in Mark (chaps. 14—15), which narrate the trial and death of the King, are a surprise. Schweitzer was correct: that gap between a non-messianic ministry and a messianic death remains a prime topic for theological as well as historical reflection.[8] Trying to define the problem away by eliminating all traces of royal tradition from the passion accounts and from the confession of Jesus as Messiah is an inadequate approach, as I hope has become clear. If our task is to understand NT Christianity and the tradition on which it is based, the only course is to begin with the cross as the moment of disclosure and then work forward and backward.

There were, of course, estimates of Jesus by his contemporaries that took little account of his passion. There are indications (e.g., in Mark 8:27–28) that estimates of Jesus as a prophet were current during his ministry. Though Helmut Koester in his thesis about christological types, spelled out first in his "One Jesus and Four Primitive Gospels," employs heuristically categories that are too neatly delineated and unnecessarily distinct from one another, he is certainly correct that people could regard Jesus as a religious figure of major importance with little consideration of the cross-resurrection kerygma.[9] In that respect, this study is decidedly one-sided. My interest is in NT tradition, for which Jesus' death and resurrection were central to the writers' conception of the gospel.

This study is limited in other respects as well. I have spent little time examining the use of scriptural material from the wisdom tradition or biblical material employed to speak of Jesus as a heavenly being, whether in terms of a heavenly intermediary or in language customarily reserved for God. Nor have I devoted attention to scriptural material used to speak about holy men and prophets. Such material is not simply derived from the confession of Jesus as Christ. The specific ministry of Jesus, particularly the extraordinary authority with which he confronted people and claimed to speak for God, demanded expression that no single category in the tradition could provide. Jesus was identified as the prophet like Moses, as Wisdom, as the principal angel; at an

---

8. Schweitzer, *Quest of the Historical Jesus,* 337–52.

9. Koester, "One Jesus and Four Primitive Gospels," in Koester and Robinson, *Trajectories,* 158–204. There are current attempts to understand Jesus that focus on his ministry almost to the exclusion of his trial and death. See, e.g., Vermes, *Jesus the Jew.*

early date, Christians insisted that God's ineffable name had been be-stowed on the exalted Christ.

The matter of date perhaps deserves comment. Many NT Christolo-gies, like those of Ferdinand Hahn and Reginald Fuller, have been structured in terms of some developmental pattern, with distinctions between early and late, Palestinian and gentile Christianity. Such views need to be qualified. Distinctions between "high" and "low" Christolo-gies, for example, may bear little relationship to date. Luke's "prophetic Christology" seems clearly to be his own construction, while the exalted view of Jesus in Philippians 2 is pre-Pauline. From the very first, Chris-tians spoke of Jesus in different ways in different settings! The language of prayer and praise was not the same as that used in preaching and teaching.[10] Reconstructing the evolution of the tradition must include form-critical analysis of the various ways of speaking about Jesus before drawing conclusions about priority of specific conceptions. Further, it has proved difficult to draw clear boundaries between Hellenistic Jew-ish Christianity and gentile Christianity. And in any case, distinctions between "early" and "late" are relative, since most major christological developments probably predate most of the NT writings.[11]

Because my task here was not to construct an NT Christology but to study the development of christological exegesis, questions about form and function have often been neglected. The development of traditions for which I have argued has been analyzed more in terms of logic than chronological sequence. The confession of Jesus as Messiah was not the only appraisal of his ministry, nor was it the earliest (see Mark 8:27–28; 14:63–64; 15:1–20). The christological interpretation of the Scriptures that underlies the NT, however, takes the confession of Jesus as Mes-siah as its point of departure. The process of evolution, if not sequen-tial, is at least reasonable and predictable. This study, if it is to be complete, requires several additional volumes to supplement what has been done here, showing how links were forged among various inter-pretive traditions.

To state it again, the confession of Jesus as Messiah is the presuppo-sition of NT Christology but not its content. The confession "Jesus is the Messiah" underlies the later use of Christ as a virtual second name for Jesus. Even at later times, the content of the term as a scriptural title could be reactualized (as in Luke–Acts), but it did not become an

---

10. Kramer, *Christ, Lord, Son of God.*
11. Hengel, *Son of God,* 2.

important feature of operative Christology. Other titles and images were used to speak of Jesus in prayer and praise; images of the exalted Lord were more obviously self-involving, implying a life of faithful response in terms of obedience. Traditions about Wisdom and angelic intermediaries became important in exploring the relationship between Jesus and the Father, as well as the relationship between the Creator and creation, explorations that were crucial aspects of social and political developments in the late Roman Empire,[12] playing a critical role in the institutional development of the Christian movement. The confession of Jesus as Messiah retained its significance in scriptural argumentation (see Justin Martyr), but was little used elsewhere.

Yet the confession of Jesus as the crucified and risen Messiah of Israel continued to have implications for relations between those who confessed Jesus and other Jewish groups. Jesus remained Israel's Messiah as well as the Savior of the Gentiles. The relationship between Jesus' ministry and God's promises to his people was and still remains a critical area for theological reflection.[13] The confession, furthermore, provided some direction and order for subsequent tradition. Control in the exegetical developments that came to be embodied in the NT and in later "orthodox" Christianity remained the tradition about Jesus of Nazareth; even when the major questions had to do with the status of the Son of God as a heavenly intermediary, reflection remained tied to Jesus. Orthodox Christianity resisted allowing him to become an incarnational principle or a disembodied heavenly figure.

The tradition about Jesus, recorded in the NT, remained a criterion for Christian speech about Jesus. And at the heart of that tradition was the story of how he had died at the hands of Pontius Pilate as King of the Jews—and how God had vindicated him as Christ, raising him from the dead. Whether Christian theologians saw in the confession of Jesus as the crucified Christ a critique of political authority or of human wisdom, a new beginning for the human family in which old barriers had been torn down or a death blow to the law as a sign of distinction

---

12. In addition to Segal's *Two Powers in Heaven,* see his "Ruler of This World: Attitudes toward Mediator Figures and the Problem of a Sociology of Gnosticism," in *Jewish and Christian Self-Definition,* vol. 2, *Aspects of Judaism in the Graeco-Roman Period,* ed. Sanders et al., 245–68. See also Meeks, *The First Urban Christians,* esp. chap. 6; idem, "The Stranger from Heaven in Johannine Sectarianism," *JBL* 91 (1972): 44–72; and Pagels, *The Gnostic Gospels.*

13. Dahl, "The Crucified Messiah and the Endangered Promises," *Word and World* 3 (1983): 251–62.

between the people of God and others, the "scandal" or "surprise" bound up with the death and vindication of the Messiah had to be accounted for. Jesus could never become a hero like others. God's grace had taken a particular form in Jesus' ministry, the specificity of which is clearly decisive even for Paul, who says little about the ministry of Jesus, as Schillebeeckx notes:

> For each *kerygma* severally displays a specific historical concern with Jesus of Nazareth. This applies even to the Pauline proclamation of Christ, concentrated on the "paschal" *kerygma,* which sees in the historical datum of Jesus' death the very core of the true humanity of the earthly Jesus. . . . Even if Paul may know little in other respects of Jesus' earthly life, of his message and conduct, it still points to the fact that he intends his *kerygma* to be grounded in a historical Jesus event, perhaps the most profoundly human thing about Jesus' whole life on earth, the fact of his trial and execution.[14]

For NT Christianity, as for Paul, the good news was inextricably bound to the historical form in which God's grace was now to be encountered, a form best captured in the little formula Paul cites in 1 Cor. 15:3–5:

> . . . that Christ died for our sins in accordance with the scriptures, that he was buried, that he was raised on the third day in accordance with the scriptures, and that he appeared . . .

---

14. Schillebeeckx, *Jesus,* 81–82.

BIBLIOGRAPHY

Aberbach, Moses, and Bernard Grossfeld. *Targum Onkelos on Genesis 49*. SBL
Aramaic Studies 1. Missoula, Mont.: Scholars Press, 1976.

Allegro, John, ed. *Discoveries in the Judean Desert of Jordan V: Qumran Cave 4*.
Oxford: At the Clarendon Press, 1968.

The Babylonian Talmud. Ed. I. Epstein. London: Soncino Press, 1935–53.

Berger, Klaus. "Die königlichen Messiastraditionen des Neuen Testaments."
NTS 20 (1973–74): 1–44.

————. "Zum Problem der Messianität Jesu." *ZTK* 71 (1974): 1–30.

————. "Zum traditionsgeschichtlichen Hintergrund christologischer Hoheitstitel." *NTS* 17 (1970–71): 391–425.

Berger, Peter. *The Sacred Canopy*. Garden City, N. Y.: Doubleday & Co., 1967.

Black, M. *An Aramaic Approach to the Gospels and Acts*. New York and London:
Oxford Univ. Press, 1967.

Bowker, John. "The Son of Man." *JTS* 28 (1977): 19–48.

————. *The Targums and Rabbinic Literature*. New York and Cambridge:
Cambridge Univ. Press, 1969.

Braude, W., trans. *The Midrash on Psalms*. New Haven: Yale Univ. Press, 1959.

Brooke, George J. *Exegesis at Qumran: 4QFlorilegium in Its Jewish Context*.
Sheffield, Eng.: JSOT Press, 1985.

————. "Qumran Pesher: Towards the Redefinition of a Genre." *RQ* 10 (1981):
483–503.

Bruce, F. F. *Biblical Exegesis in the Qumran Texts*. Grand Rapids: Wm. B.
Eerdmans, 1959.

Bultmann, Rudolf. *History of the Synoptic Tradition*. Trans. J. Marsh. New
York: Harper & Row, 1963.

Cadbury, Henry. "The Speeches in Acts." In *The Beginnings of Christianity*, ed.
S. Foakes-Jackson and K. Lake, 5:402–26. London: Macmillan & Co., 1933.

————. "The Titles of Jesus in Acts." In *The Beginnings of Christianity*, ed.
Foakes-Jackson and Lake, 1:354–74.

Casey, Maurice. *Son of Man*. London: SPCK, 1979.

Childs, Brevard. "Psalm Titles and Midrashic Exegesis." *JSS* 16 (1971): 137–50.

Chilton, Bruce. *A Galilean Rabbi and His Bible.* Wilmington, Del.: Michael Glazier, 1984.

———. *The Glory of Israel: The Theology and Provenience of the Isaiah Targum.* JSOTSup 23. Sheffield, Eng.: JSOT Press, 1983.

Christiansen, I. *Die Technik der allegorischen Auslegungswissenschaft.* Tübingen: J. C. B. Mohr (Paul Siebeck), 1969.

Colpe, Carsten. "ho huios tou anthrōpou." *TDNT* 8 (1972): 400–477.

Dahl, Nils A. *The Crucified Messiah.* Minneapolis: Augsburg Pub. House, 1974.

———. "The Crucified Messiah and the Endangered Promises." *Word and World* 3 (1983): 251–62.

———. *Jesus in the Memory of the Early Church.* Minneapolis: Augsburg Pub. House, 1976.

———. *Studies in Paul.* Minneapolis: Augsburg Pub. House, 1977.

Dahl, Nils A., and Alan Segal. "Philo and the Rabbis on the Names of God." *JSJ* 9 (1979): 1–28.

Dibelius, Martin. *From Tradition to Gospel.* Trans. B. L. Woolf. New York: Charles Scribner's Sons, 1935.

———. *Studies in the Acts of the Apostles.* Trans. M. Ling. New York: Charles Scribner's Sons, 1956.

Dodd, C. H. *According to the Scriptures.* London: James Nisbet & Co., 1952.

Dupont-Sommer, André. *The Essene Writings from Qumran.* Trans. G. Vermes. Cleveland: World Pub. Co., 1961.

Fishbane, Michael. *Biblical Interpretation in Ancient Israel.* Oxford: At the Clarendon Press, 1985.

Fitzmyer, Joseph A. *A Wandering Aramean: Collected Essays.* SBLMS 25. Missoula, Mont.: Scholars Press, 1979.

Fuller, R. *The Foundations of New Testament Christology.* New York: Charles Scribner's Sons, 1965.

Gelston, A. "A Sidelight on the 'Son of Man.'" *SJT* 22 (1969): 189–96.

Gese, Hartmut. "Psalm 22 und das Neue Testament: Der älteste Bericht vom Tode Jesu und die Entstehung des Herrenmahles." *ZTK* 65 (1968): 1–22.

Ginzburg, L. *Eine unbekannte jüdische Sekte.* New York: G. Olms, 1922.

Goldin, Judah. *Song at the Sea: Being a Commentary on a Commentary in Two Parts.* New Haven: Yale Univ. Press, 1971.

Green, W. S., ed. *Approaches to Ancient Judaism: Theory and Practice.* Brown Judaic Studies 1. Missoula, Mont.: Scholars Press, 1978.

Gundry, R. *The Use of the Old Testament in St. Matthew's Gospel.* Leiden: E. J. Brill, 1967.

Haenchen, Ernst. *The Acts of the Apostles.* Trans. H. Anderson. Philadelphia: Westminster Press, 1971.

———. *Der Weg Jesu.* Berlin: Walter de Gruyter, 1968.

Hahn, Ferdinand. *The Titles of Jesus in Christology.* Trans. H. Knight and G. Ogg. Cleveland: World Pub. Co., 1969.

Hammerton-Kelly, R. G. "Some Techniques of Composition in Philo's Allegorical Commentary with Special Reference to *De Agricultura.*" In *Jews, Greeks, and Christians,* ed. R. G. Hammerton-Kelly and R. Scroggs, 45–56. Leiden: E. J. Brill, 1976.

Hanson, R. P. C. *Allegory and Event.* Richmond: John Knox Press, 1959.

Harvey, A. E. *Jesus and the Constraints of History*. Philadelphia: Westminster Press; London: Gerald Duckworth & Co., 1982.

Hay, David. *Glory at the Right Hand: Psalm 110 in Early Christianity*. SBLMS 18. Nashville: Abingdon Press, 1973.

Hegermann, H. *Jesaia 53 in Hexapla, Targum, und Peschitta*. Gütersloh: Bertelsmann, 1954.

Hengel, Martin. *The Atonement: The Origin of the Doctrine in the New Testament*. Trans. John Bowden. Philadelphia: Fortress Press; London: SCM Press, 1981.

_____. *Judaism and Hellenism*. Trans. John Bowden. Philadephia: Fortress Press; London: SCM Press, 1974.

_____. *The Son of God: The Origin of Christology and the History of Jewish-Hellenistic Religion*. Trans. J. Bowden. Philadelphia: Fortress Press; London: SCM Press, 1976.

Hill, David. "'Son of Man' in Psalm 80 v. 17." *NovT* 15 (1973): 261–69.

Hooker, Morna. *Jesus and the Servant*. London: SPCK, 1959.

Horbury, William. "The Messianic Associations of 'the Son of Man.'" *JTS* 36 (1985): 34–55.

Horst, P. W. van der. "Moses' Throne Vision in Ezekiel the Dramatist." *JJS* 34 (1983): 21–29.

Howard, G. "The Tetragram and the New Testament." *JBL* 96 (1977): 63–83.

Jacobson, H., ed. *The Exagogue of Ezekiel*. New York and Cambridge: Cambridge Univ. Press, 1983.

Jeremias, Gerd. *Der Lehrer der Gerechtigkeit*. SUNT 2. Göttingen: Vandenhoeck & Ruprecht, 1963.

Jeremias, Joachim. *The Eucharistic Words of Jesus*. Trans. N. Perrin. Philadelphia: Fortress Press, 1977; London: SCM Press, 1966.

_____. *New Testament Theology*. Vol. 1, *The Proclamation of Jesus*. Trans. J. Bowden. New York: Charles Scribner's Sons; London: SCM Press, 1971.

_____. "pais theou." *TDNT* 5 (1972): 677–717.

Jervell, J. *Luke and the People of God*. Minneapolis: Augsburg Pub. House, 1972.

Jonge, M. de. "The Use of the Word 'Anointed' in the Time of Jesus." *NovT* 8 (1966): 132–33.

Juel, Donald. *Luke-Acts: The Promise of History*. Atlanta: John Knox Press, 1983.

_____. *Messiah and Temple: The Trial of Jesus in the Gospel of Mark*. Missoula, Mont.: Scholars Press, 1977.

_____. "The Servant-Christ." *SWJT* 21 (1979): 7–22.

_____. "Social Dimensions of Exegesis: The Use of Psalm 16 in Acts 2." *CBQ* 43 (1981): 543–56.

Käsemann, Ernst. *Commentary on Romans*. Trans. W. Bromiley. Grand Rapids: Wm. B. Eerdmans, 1980.

_____. *Essays on New Testament Themes*. Trans. W. G. Montague. London: SCM Press, 1964.

Keifert, Pat. "Mind Reader and Maestro: Models for Understanding Biblical Interpretation." *Word and World* 1 (1981): 153–68.

Kelsey, David. *The Uses of Scripture in Theology*. Philadelphia: Fortress Press, 1975.

Klinzing, G. *Die Umdeutung des Kultus in der Qumrangemeinde und im Neuen Testament.* SUNT 7. Göttingen: Vandenhoeck & Ruprecht, 1971.

Klostermann, E. *Das Markusevangelium.* HNT. Tübingen: J. C. B. Mohr (Paul Siebeck), 1950.

Koester, Helmut, and J. M. Robinson. *Trajectories through Early Christianity.* Philadelphia: Fortress Press, 1971.

Kramer, Werner. *Christ, Lord, Son of God.* Trans. B. Hardig. London: SCM Press, 1966.

Kugel, James, and Rowan Greer. *Early Biblical Interpretation.* Philadelphia: Westminster Press, 1986.

Küng, Hans. *On Being a Christian.* Trans. Edward Quinn. Garden City, N. Y.: Doubleday & Co., 1976.

Kurz, William. "The Function of Christological Proof from Prophecy in Luke and Justin." Diss., Yale Univ., 1976.

Lane, William. *The Gospel according to Mark.* NICNT. Grand Rapids: Wm. B. Eerdmans, 1974.

Le Deaut, R. "Apropos a Definition of Midrash." *Int* 25 (1971): 259–82.

Leiman, Sid. *The Canonization of Hebrew Scriptures.* Hamden, Conn.: Archon Books, 1976.

Levey, Samson. *The Messiah: An Aramaic Interpretation.* Cincinnati: Hebrew Union College, Jewish Institute of Religion, 1974.

Lindars, Barnabas. *Jesus Son of Man.* Grand Rapids: Wm. B. Eerdmans; London: SPCK, 1983.

———. *New Testament Apologetic.* London: SCM Press, 1961.

Linnemann, Eta. *Studien zur Passionsgeschichte.* Göttingen: Vandenhoeck & Ruprecht, 1970.

Loevestam, E. "Die Davidssohnsfrage." *SEA* 27 (1962): 72–82.

———. *Son and Savior.* Lund: C. W. K. Gleerup, 1961.

Mack, Burton. *Logos und Sophia: Untersuchungen zur Weisheitstheologie im hellenistischen Judentum.* SUNT. Göttingen: Vandenhoeck & Ruprecht, 1973.

McNamara, M. *The New Testament and the Palestinian Targum to the Pentateuch.* Rome: Pontifical Biblical Institute, 1966.

———. *Targum and Testament.* Shannon: Irish Univ. Press, 1972.

Matera, Frank. *The Kingship of Jesus.* SBLDS 66. Chico, Calif.: Scholars Press, 1982.

Maurer, Christian. "Knecht Gottes und Sohn Gottes im Passionsbericht." *ZTK* 50 (1953): 1–38.

Meeks, Wayne. *The First Urban Christians.* New Haven: Yale Univ. Press, 1983.

———. *The Prophet-King.* Leiden: E. J. Brill, 1967.

———. "The Stranger from Heaven in Johannine Sectarianism." *JBL* 91 (1972): 44–72.

Mekilta de Rabbi Ishmael. Ed. J. Lauterbach. Philadelphia: Jewish Pub. Soc. of America, 1949.

The Mekilta of R. Simeon ben Yochai. Ed. J. Lauterbach. Philadelphia: Jewish Pub. Soc. of America, 1933.

Midrash Rabbah. Trans. H. Freeman. London: Soncino Press, 1939.

Nagata, T. "Phil. 2:5–11: A Case Study in the Contextual Shaping of Early Christology." Diss., Princeton Theol. Sem., 1981.

Neusner, Jacob. *Midrash in Context: Exegesis in Formative Judaism.* Philadelphia: Fortress Press, 1983.

Nickelsburg, G. *Jewish Literature between the Bible and the Mishnah.* Philadelphia: Fortress Press, 1981.

_____. *Resurrection, Immortality, and Eternal Life in Intertestamental Judaism.* Cambridge: Harvard Univ. Press, 1972.

Nickelsburg, G., and M. Stone. *Faith and Piety in Early Judaism.* Philadelphia: Fortress Press, 1983.

Oswald, Julius von. "Die Beziehungen zwischen Psalm 22 und dem vormarkinischen Passionsbericht." *ZTK* 101 (1979): 53–66.

Pagels, Elaine. *The Gnostic Gospels.* New York: Random House, 1979.

Peddinghaus, Carl. "Die Entstehung der Leidensgeschichte: Eine traditionsgeschichtliche und historische Untersuchung des Werdens und Wachsens der erzählenden Passionstradition bis zum Entwurf des Markus." Diss., Univ. of Heidelberg, 1965.

Perrin, N. "Mark 14:62: The End Product of a Christian Pesher Tradition?" *NTS* 12 (1966): 150–55.

_____. *What is Redaction Criticism?* GBS. Philadelphia: Fortress Press, 1969.

Petersen, Norman. *Literary Criticism for New Testament Critics.* GBS. Philadelphia: Fortress Press, 1978.

Porton, Gary. "Defining Midrash." In *The Study of Ancient Judaism,* ed. J. Neusner, 55–92. New York: Ktav, 1981.

_____. *The Traditions of R. Ishmael.* Leiden: E. J. Brill, 1976–82.

_____. *Understanding Rabbinic Midrash.* Hoboken, N. J.: Ktav, 1985.

Ruppert, L. *Jesus als der leidende Gerechte? Der Weg Jesu im Lichte eines alt- und zwischentestamentlichen Motives.* SB 59. Stuttgart: Katholisches Bibelwerk, 1972.

Sandmel, Samuel. "The Haggadah within Scripture." *JBL* 80 (1961): 105–22.

Schillebeeckx, Edward. *Christ: The Experience of Jesus as Lord.* New York: Seabury Press, 1980.

_____. *Jesus: An Experiment in Christology.* Trans. H. Haskins. New York: Seabury Press, 1979.

Schmid, Josef. *The Gospel according to Mark.* Trans. K. Conden. Regensburger New Testament. New York: Mercier Press, 1968.

Schürer, Emil. *The History of the Jewish People in the Age of Jesus Christ.* Ed. Geza Vermes, Fergus Millar, and Matthew Black. Edinburgh: T. & T. Clark, 1973–1987.

Schweitzer, Albert. *The Quest of the Historical Jesus.* Trans. W. Montgomery. New York: Macmillan Co., 1948.

Schweizer, Eduard. *The Good News according to Mark.* Trans. D. Madvig. Richmond: John Knox Press, 1970.

Seeligman, I. E. "Voraussetzungen der Midrashexegese." *VTSup* 1 (1953): 150–81.

Segal, Alan. *Rebecca's Children.* Cambridge: Harvard Univ. Press, 1985.

_____. "Ruler of This World: Attitudes toward Mediator Figures and the Problem of a Sociology of Gnosticism." In *Jewish and Christian Self-Definition,* vol. 2, *Aspects of Judaism in the Graeco-Roman Period,* ed. E. P. Sanders et al., 245–68. Philadelphia: Fortress Press, 1981.

————. *Two Powers in Heaven.* Leiden: E. J. Brill, 1977.

Seidelin, Paul. "Der 'Ebed Jahwe' und die Messiasgestalt im Jesajatargum." *ZNW* 35 (1936): 194–231.

Spiegel, Shalom. *The Last Trial.* Trans. Judah Goldin. New York: Schocken Books, 1969.

Stendahl, Krister. "Interpretation." *IDB.*

————. *The School of St. Matthew.* Philadelphia: Fortress Press; Lund: C. W. K. Gleerup, 1954.

Stone, Michael. *Scripture, Sects, and Visions: A Profile of Judaism from Ezra to the Jewish Revolts.* Philadelphia: Fortress Press, 1980.

Strugnell, John. "Notes en marge du volume V des Discoveries in the Judean Desert of Jordan." *RQ* 29 (1970): 163–276.

Suhl, Alfred. *Die Funktion der alttestamentlichen Zitate und Anspielungen im Markusevangelium.* Gütersloh: Gütersloher Verlagshaus, 1965.

Sundberg, Alan. *The Old Testament and the Early Church.* Cambridge: Harvard Univ. Press, 1964.

Tannehill, Robert. "The Disciples in Mark: The Function of a Narrative Role." *JR* 57 (1977): 386–405.

————. "The Gospel of Mark as Narrative Christology." *Semeia* 16 (1979): 57–95.

The Targum of Isaiah. Trans. J. F. Stenning. Oxford: At the Clarendon Press, 1949.

Taylor, Vincent. *The Gospel according to St. Mark.* London: Macmillan & Co., 1952.

Theisohn, J. *Der Auserwählte Richter.* Göttingen: Vandenhoeck & Ruprecht, 1975.

Vermes, Geza. *The Dead Sea Scrolls in English.* 2d ed. New York: Penguin Books, 1975.

————. *The Dead Sea Scrolls: Qumran in Perspective.* Philadelphia: Fortress Press, 1982.

————. *Jesus and the World of Judaism.* Philadelphia: Fortress Press, 1983.

————. *Jesus the Jew: A Historian's Reading of the Gospels.* Philadelphia: Fortress Press, 1981; London: William Collins Sons, 1973.

————. *Post-Biblical Jewish Studies.* Leiden: E. J. Brill, 1975.

————. *Scripture and Tradition in Judaism.* 2d ed. Leiden: E. J. Brill, 1973.

Vielhauer, Philipp. *Aufsätze zum Neuen Testament.* Munich: Chr. Kaiser Verlag, 1965.

Werner, Martin. *Die Entstehung des christlichen Dogmas.* Bern: Paul Haupt Verlag, 1941.

Wilcox, Max. "The Promise of the 'Seed' in the New Testament and the Targumim." *JSNT* 5 (1979): 2–20.

Williams, Samuel. *Jesus' Death as Saving Event: The Background and Origin of a Concept.* HDR 2. Missoula, Mont.: Scholars Press, 1975.

Woude, A. S. van der. *Die messianischen Vorstellungen der Gemeinde von Qumran.* Assen, Neth.: Van Gorcum, 1957.

Wright, Addison G. *The Literary Genre Midrash.* New York: Alba House, 1967.

Yadin, Y. "A Midrash on 2 Sam. vii and Ps. i–ii (4QFlorilegium)." *IEJ* 9 (1959): 95–98.

York, A. D. "The Dating of Targumic Literature." *JSJ* 5 (1974): 49–62.

INDEX
OF PASSAGES